ACQUITTALS IN THE SPANISH INQUISITION

The Spanish Inquisition has become such a byword for injustice that many forget it was also a judicial system capable of acquittal. This study of more than 67,000 trials uncovers over 2,500 formal acquittals, more than 6,600 suspended trials, and nearly 2,100 with unknown or no recorded outcomes.

The inquisitors were jurists who frequently held other judgeships before and after their tenure and used the same evidentiary rules as other Spanish courts. If every acquittal may be taken as an admission of error, the Spanish Inquisition admitted its errors thousands of times, occasionally even putting them on public display at the *autos de fe*. An acquittal can also be taken as a sign that the inquisitors did not wish to punish the innocent and that while they were quick to arrest and charge people on flimsy evidence, they were too conscientious to convict them without further proof. However, it is also clear that the Holy Office at times did bend, twist, or even break the law when it suited it in order to secure a conviction.

This book is aimed at students, scholars, and general readers seeking a nuanced understanding of the Spanish Inquisition and its workings.

Gunnar W. Knutsen is Professor of Early Modern History at the University of Bergen. He worked for the University of Oslo from 1996 to 2009 before moving to Telemark University College and then to the University of Bergen in 2014. He is an associated researcher at ENS-Lyon.

ACQUITTALS IN THE SPANISH INQUISITION

Gunnar W. Knutsen

Routledge
Taylor & Francis Group
LONDON AND NEW YORK

Designed cover image: Pedro Berruguete, *Saint Dominic Presiding over an Auto da fe* (c. 1495). Magite Historic/Alamy Stock Photo.

First published 2025
by Routledge
4 Park Square, Milton Park, Abingdon, Oxon OX14 4RN

and by Routledge
605 Third Avenue, New York, NY 10158

Routledge is an imprint of the Taylor & Francis Group, an informa business

British Library Cataloguing-in-Publication Data
A catalogue record for this book is available from the British Library

Library of Congress Cataloging-in-Publication Data
Names: Knutsen, Gunnar W., 1968– author.
Title: Acquittals in the Spanish Inquisition / Gunnar W. Knutsen.
Description: Abingdon, Oxon [UK] ; New York, NY : Routledge Taylor & Francis Group, 2024. | Includes bibliographical references and index.
Identifiers: LCCN 2024029465 (print) | LCCN 2024029466 (ebook) | ISBN 9781032596662 (hardback) | ISBN 9781032596679 (paperback) | ISBN 9781003455691 (ebook) | ISBN 9781040182789 (adobe pdf) | ISBN 9781040182802 (epub)
Subjects: LCSH: Acquittals—Spain—History. | Criminal procedure—Spain—History. | Criminal justice, Administration of—Spain—History. | Inquisition—Spain—History.
Classification: LCC KKT4744 .K58 2024 (print) | LCC KKT4744 (ebook) | DDC 272/.6—dc23/eng/20240626
LC record available at https://lccn.loc.gov/2024029465
LC ebook record available at https://lccn.loc.gov/2024029466

ISBN: 978-1-032-59666-2 (hbk)
ISBN: 978-1-032-59667-9 (pbk)
ISBN: 978-1-003-45569-1 (ebk)

DOI: 10.4324/9781003455691

Typeset in Sabon LT Pro
by Apex CoVantage, LLC

CONTENTS

FIGURES

TABLES

PREFACE

A great number of people have aided me in writing this book, which has taken several years longer than I originally envisaged. The first thank you goes to my old friend and mentor Gustav Henningsen, who unfortunately passed away when this book was being prepared for publication. Gustav was a source of inspiration for all my work on the Spanish Inquisition. In 1997, he gave me access to the card file index of *relaciones de causas* that first alerted me to the massive number of acquittals in the Spanish Inquisition, and many years later made it possible to study them. I have received generous advice and valuable data on Toledo from Jean Pierre Dedieu, who invited me to work with him at ENS-Lyon on several occasions in 2012 and 2013, for the academic year during my sabbatical in 2017–2018, in 2021, and again in 2023. Like his friend Gustav Henningsen, he has continued to be an important source of information, advice, and inspiration after his retirement. There is probably nobody who knows more about historical databases than him. I am also greatly indebted to the *Institut d'Asie Orientale* and the ENS-Lyon, and the many wonderful colleagues there who have accepted me as a member of their laboratory and hosted me when I came to work with Dedieu. William Monter generously read and commented on an early article draft of what later became a book project. Mauricio Drelichman and I cooperated on a related project that allowed us to expand the data in the Early Modern Inquisition Database (EMID) significantly. David González Agudo, Ana Vargas Martínez, and in particular Ignacio Sánchez Ayuso have done a massive job as research assistants, registering data from tens of thousands of trials for us. Pablo Pérez García, Pedro Ortego Gil, Sergio Urzainqui, María Jesús Zamora, and Bruno Pomara have generously given me references and suggested relevant literature. Ignazio Panizo has been a great help at the

Archivo Histórico Nacional. Rafael Benitez Sánchez Blanco has been a stimulating sounding board for my many thoughts and questions on acquittals in the Inquisition. I am greatly indebted to him, to Jorge Catalá, and the rest of the *Departamento de history moderna* at the University of Valencia who have accepted me as one of their own on my research stays there. Giovanna Fiume helped me resolve doubts about the *absolución ad cautelam*. Telemark University College and the University of Bergen have funded the research that went into this book, and I am grateful to have received the opportunity to pursue this project during my tenure at both institutions.

All translations in this book are my own, and I am the sole responsible for any and all errors in this as in any other matter in the book. I have consistently referred to all those tried by the Inquisition as male, except when dealing with a named female defendant, for the simple reason that three-fourths of those tried are identified in the sources as males.

Researching and writing this book took me more than a decade. In those years I married, became a father, had a brush with death, and was hospitalized more than once. When I finally had a finished manuscript and a book contract, my father died, and within two months of him, two of the friends who have meant the most to me as a historian, Friso Ross and Gustav Henningsen. They are dearly missed, and I dedicate this book to them.

1

INTRODUCTION

Background

The problem

In February 1566, the Spanish Inquisition's tribunal in Toledo voted to acquit Juan Beltramo from the charge of Lutheranism. He was left in jail for another three days before he was called from his cell and asked by the inquisitor 'if he had remembered anything [new] concerning his case'. Only when he had answered in the negative and it was obvious that he had nothing to confess was the sentence of acquittal read to him, whereupon 'he threw himself at the feet of the lord inquisitor'.[1]

Even more dramatically, the Flemish soldier in Habsburg service, Simón Maestrich from Maastricht was acquitted the same year in the same tribunal after having been tortured without confessing to the Lutheranism he had been charged with. When he was brought from his cell four days after the torture and questioned if he had remembered anything new concerning his case, he started crying and said that he remembered nothing new and 'would never remember things he had never said or done'. His sentence of acquittal was then read to him 'and he went down on his knees and thanked the lords inquisitors very much'.[2]

Such riveting scenes as we saw in the cases of Juan Beltrano and Simón Maestrich and the acquittal of a defendant in the Spanish Inquisition may seem surprising to the reader with little or no first-hand knowledge of documents from the Holy Office. After all, the Spanish Inquisition was geared towards generating confessions and convictions. From the polemical literature of the sixteenth century to the historiography of the twentieth and twenty-first centuries, authors have stressed the Inquisition's search for convictions and confessions, both as a way of saving souls and as a tool for self-justification.

DOI: 10.4324/9781003455691-1

This, in turn, has generated one of the greatest misperceptions of the Spanish Inquisition, which is that, in the words of a major contemporary Hispanist, 'it was extremely rare for an inquisitorial trial to end with a sentence of acquittal'.[3] For those who believe that the Inquisition never acquitted anyone, the number of acquittals contained in the sources must be surprising. Of the 67,201 trials between 1480 and 1820 examined for this study, more than 11,000 ended in some form of non-conviction, as shown in Table 1.1.[4] Of these, 2,529 trials ended with a formal acquittal, usually formulated as an *absolución de la instancia*.[5] Based on an assumption that the total number of court cases must have been somewhere in the region of 130,000 trials, we can expect that at least 4,000 of them will have ended in a formal acquittal.

This was an unexpected finding, and it didn't generate much interest when shared with others working on the Spanish Inquisition. Gustav Henningsen said, 'I'm not really interested in the Spanish Inquisition, I'm interested in the sources it has produced and what they say about witchcraft beliefs'. Jean Pierre Dedieu was flat-out sceptical and had to be almost physically restrained in his office chair to make him see how many acquittals there were. On that sunny day in Lyon in 2013, he became a man transfixed, repeating to himself 'I could never imagine they were so many, I could never imagine they were so many' over and over again as he scrolled down the list of acquittals. I had much the same feeling of wonder myself when I first realized the number of actual acquittals.

As Table 1.1 shows, acquittals were far from the only way of ending a trial without a conviction, and, indeed, not the most common. Suspensions and simply dropped trials form the majority of the recorded non-convictions. As many as 10 per cent of all trials were suspended.

The persistent belief that the Spanish Inquisition never acquitted the accused is almost as old as the institution itself. It arose, perhaps, during the first years of the Inquisition's activities in Spain, which were by far the bloodiest of its existence. This belief in the Inquisition as a deadly institution with no escape became an integral component of the black legend of the Spanish as an exceptionally cruel people.[6] Together with the view of the Spanish as slovenly and dishonest, it has persisted as a stereotype of Spanish history up to our times, though perhaps less prominent in recent years.[7]

TABLE 1.1 Trial outcomes 1480–1820, known trials

Acquittals	*Suspensions*	*Unknown*	*Convictions*[1]	*Total*
2,529	6,601	2,099	55,972	67,201

Note.

1 This includes those simply ordered to pay the Inquisition's costs or to be reprehended, without any formal finding of guilt. In other words, this is the maximum number we obtain if we stretch our definition of conviction to the utmost.

The best model for the history of trial activities of the Spanish Inquisition is Jean Pierre Dedieu's concept of four seasons, of which the first and bloodiest lasted until 1525.[8] As Dedieu duly noted, these are also the least well-documented years of the Holy Office in Spain. At the same time, this is the period on which most common assumptions about the institution are based, at least outside specialist circles. The next three centuries of its existence offer abundant sources showing a judicial system that dealt with a wide range of offenses and relatively rarely passed death sentences. The trials studied in this book come from all periods of the Spanish Inquisition's existence, covering 340 years. However, the majority date from what Dedieu calls the second and third seasons of the Spanish Inquisition, the years from 1525 to 1725. The sources show that in this period, the Holy Office in Spain was in fact almost as likely to acquit as to execute its defendants. Among the cases from that period in this sample, 1,373 were sentenced to die in person, while another 1,485 were to be burned in effigy. In total, 2,421 were acquitted *de la instancia* in the same period. The majority of defendants were convicted and sentenced to other forms of punishment.

Despite its emphasis on securing confessions,[9] the Holy Office had always known that not every defendant was guilty, and it always had rules regulating such cases. However, the problem of innocent defendants became painfully clear for the institution in 1507, when the scandalous Cordoba trials overseen by the inquisitor Diego Rodriguez Lucero forced the resignation of Torquemada's successor Deza as Inquisitor-General. There was after this an awareness that many innocent persons who had been reported as suspicious should never have been arrested or prosecuted. Yet even in this situation, it was decided that those convicted by Lucero should be considered correctly judged, even though the matter of these trials and convictions continued to be raised for decades.[10]

A formal trial in the Inquisition only started after evidence had been gathered and examined, a process which meant that the vast majority of those reported to the Holy office never suffered prosecution. This previous evaluation of proof by the inquisitors was the reason why an inquisitorial trial started with the presumption of guilt: It was only meant to commence when there in fact was sufficient evidence to have reason to believe that the defendant was guilty. This is the source of much misunderstanding, as it is often taken as evidence of the Inquisition's eagerness to consider every denounced person guilty. While there is no doubt that the Holy Office was hostile to religious and ethnic minorities, the presumption of guilt was in fact a legal device for a trial that commenced only after the gathering and preliminary assessment of legal evidence. On the other hand, it was also in part due to the fact that a trial only started after the collection and evaluation of evidence that indicated guilt that the trial itself came to be geared towards generating confession and conviction. Indeed, one might very well be excused for thinking that such a system did not allow for acquittals. Even a brief acquaintance with the sources will disabuse the researcher of any such notions. The Spanish Inquisition did in fact acquit several thousand defendants that the inquisitors themselves earlier had considered probably guilty based on the preliminary evidence collected against them.

The standard of proof required for the presumption of guilt was defined as 'half proof', equivalent to one adult eyewitness who could testify to the full crime. For a conviction, 'full proof' was needed, meaning two adult eyewitnesses to the actual crime, or a confession by the defendant.[11] Although the loss of much of the Spanish Inquisition's archives means we will never know the percentage for certain, the vast majority of denunciations never led to a formal trial, because there was not enough evidence to warrant further proceedings. To know this with certainty, we would have to compare the records of trials with the books of denunciations. These have only been preserved in exceptional cases in Spain. In neighbouring Portugal, they have been preserved to a much higher degree, and studies have shown that as few as 5 per cent of all denunciations led to trials.[12] Another way of looking at it would be to study the preserved reports from the inquisitors' visitations of the inquisitorial districts. These have been largely ignored by historians, precisely because they produced few trials.[13] They did, however, produce large numbers of denunciations that were never followed up. Using these and surviving denunciation protocols, Jean Pierre Dedieu calculated that some 5 to 7 per cent of denunciations in Toledo led to trials.[14] The few studies that have been done thus point towards the same direction: slightly more than one in 20 denunciations led to a trial. Clearly, the selection of which denunciations to investigate and bring to trial was one of the key moments in the development of a trial, and with 20 cases to choose among for each one that actually went to trial, we must expect that the inquisitors chose cases where they believed that guilt could be legally proven. This is a key point that we shall return to more than once. The undocumented process of selection of cases from the lost books of denunciations for trials whose records have come down to us is a phenomenon we can only study through its effects in terms of trials held, except when it caused such disruption that it generated conflict. The best illustration of this is perhaps the Barcelona tribunal's fiscal who wrote a series of scathing letters protesting the inquisitors' refusal to prosecute alleged witches in 1620.[15] Without these letters, we might not have known that these cases were ever brought to the tribunal's attention and the evidence produced in secular courts evaluated by the Inquisition since the inquisitors decided that there was no proof of any crime pertaining to the Holy Office and refused to prosecute the alleged witches.[16]

Although they took care to select winnable cases, the inquisitors recognized that some defendants would in fact be cleared after a formal trial, and the Spanish Inquisition's rules and regulations did indeed contain instructions on how to handle such acquittals.

Inquisitorial trials were held in secret and were followed by lavish public punishment ceremonies known as *auto de fe*.[17] It is well known that the Inquisition placed great weight on the public reading of sentences and punishments as a conclusion to the secret trials, but it is far less well known that there was a rarely used ritual for showing those acquitted in addition to those convicted.[18] One of the reasons often given for claiming that the Holy Office never acquitted anyone is that it would never admit to being wrong.[19] By that logic, the Holy Office should not have burned escaped convicts in effigy, which it routinely did, even though this signalled the institution's inability to capture prominent heretics.[20] In fact, the Inquisition had a fully developed ritual for publicly and theatrically showing the innocence of acquitted defendants and used this to showcase its own fairness, rather than admitting any error or wrongdoing. The acquitted walked in the same solemn procession before the *auto da fe* as those who had been convicted, but not together with them,[21] either preceding them or walking at the end with the royal delegation and other notables. In 1566, for example, a Frenchman who was acquitted by the Holy Office was paraded at the *auto da fe* in Barcelona 'with a laurel wreath on his head and a palm frond in his hands' in clear contrast to the decorated *sambenitos* and pointed hats worn by the convicts who carried candles in their hands.[22] A century and a half later, in Valladolid in 1704, we have the example of Francisco Rodriguez, who 'appeared at the *auto da fe* with palm fronds and listened to his sentence', and the next day 'he rode a white horse with the same palm fronds alongside the ministers of the Holy Office, behind the false witnesses' who had caused his prosecution.[23]

The Holy Office did, however, rarely use this option to make a public showing of its own 'justice and clemency' in the case of living defendants, and the dead were rarely acquitted.[24] Yet, the instructions issued by Inquisitor General Valdés' in 1561 state that the acquittal of a deceased defendant should always be read at an *auto da fe*, while acquittals of the living should only be published at an *auto* if the defendant explicitly requested it.[25] These instructions were not dead letters. The Greek Domingo Golada died during the course of his trial in Barcelona. On 8 September 1602, his name and 'his memory and reputation' were publicly cleared and his sentence of acquittal was read aloud at the *auto da fe* in Barcelona that day.[26] Few of the living appear to have made such a request to have their sentence read aloud, and we do not know how many were even aware that this option was available for them. In some cases, we can see that they were given a choice. For example, Juan Note Pascual 'did not want the sentence read at the *auto* [*de fe*]' after he was acquitted of bigamy in Murcia in 1571, perhaps because his acquittal was based on the finding that 'his first marriage was not fully proven' and he did not want to attract attention and possibly new witnesses to the case.[27]

Others chose to signal their acquittal in the most public way possible, as we saw in Barcelona in 1566. In Cartagena de India in 1650, the Augustinian friar Francisco de Amaya had his acquittal read aloud at the *auto de fe*, thus letting everyone know that he had in fact not uttered any heresies, as he had been accused of.[28] In Lima, in 1639, the acquitted Old Christians who had been implicated in the infamous 'great conspiracy' of Judaizers spanning the breath of the Spanish empire marched at the end of the procession, with the royal delegation rather than with the convicts.[29]

Most of those acquitted never took part in an *auto da fe* and were simply sworn to secrecy and then released from jail without further ceremony, or they were set free after a private admonition or reprimand. Even so, an inquisitorial trial marked them with infamy, since 'imprisonment was remembered and handed down through generations while the fact of its being causeless was forgotten'.[30] It might also cause financial ruin even to the innocent since the accused were required to pay for their own upkeep in prison during their trials.[31]

This study

Following the introduction, this book is divided into three chapters and a conclusion. The first sets out the way the Spanish Inquisition was organized and operated, as well as the legislation regulating its activities. It takes as its point of departure the Inquisition's search for conviction whenever a formal trial was initiated. This forms the background for the next section, which answers the question of the ways in which a trial in the Spanish Inquisition could end if there was no conviction. There were several ways in which an inquisitorial trial might end without a conviction, and not all of them were regulated by the legislation studied in the first section. In addition to outright acquittals, the documentation shows that the Spanish Inquisition also used formal suspensions, simply dropped some cases with no recorded outcome, and cautiously absolved a significant number of defendants by lifting any ecclesiastical censures they might have incurred without acquitting them, as we shall see later. The final chapter then looks at the formal acquittals. It answers the questions of who were acquitted, of what charges, when, and where. This is based on the study of some 2,529 recorded acquittals out of 67,201 trials registered in Early Modern Inquisition Database (EMID) at the time of writing. While the loss of significant amounts of archival material makes statistical study of inquisitorial activity in Spain challenging, the sheer number of documented trials and acquittals allows us to make some approximations. We then go into the question of why these trials ended in acquittals, looking both at the means of defence available for the defendant and the reasons given by the Holy Office when recording acquittals. The conclusion asks what the consequences of an acquittal were, and what to make of the relationship between acquittals, which were usually conditional, and the formal suspension of trials.

Historiography

In the great and varied historiography of the Spanish Inquisition, acquittals are virtually absent, despite five centuries of writing and two centuries of scholarship that continue to expand at a rapid pace. Works on the Holy Office have been published almost from the founding years of the institution. A number of books were written by the Spanish Inquisition's own men, including both hagiographies[32] and the first critical history based on primary sources.[33] Some of those persecuted by the Holy Office left their own early verdict on the institution and its history.[34] Acquittals, naturally enough, was not a subject they wrote about.

That acquittals have also failed to attract the attention of Inquisition scholars is in some ways easier to explain than the paucity of research on early modern acquittals in general. It can, perhaps, in part be explained by the relatively low percentage of acquittals and suspensions, which are only visible if one works with large amounts of data, while more recent historiography has tended to favour a more qualitative approach based on much smaller documentary bases.

A contributing factor has probably been looking at the subjects that have interested us – the researchers working on Inquisition documents. Generalizing broadly – perhaps excessively – one may say that the majority of scholars working on the Spanish Inquisition can be divided into two groups with distinct interests and motivations underlaying their research. The first group has primarily been interested in the Spanish Inquisition as a repressive system, frequently motivated by a conviction that this was one of the first attempts at total and comprehensive control of a population's beliefs and convictions. The Holy Office has thus been seen as a predecessor of and inspiration for authoritarian impulses and regimes of the twentieth century, though the focus on the repressive apparatus can be traced back to José Antonio Llorente's *Histoire critique de l'Inquisition espagnole*, published in four volumes in 1817 and 1818.[35] Llorente had been commissary and secretary to the Holy Office. He thus had both first-hand experience and access to extensive primary sources as he wrote what is considered the first scholarly history of the Spanish Inquisition. As with the many later students of the Inquisition as a repressive system over the next two centuries, he paid scant attention to the subject of acquittals, which is a perfectly understandable thing to do since convictions are much more obvious expressions of repression. While reasonable, this does perhaps overlook how the many cases that ended in a suspension or an acquittal or were dropped or simply never developed into a formal trial after the first questioning of witnesses also contributed to a sense of vulnerability and hence self-censorship. Starr-Lebeau notes how an Inquisition directed at *conversos* in Guadalupe in 1485 also quieted Old Christians, 'through the indirect force of an institution like the Inquisition which was not specifically directed against them'.[36] In this perspective, one might well argue that even acquittals and absolutions contributed to repression. The insistence on inquisitorial intervention before allowing Protestants to convert to Catholicism in Spain meant that new converts were put in a position of palpable vulnerability before being allowed into the fellowship of believers, clearly showing them the danger of any future deviation from Spanish Catholic orthodoxy.[37]

The second group of scholars have been using the Inquisition's documents to study early modern Spanish culture, both elite and popular, in particular, those aspects of it that the Holy Office set out to combat and change: religious as well as other minorities, sometimes dubbing these 'counter-cultures' or 'sub-cultures'. This trend came to the fore in the 1960s and 1970s, reflecting the contemporary advances in social and cultural history elsewhere, and contributing greatly to what has since been known as 'history from crime'. These researchers have frequently little real interest in the Holy Office itself as an institution, only in the documents it produced which are used to create an image of what it was that the Inquisition investigated and punished.[38] When the main interest is what the Inquisition tried to repress and punish, it is no wonder that the trials of the manifestly innocent are of little interest. For example, if the researcher is interested in Lutherans in Spain, he or she is unlikely to spend much time on those who convinced the Inquisitors that they were completely orthodox Catholics who knew nothing of Luther's teaching. There are therefore some very good reasons why many historians have had little to say of acquittals in the Spanish Inquisition. As this book was being researched in Madrid, this pattern could be seen very clearly in the archive: in *legajo* 133 of the Inquisition section in the National archive, another researcher who was there a few weeks before one of the present author's visits had ordered copies of virtually every trial for Judaism – except for those that ended in acquittals!

Naturally, other scholars have had an interest in the Inquisition itself, or in its treatment of a single offence without necessarily viewing it as uniquely repressive, but they form a minority in the published scholarship and have come to the fore in the last decade or so. The present author had no particular interest in acquittals until discovering that there were so many of them in 2012 and then had problems getting members of the older generation of Inquisition specialists to take the subject seriously.

Nevertheless, acquittals have not been completely absent from the historiography. A number of extensive studies of individual tribunals have appeared in the course of the last 30 years, frequently incorporating statistics based on the *relaciones de causas* as pioneered by Gustav Henningsen and his collaborator Jaime Contreras.[39] These usually mention the number and rate of acquittals, even if they do not dwell on the subject. An example is Contreras himself, whose study of the Holy Office in Galicia showed that 18.5 per cent of the accused were acquitted or absolved, without doing much more with that information.[40] Cristian Berco's study of sodomy trials also mentions acquittals, notably the higher acquittal rate of foreign than of Spanish defendants,[41] while the present author has noted the significant number of acquittals in trials for superstition in the Holy Office in Barcelona.[42]

Over the years, this literature has established that the number of acquittals must have been substantial, yet it seems as if several thousand acquittals and absolutions do not make an impact on the interpretation of the Holy Office even when they are known. For instance, in his widely used textbook on the Spanish Inquisition, Henry Kamen writes that 'the number of acquittals were few' – immediately after drawing on Jaime Contreras' work to note that 18.5 per cent of the defendants in Galicia were in fact 'absolved'.[43] This is a commonly stated view that the number of acquittals was few. Common is also the conflation of acquittals *de la instancia* and absolutions *ad cauthelam*, a distinction we will discuss more fully later. Here it should be simply noted that they are not the same: one is a finding that guilt in the alleged law-breaking has not been proven, and the other is a lifting of whatever ecclesiastical censures may have been incurred. Stephen Haliczer likewise asserts that the number of exonerations was low when he states that between '1478 and 1530, the Valencia tribunal only handed down 12 absolutions out of 1,862 sentences' (based solely on fiscal records). However, he omits to mention that the same tribunal handed down at least 71 acquittals and 221 absolutions in 4,999 cases during the next 180 years. Hence, he concludes that 'outright acquittal was rather uncommon in the Inquisition' and repeats the old speculation that this may be 'because it [an acquittal] constituted an admission that the tribunal was wrong to prosecute the case'.[44]

Given that we now can document more than two and a half thousand acquittals among the documented cases, an equal number of cautious absolutions, and even a higher number of suspensions, we must ask how modern historians got this so wrong. Perhaps it is simply a matter of perspective, as the numbers and rates of detected acquittal varied a great deal over time, between tribunals and from one type of offence to another. Those historians working on witchcraft, for example, will see documents indicating relative lenience and a high number of acquittals, certainly compared to other European countries. Those studying Judaizers, on the other hand, will see few trials ending in acquittals, and a great deal of brutality. These differences are, of course, bound to influence how we see the Holy Office. Another reason is the great importance of Jean-Pierre Dedieu's study of the Inquisition of Toledo which has become one of the most important works referred to by later Inquisition scholars.[45] Absolutions and acquittals are scarcely mentioned in his study. Another important work which is still one of the cornerstones of Inquisition research more than a hundred years after its original publication is the classic four-volume study by Henry Charles Lea.[46] Lea wrote long before the advanced statistical analyses that were introduced in the 1970s, and his impressionistic conclusion (based on extensive reading of sources) was that the Inquisition rarely acquitted anybody.[47] Thus, some of the core studies that have shaped conceptions in the field of Inquisition studies dismiss acquittals as barely relevant to the study and understanding of the Spanish Inquisition.

Historical research on acquittals in other judicial systems in early modern Europe is also relatively limited. Acquittals are frequently mentioned only as a result of the prosecution's failure to prove its case – much like the inquisitors liked to write their sentences of acquittal, where they, after leading the investigation and assembling the evidence, would state that the fiscal had failed to make his case! In effect, then, the historian adopts the language of the courts and frequently accepts the judges' self-serving version of events. This essentially negative view of acquittals as a failure to prove a case also makes the subject seem less appealing to those interested in relations of power, since acquittals are or appear to be poor expressions of the courts' role in disciplining popular culture, the repression of minorities or other such areas of study where judicial records have played a prominent role. More attention has been given to some of the reasons for acquittals, such as insanity,[48] and while a very great deal has been written on the most important form of evidence in early modern court rooms, the testimony of witnesses, most of that literature is centred on contemporary issues.[49]

The numerous different jurisdictions that made up the early modern Spanish judicial system have seen a great deal of interest during the last four decades, producing a number of fine studies in several languages. Nonetheless, only a single article appears to have come to light which deals with the issue of acquittals,[50] while a number of monographs touch on the issue. Even so, a couple of things are worthy of note. One clear trend is a higher number of acquittals in secular courts than in the Spanish Inquisition.[51] Another important distinction is the use of full and formal acquittals, in addition to conditional acquittals. As we shall see later, the Spanish Inquisition insisted on conditional acquittals as a matter of principle. On the other hand, the Holy Office was much more likely to formally suspend a case than were secular courts.

Inquisitorial law

The legislation of the Spanish Inquisition is surprisingly difficult to get to grips with. Not only is there an absence of any single authoritative law or collection of legislation, but the organic nature of inquisitorial legislation also means that it evolved over centuries with differences between the various tribunals. As Lynn says, '[I]nquisitors drew upon a circulating body of procedural guidelines and in turn sought to revise these in the face of a range of experiences in the world'.[52]

When the Spanish Inquisition was founded in 1478, the first inquisitors used the same legal sources as their medieval predecessors[53]: Canon law and inquisitors' manuals, most famously that of Bernard Gui. However, the Spanish Inquisition was very different from the medieval Inquisitions. Unlike them, it was a permanently established organization with fixed tribunals, permanent staff, and a hierarchical structure with a central council, *la Suprema*, led by an inquisitor general. Furthermore, the main target of this new Inquisition was not Christian heretical groups such as the Waldenses but recent converts from Judaism. These differences necessitated new legislation to address the many situations that were not covered in the existing texts.[54] Thus, a flurry of new legislation appeared from Torquemada and his council.

A similar situation developed in Italy after the establishment of the Roman Inquisition in 1542. As Jeremy Black writes, the Italian 'post-1542 tribunals developed legal procedures, followed basic rules and patterns. Full-time inquisitors and their assistants, facing more numerous and more complex cases, needed to follow clearer pathways for their own advantage and convenience'.[55] The by-laws issued by the Portuguese Inquisition were more coherent and orderly than those in Spain, yet they were 'relatively laconic' in terms of instructions when it came to conducting actual trials.[56] In fact, in both the Spanish and Portuguese Inquisitions, more attention in both instructions and ordinances appears to have been focused on organization, administration, and economy than on trial procedures, sentencing, and punishment.

Despite Torquemada's reputation for ruthless and bloody persecution of Judaizers, most of the legislation issued during his tenure as inquisitor general dealt with bureaucratic and economic issues.[57] Further instructions followed from his successors. These were later supplemented with so-called *cartas acordadas* which were letters sent to one or more tribunals setting out how they were to proceed in determined circumstances, frequently as a result of doubts raised by the local tribunals themselves in letters to Madrid. This ad hoc way of resolving doubts and issuing instructions on an individual basis without sending them to all tribunals or compiling them in collections created problems, since every tribunal now had a different set of instructions and legislation. Eventually it became clear to the inquisitor general and the *Suprema* that even they lacked a full and complete collection of all instructions issued to the various tribunals over the centuries. Local tribunals were even ordered to search their archives and remit copies to Madrid of instructions that they had previously received from the *suprema*.[58] This lack of authoritative collections combined with local and temporal variation frequently makes it difficult to ascertain exactly what was the judicial basis for sentences passed in the Spanish Inquisition.

Sources of law

With such an eclectic collection of legislation, it is no surprise that a number of scholars have been working to study the various forms of laws and instructions of the Spanish Inquisition. However, the best systematic study of Spanish inquisitorial jurisprudence is still Jean Pierre Dedieu's 1987 article.[59] Dedieu sees the Inquisition's legislation as comprising four different levels. At the first level was the *ius commune*,[60] the collection of rules and techniques based on Roman law and canon laws that all law students of the period learnt during their studies. These were the legal bases that judges normally used, reducing the national law codes to a subsidiary role.[61] Above this, he puts the canon law texts promulgated by the papacy, principally the *Liber Sextus* (1298) and the *Clementines* (1317), which were the formal foundations of inquisitorial law in the entire Catholic world.[62] These defined the jurisdiction of the Holy Office and its procedure insofar as it deviated from the *ius commune*, and they constituted what is, properly speaking, inquisitorial law. The instructions issued by Torquemada and his successors up to 1561 form a third level.[63] These were both more precise and less extensive than canon law and the *ius commune*, and they only applied to the tribunals of the Spanish Inquisition. Their main focus was on particularly important subjects, possible points of interest and of conflict, as well as the new issues that cropped up with the innovation of permanently established tribunals with fixed buildings and a permanent bureaucracy that instead of Medieval heretical sects mostly prosecuted alleged Judaizers, crypto Muslims, Protestants after the reformation changed Europe's religious landscape, and massive numbers of ordinary Catholic Spaniards who had somehow transgressed by blaspheming, swearing or in other ways broken with Catholic doctrine, frequently unwittingly so. As a fourth level, Dedieu posits the *cartas acordadas* which as mentioned earlier contained resolutions of individual matters, cases or doubts, that created new rules without being incorporated into new sets of instructions issued by the inquisitor general. Legislation on these different levels coexisted, even when they contradicted each other, and the judges would use whichever piece of legislation they found appropriate (or even knew about).[64] This, of course, was not unlike the situation in secular courts in Spain, and indeed, other parts of Europe using the *ius commune*.

The four levels outlined earlier formed a hierarchy, with the *cartas acordadas* taking primacy over the instructions, which again were given precedence over the basic canon law texts, while the whole edifice rested on the foundations of the *ius commune*. Such a complex mass of legislation was difficult to handle, and after the mid-sixteenth century, there was probably no person who ever knew the totality of the legislation of the Spanish Inquisition. It is important to stress the enormous amounts of documents produced by the Holy Office over the centuries.

The individual tribunals tried to overcome the difficulty of the piecemeal legislation by compiling their own sets of alphabetically ordered handwritten collections of instructions called *abecedarios*,[65] and style manuals and copy books with instructions on how to proceed in interrogations, write down trial records, and so on. This further fragmented the legal basis on which the various tribunals operated and gave every regional Inquisition a slightly separate style as it followed different manuals and *abecedarios*. This was somewhat offset by the later practice of various tribunals exchanging copies of their *abecedarios*. Two sets of instructions (known as 'the old instructions' and 'the new instructions') and three compilations of instructions including both ('the old instructions' and 'the new instructions') were printed in limited print runs between 1536 and 1667.[66] A guide to inquisitorial procedure called *Orden de procesar en el Santo Oficio* was printed in 1607.[67] These were the only printed instructions in the 350 years of the institution's history, and each was printed in runs estimated to consist of only 200 copies.[68] Furthermore, the compilations did not include any instructions issued after 1576.[69] Thus, even these attempts to distribute uniform copies of instructions were far from ever creating a single accessible and complete corpus of legislation. Indeed, they illustrate the problem, since the printed books were in fact collections of earlier handwritten instructions.

The practice of letting local positions such as notaries be passed on for generations within a single family caused a great deal of continuity in how business was conducted within each tribunal, and the lack of a single code of law valid in all tribunals made this even more pronounced since it forced a greater reliance on the locally produced compilations. These were usually the private property of the men who produced them, or their heirs, so that there was a self-reinforcing tendency towards greater variations and local traditions carried by the local personnel at each tribunal and not under formal control of the institution itself,[70] counteracting the efforts of the *Suprema* to centralize and standardize the Spanish Inquisition. With such a disparate selection of laws and regulations, it is no wonder that the inquisitors appear to have used the *ius commune* from their studies as the basis for much of their activity. The procedures followed by the Spanish Inquisition left them a great deal of room to manoeuvre, leaving them relatively free to conduct trials as they saw fit. This was not exceptional in Spain, or indeed, in early modern Europe. The inquisitors, as we shall see later, belonged to the *letrado* elite, steeped in Roman and canon law, and they knew the doctrine of 'arbitrary justice' known as *arbitrium* well from their law studies. French *parlements* also dealt in 'arbitrary justice', exercising their *arbitrium* in such a way that the judges were left wide discretion in how to settle the cases brought before them. Indeed, William Monter informs us, Pierre Lizet, the 'bibliophilic head of the French court system owned no collections of French royal edicts'.[71] The law of the land was quite literally not what the judges used to pass sentences: 'Reading royal decrees therefore tells us almost nothing about how criminal justice was actually administered in early modern France'.[72] It would be exaggerated to say the same about the Spanish Inquisition, but one does not get a full understanding of the real world functioning of the Holy Office in Spain by reading its rules and regulations, and one is faced with the added question of which rules and regulations to read in the sprawling mass of legislation that has come down to us.

In the case of the Holy Office as well as in secular courts in Spain, as in Italy, and, indeed as in France, the importance of the *ius commune* was that it 'radiated juridical logic, juridical concepts, and the terminology and mechanisms of legal reasoning – in short, the jurists', hence the judges', modes of being'. It 'informed every act and every opinion of the agents of justice because it penetrated the jurists' reasoning mechanisms and because its language was the vehicle for all ideas'.[73] Julian H. Franklin makes much the same point in his study of France, where it is claimed that the *ius commune* was never accepted as 'fully accepted by the French as an immediately binding common law' as it had been in Italy and Spain. Yet even Hotman, 'the most militant of the anti-Romanists' among French jurists, had to accept that 'Roman legal institutions had deeply affected practice, and even where practice was divergent the general categories of Roman jurisprudence were the basis of interpretation' for French lawyers.[74] It was precisely this common legal tradition based on Roman and canon law that informed the decisions made by the inquisitors who could never escape the imprint of their education. Like all other contemporary judges, they were bound up in the modes of thinking and arguing, and indeed in the very language of the *ius commune* in a way that they neither could nor attempted to escape even when they were applying a different set of laws and instructions. Indeed, just as Pedro Ortego Gil points out for judges in secular courts,[75] the inquisitors rarely speak about the law (*ley*) in their trial documents. Instead, they speak about justice (*derecho*). The law was not very significant, *derecho* was.

Sources to trials

The study of acquittals must by necessity start with the examination of judicial sources: trials, trial summaries, voting records, legislation and instructions issued to the courts, legal manuals, handbooks, and letters requesting and giving information on individual trials and thorny legal problems. Unfortunately, the archives of the Spanish Inquisition suffered destruction during a number of French invasions from the sixteenth to nineteenth centuries.[76] Most of the documentation from the Inquisition's central council, the *Suprema*, has survived, while the archives of many local tribunals have been lost in their entirety. A number of documents from the small Inquisition of the Canary Islands that were previously in private hands have been turned over to the *Museo de las Canarias*. These apart, only from Mexico, Cuenca, Toledo, and to a lesser degree Valencia and Zaragoza, have documents from the local tribunals been preserved in significant numbers.[77] This means that we have a limited number of *procesos*, original trial records. We have hardly any books of denunciations, and very few books of voting records where decisions on cases were written down as they were made, before those decisions were later recorded in the trial records. We do have a large number of cases, summaries, *relaciones de causas*, which have been preserved because they were sent to the *Suprema* in Madrid. The *procesos* and the *relaciones* are the two sources that form the mainstay of the study of inquisitorial sentencing in this book. The *relaciones de causas* are our only source to the trials in most tribunals, while the fact that they form a relatively large and long series of reports of activity sent in with regularity from all tribunals (even Cuenca, which was absent in Henningsen's study) makes it possible to calculate how much has been lost on the basis of the lacunae in the preserved documents.[78] Here also we have losses, due to the ravages of time, and the misplacement of documents in the archive in both historic and recent times, but nothing like that suffered by the archives of the local tribunals. The preserved *relaciones de causas* which have been located in the preparations for this book contain almost 64,000 trials. The *procesos* make up a fraction of that number, fewer than 4,000 in total. Hundreds of these are also known through the *relaciones de causas*.

The few preserved books of voting records have also been consulted, yet their value for this investigation has been disappointing since they rarely record the reason for the votes cast. Fiscal records have also been preserved to some degree, but they tend to be of limited value in the study of acquittals since these sentences rarely involved pecuniary elements. When sequestered property was sold off to pay for the defendant's upkeep during a trial, both the sequestration and sale were recorded in documents that give no information of the eventual sentence issued later. More important for this study has been the mass of instructions, *cartas acordadas* and other pieces of legislation which are discussed in the next chapter. These have been preserved in great numbers and little order, which means that they have been useful but difficult to work with.

Finally, letters are an important source of the functioning of the Spanish Inquisition. The inquisitors were great letter writers, personally writing a number of letters every day. Tens of thousands of these have been preserved while an even greater number have probably been lost. Many, perhaps all, those sent to the *Suprema* appear to have been preserved, most of them collected in loose boxes or bound volumes, while others have been misfiled. They often contain information kept out of the official trial records, and this is where we can find doubts about sentencing and guilt, even appeals on behalf of convicts by the inquisitors to the monasteries where the convicts were kept in reclusion,[79] requests for instructions, and traces of informal actions and of formal interrogations that entered protocols long lost or which never resulted in formal trials reported in the *relaciones*. Naturally, they also contain information about lost *procesos* which were reported in *relaciones* that nobody today can find. Equally obvious, it is impossible to go through all of them, at least in detail. The present author searched all the letters to and from Barcelona and Valencia before 1700 for mentions of trials for superstitions for an earlier book.[80] That alone took several months, and doing the same for all letters from all tribunals through their entire existence would take years if not decades if searching more broadly than for a single type of trials. Indeed, the richness of the documentation sometimes makes one despair of working with it. It was precisely the explosive increase in the number and length of *relaciones de causas* after 1700, when they were submitted monthly rather than yearly, that made Gustav Henningsen decide to limit his registration to the sixteenth and seventeenth centuries.[81]

Navigating such a mass of documents is a difficult task and one that could not have been realistically undertaken without access to EMID. EMID has both made it possible to locate and read 2,529 acquittals among more than 67,000 trials, and to put those exonerations in context by comparing them statistically to the much more numerous convictions. It thus depends on EMID's two main uses: as a detailed archival guide and as a source for more complete statistics of the activities of the Holy Office in Spain. Despite the extensive destruction of its archives, the Spanish Inquisition has bequeathed massive amounts of archival material to historians, so much that it can be difficult to find what we are looking for.

The modern researcher is not the first to note the overwhelming mass of documents produced by the Holy Office. The man in charge of putting the *Suprema*'s archive in order on the Inquisition's reestablishment after the French occupation ended in 1814 wrote complaining that an 'immense number of documents' in the archive were '*in caos*'. 'There is a multitude of folio books in many cabinets' wrote the despairing archivist, Thulian Ruíz de Reajar, adding that many were from the time of the Inquisition's foundation, others from territories long lost such as Sicily and Sardinia, fiscal records that 'because of their antiquity were in a useless state' and many trials 'against defendants whose remembrance is entombed under oblivion'. When complaining about the high number of uncatalogued sources, today's historians should remember that it could have been very different: Thulian Ruíz de Reajar recommended burning the archive.[82]

Notes

1 *Proceso* in AHN, Inq. Leg, 199, exp. 39.
2 *Proceso* in AHN, Inq, Leg, 112, exp. 15.

3 Joseph Pérez, *The Spanish Inquisition: A History* (London: Profile Books, 2004), 148–49.
4 The quantitative data for this study come from the Early Modern Inquisition Database (EMID), which, at the time of writing, contained data on 67,201 trials in the Spanish Inquisition, based on the source types outlined earlier. Trial data has been carefully classified and coded for a number of variables, including sentencing data.
5 For the various types of acquittals used by the Spanish Inquisition, see Chapter 4.
6 For the black legend, see, for example, J. N. Hillgarth, *The Mirror of Spain, 1500–1700: The Formation of a Myth* (Ann Arbor: University of Michigan Press, 2000); Charles Gibson, *The Black Legend: Anti-Spanish Attitudes in the Old World and the New* (New York: Knopf, 1971); William S. Maltby, *The Black Legend in England: The Development of Anti-Spanish Sentiment, 1558–1660* (Durham, NC: Duke University Press, 1971); Ricardo García Cárcel, *la leyenda negra: Historia y opinion* (Madrid: Alianza, 1998); Consuelo Maqueda Abreu, "Extranjeros, Leyenda Negra e Inquisición," *Revista de la Inquisición*, no. 5 (1996); Miguel Molina Martinez, *la leyenda negra* (Madrid: Nerea, 1991).
7 Ruth MacKay, *'Lazy, Improvident People': Myth and Reality in the Writing of Spanish History* (Ithaca, NY: Cornell University Press, 2006).
8 Jean Pierre Dedieu, "Les quatre temps de l'Inquisition," in *L'Inquisition espagnole, XVe–XIXe siècle*, ed. Bartolome Bennassar (Paris: Hachette, 1979).
9 The Inquisition's pronounced emphasis on confession stemmed from the dual nature of the Inquisition trial as seeking both judicial and penitential truths, and aiming to reintegrate the heretic into the Catholic church, if possible. See Jean Pierre Dedieu and Gunnar W. Knutsen, "La cause de foi dans l'Inquisition espagnole," *Annales*, no. 1 (2023): 1–26.
10 This incident still merits a fuller study. See Henry Kamen, *The Spanish Inquisition: A Historical Revision* (New Haven, CT: Yale University Press, 1997), 72–74; John Edwards, "Trial of an Inquisitor: The Dismissal of Diego Rodriguez Lucero, Inquisitor of Cordoba, in 1508," *Journal of Ecclesiastical History* 37, no. 2 (1986); Ana Christina Cuadro García, "Acción inquisitorial contra los judaizantes en Córdoba y crisis eclesiástica (1482–1508)," *Revista de historia moderna: Anales de la Universidad de Alicante*, no. 23 (2003); John Edwards, *The Inquisitors: The Story of the Grand Inquisitors of the Spanish Inquisition* (Stroud: Tempus, 2007), 41–55; Henry Charles Lea, *A History of the Inquisition of Spain*, 4 vols, vol. 1 (New York: Macmillan Co., 1906–08), 189–211.
11 María Paz Alonso Romero, *El proceso penal en Castilla (siglos XIII–XVIII)* (Salamanca: Ediciones Universidad de Salamanca, 1982), 228–34; Jean Pierre Dedieu, "L'Inquisition et le droit. Analyse formelle de la procedure inquisitoriale en cause de foi," *Melanges de la Casa de Velázquez* 23 (1987): 234–37; Henry Charles Lea, *A History of the Inquisition*, vol. 2, 561–63, 569–71; Giorgia Alessi Palazzolo, *Prova legale e pena la crisi del sistema tra evo medio e moderno*, Storia e diritto (Napoli: Jovene, 1979).
12 José Pedro Paiva, *Bruxaria e superstição num país sem 'caça às bruxas' 1600–1774*, 2nd ed. (Lisboa: Editorial Notícias, 2002), 208. Jeremy Black likewise suggests that many denunciations were never followed up by the Roman Inquisition, though the figures he suggest are both much higher and less certain than Paiva's. Christopher F. Black, *The Italian Inquisition* (New Haven, CT: Yale University Press, 2009), 72, 134.
13 For a recent attempt to utilize these, see Juan Ignacio Pulido Serrano and William Childers, *la Inquisición vista desde abajo: testificaciones de gente corriente ante el Santo Oficio*, ed. Juan Ignacio Pulido Serrano and William Childers (Iberoamericana, 2020).

14 Jean-Pierre Dedieu, *L'Administration de la foi: L'Inquisition de Tolède (XVIe–XVIIIe siécle)* (Madrid: Casa de Velázquez, 1989), 282.
15 Various letters from fiscal Paniuagua in BN, MS2440.
16 For these trials, see Gunnar W. Knutsen, *Servants of Satan and Masters of Demons: The Spanish Inquisition's Trials of Superstition, Valencia and Barcelona, 1478–1700* (Turnhout: Brepols, 2009); Agustí Alcoberro, "Cacera de bruixes, justícia local i Inquisició a Catalunya, 1487–1643: alguns criteris metodològics," *Pedralbes* II, no. 28 (2008).
17 Francisco Bethencourt, "The Auto da Fe: Ritual and Imagery," *Journal of the Warburg and Courtauld Institutes* 55 (1992); Maureen Flynn, "Mimesis of the Last Judgment: The Spanish Auto de Fe," *Sixteenth Century Journal* 22, no. 2 (1991); Consuelo Maqueda Abreu, *El auto da fe* (Madrid: Ediciones Istmo, 1992); Doris Moreno Martínez, "Una apacible idea de la gloria: El auto da fe barroco y sus escenarios simbólicos," *Manuscrits: Revista d'història moderna*, no. 17 (1999); Henry Charles Lea, *A History of the Inquisition of Spain*, 4 vols, vol. 3 (New York: Macmillan Co., 1906–08), 209–29; Francisco Bethencourt, *The Inquisition: A Global History, 1478–1834*, trans. Jean Birrell (Cambridge: Cambridge University Press, 2009), 246–315.
18 Lea, *A History*, vol. 2, 561; Lea, *A History*, vol. 3, 108; Bethencourt, *The Inquisition*, 280–81.
19 This can be traced back to contemporary critics and even autobiographical texts from those tried by the Inquisition, such as the Frenchman Dellon's story of his experiences with the Portuguese Inquisition in Goa. His book has been published in numerous editions and translations since its first appearance in 1687. The best modern edition is Charles Amiel and Anne Lima, eds., *L'Inquisition de Goa: la relation de Charles Dellon (1687)*, Collection Magellane (Paris: Editions Chandeigne, 1997).
20 French *parlements* avoided public punishment of effigies for this very reason. William Monter, *Judging the French Reformation: Heresy Trials by Sixteenth-Century Parlements* (Cambridge, MA: Harvard University Press, 1999), 4.
21 Maqueda Abreu, *El auto de fe*, 233.
22 Quoted in William Monter, *Frontiers of Heresy: The Spanish Inquisition from the Basque Lands to Sicily* (Cambridge: Cambridge University Press, 1990), 109.
23 AHN, Inq, Leg 3250, *relación de causas* from the *auto da fe* in Valladolid of 14 December 1704.
24 There are nine such cases presently recorded in EMID: all for Judaizing. Seven are from Cuenca in 1556, one from Llerena in 1580–81, and one from Logroño in 1615–16.
25 Valdés' instructions issued in Toledo 1561, article 62.
26 AHN, Inq, Lib 731, fols. 427v–429v.
27 AHN, Inq, Leg. 2022, exp. 5, fol. 4v.
28 AHN, INQ, lib. 1021, fols. 235r–269v.
29 Ana E. Schaposchnik, *Under the Eyes of the Inquisition: Crypto-Jews in the Ibero-American World (Peru, 1600s)* (Madison: University of Wisconsin, 2008), 134–35.
30 Lea, *A History*, vol. 1, 357.
31 This was another inheritance from the Medieval Inquisitions: James B. Given, *Inquisition and Medieval Society: Power, Discipline, and Resistance in Languedoc* (Cornell University Press, 2001), 62.
32 See, for example, L. Paramo, de origine et progressu officii sanctae Inquisitionis ejusque dignitate et ulititate, de Romani pontificis potestate et delegta inquisitorum edicto fidei et ordine judiciaris sancti officii quaestiones decem (Typographia Regia, 1598).

33 J.A. Llorente, *Histoire critique de l'Inquisition d'Espagne*, 4 vols. (chez Treuttel et Wurtz . . . [chez] Delaunay . . . [chez] P. Mongie ainé, 1817–1818).
34 See, for example, Nicolas Castrillo Benito, *El 'Reginaldo Montano': Primer libro polemico contra la Inquisición española* (Madrid: CSIC, 1991).
35 Originally published in French in Paris, it has continued to appear in new editions in Spanish up to our day. The twin factors of Llorente's personal experience with inquisitorial proceedings and his access to sources that later have been lost assures the continued relevance of his work. An abridged version appeared in English in 1826: Juan Antonio Llorente, *The History of the Inquisition of Spain, from the Time of Its Establishment to the Reign of Ferdinand VII: Composed from the Original Documents of the Archives of the Supreme Council and from Those of Subordinate Tribunals of the Holy Office* (G.B. Whittaker, 1826).
36 Gretchen D. Starr-LeBeau, *In the Shadow of the Virgin: Inquisitors, Friars, and Conversos in Guadalupe, Spain, Jews, Christians, and Muslims from the Ancient to the Modern World* (Princeton, NJ: Princeton University Press, 2003), 257.
37 This was not only exclusive to Spain but also practised in Italy and Portugal. For Italy, see, for example, Irene Fosi, *Convertire lo straniero forestieri e Inquisizione a Roma in età moderna* (Roma: Viella, 2011).
38 A prime example is Gustav Henningsen himself, who even devised the first statistical study of the Spanish Inquisition – the *relaciones de causas* project – principally as a way to identify and locate information on trials for witchcraft, his real interest.
39 These have been published a number of times, most recently in Gustav Henningsen, "The Database of the Spanish Inquisition," in *Vorträge zur Justizforschung, Geschichte und Theorie, band* 2, ed. Heinz Mohnhaupt and Dieter Simon (Frankfurt am Main: Vittorio Klostermann, 1993).
40 Jaime Contreras, El Santo Oficio de la Inquisición en Galicia, 1560–1700. Poder, *Sociedad y cultura* (Madrid: Akal Editor, 1982), 550. Note that Contreras here does not distinguish between absolution ad cautelam and absolución de la instance. More on this distinction in Chapter 3.
41 Cristian Berco, *Sexual Hierarchies, Public Status: Men, Sodomy, and Society in Spain's Golden Age* (Toronto: University of Toronto Press, 2007).
42 Knutsen, *Servants of Satan.*
43 Kamen, *The Spanish Inquisition*, 199. The number of acquittals he quotes comes from Contreras, El Santo Oficio de la Inquisición en Galicia, 1560–1700. Poder, *Sociedad y cultura*, 550.
44 Stephen Haliczer, *Inquisition and Society in the Kingdom of Valencia 1478–1834* (Berkeley: University of California Press, 1990), 80.
45 Dedieu, L'Administration de la foi.
46 Henry Charles Lea, *A History of the Inquisition.*
47 Lea, *A History of the Inquisition*, vol. 3, 106–08.
48 See, for example, Daniel N. Robinson, *Wild Beasts and Idle Humours: The Insanity Defense from Antiquity to the Present* (Cambridge, MA; London: Harvard University Press, 1996).
49 For example, one recent summing up of contemporary witness research (dubbed a 'consensus study report') has as an explicit aim to 'increase the chances that accurate identifications are made'. National Research Council, *Identifying the Culprit: Assessing Eyewitness Identification* (Washington, DC: The National Academies Press, 2014). A good starter, while somewhat dated, is David Frank Ross, J. Don Read, and Michael P. Toglia, eds., *Adult Eyewitness Testimony: Current Trends and Developments* (Cambridge: Cambridge University Press, 1994).
50 Pedro Ortego Gil, "Innocentia praesumpta: absoluciones en el Antiguo Régimen," *Cuadernos de Historia del Derecho*, no. 10 (2003).

51 As noted by Pablo Pérez García: Pablo Pérez García, "Perspectivas de análisis del proceso penal en el Antiguo Régimen: el procedimiento ordinario de Valencia Foral (ss XVI y XVII)," *Clío & Crímen: Revista del Centro de Historia del Crimen de Durango*, no. 10 (2013): 81.
52 Lynn, Between Court and Confessional, 28.
53 In fact, there were still inquisitors active under the old system in the crown of Aragon when the new centralized Inquisition was introduced there, meaning that there was some overlap. Lea, *A History*, vol. 1, 230.
54 For the medieval origins of inquisitorial proceedings, see Kelly, "Inquisition and the Prosecution"; Henry Ansgar Kelly, "The Right to Remain Silent: Before and After Joan of Arc," *Speculum* 68 (1993); Henry Ansgar Kelly, "Lollard Inquisitions: Due and Undue Process," in *The Devil, Heresy and Witchcraft in the Middle Ages: Essays in Honor of Jeffrey B. Russell*, ed. Alberto Ferreiro (Leiden: Brill, 1998).
55 Black, *The Italian Inquisition*, 56.
56 Elvira Mea, "O Santo Ofício português: da legislação à prática," in *Estudos em homenagem a João Francisco Marques*, ed. Luís António de Oliveira Ramos, Jorge Martins Ribeiro, and Amélia Polónia (Porto: Universidade do Porto. Faculdade de Letras, 2001).
57 González Novalin, "Las instrucciones de la Inquisición."
58 See, for example, the documents published in Henningsen, *The Salazar Documents*, 368–79.
59 Dedieu, "L'Inquisition et le droit."
60 Bellomo, *The Common Legal.*
61 Alonso Romero, *El proceso penal.*
62 Despite a large number of books on canon law, there is no complete edition of all these texts. Canon law did, of course, precede the inquisitorial procedure, and it also outlived it, being still in vigour today, indeed being updated.
63 The modern edition by Jiménez Monteserín has been superseded by the availability online of Gaspar Isidro de Argüello's collection from 1630. Miguel Jiménez Monteserín, *Introducción a la Inquisición española: documentos básicos para el estudio del Santo Oficio*, Biblioteca de visionarios, heterodoxos y marginados Segunda serie (Madrid: Editorial Nacional, 1981). de Argüello, *Instrucciones.*
64 Jonathan Seitz describes a somewhat similar situation for the Holy Office in Venice in his study of witchcraft trials: 'The Roman Inquisition was a relatively new institution with incomplete and sometimes conflicting guidance available to inquisitors facing the conflicting testimony of recalcitrant or dishonest witnesses, ambiguous evidence, and the variant approaches to discerning the supernatural one observes in these trials'. Jonathan Seitz, *Witchcraft and Inquisition in Early Modern Venice* (Cambridge: Cambridge University Press, 2011), 196.
65 Francisco Luque Muriel, "Los abecedarios como fuente para estudio de la legislacion," in *Perfiles juridicos de la Inquisición española*, ed. José Antonio Escudero (Madrid: Instituto de Historia de la Inquisición, Universidad Complutense de Madrid, 1989).
66 de Argüello, *Instrucciones.*
67 Garcia, Orden de processar en el Santo Oficio, recopilado de las instrucciones antiquas y modernas.
68 However, a number of inquisitors' manuals printed in Italy also circulated in Spain. Indeed, Spanish Inquisitors such as Simancas published instructions and other writings on the Inquisition in Latin in Italy. Lynn, *Between Court and Confessional.*
69 Gustav Henningsen, "la legislación secreta del Santo Oficio," in *Perfiles juridicos de la Inquisición española*, ed. José Antonio Escudero (Madrid: Instituto de Historia de la Inquisición, Universidad Complutense de Madrid, 1989).

70 Compare this with the Paris Parliament, where the tradition was carried forth by the judges themselves in a similar process: 'From father to son, from father-in-law to son-in-law, the traditions of the Parlement were instilled into successive generations and material mementoes – family portraits, books and manuscripts – were carefully preserved and handed on to each succeeding heir'. J. H. Shennan, *The Parlement of Paris* (London: Eyre & Spottiswoode, 1968).
71 Monter, *Judging the French Reformation: Heresy Trials by Sixteenth-Century Parlements*, 57–58. By the eighteenth century, on the other hand, the judges of the Paris Parlement did own extensive collections of royal decrees. Shennan, *The Parlement of Paris*, 133–34.
72 Monter, *Judging the French Reformation: Heresy Trials by Sixteenth-Century Parlements*, 20. In a similar vein, Fredrick II of Sicily never put his own law code, the *Liber Augustalis*, on the curriculum when he reformed the law school in 1224. Instead, the students studied Roman and canon law. Such was the importance of the *ius commune*. Bellomo, *The Common Legal*, 94.
73 Bellomo, *The Common Legal*, 90–91.
74 Julian H. Franklin, *Jean Bodin and the Sixteenth-Century Revolution in the Methodology of Law and History* (New York: Colombia University Press, 1963), 37, 40, 51.
75 Ortego Gil, "El arbitrio de los jueces inferiores: su alcance y limitaciones," 138.
76 The best overview of the preserved sources remains Gustav Henningsen, "The Archives and Historiography of the Spanish Inquisition," in *The Inquisition in Early Modern Europe. Studies on Sources and Methods*, ed. Gustav Henningsen and John Tedeschi (Dekalb: Northern Illinois University Press, 1986). To this needs to be added later discoveries of sources in Valencia, and the deposit of previously privately held documents in the *Museo de Canarias*. Luis Alberto Anaya Hernández and Francisco T. Fajardo Spínola, "Los estudios sobre la Inquisición de las Islas Canarias. Estado de la cuestión y perspectivas," in *Actas de la II Reunión Científica de la Asociacion Española de Historia Moderna Moratalla 1992* (1993). José María Cruselles Gómez, "la primera contabilidad inquisitorial. El fondo del Archivo del Reino de Valencia (1482–1527)," in *En el primer siglo de la Inquisición Española: fuentes documentales, procedimientos de análisis, experiencias de investigación* (València: Universitat de València, 2013, 2013).
77 Henningsen, "The Archives and Historiography."
78 Henningsen, "The Database."
79 Gunnar W. Knutsen, "Where Did the Witches Go? Spanish Witches After Their Trials," in *Pathways of the Past: Festschrift to Sølvi Sogner on Her 70th Anniversary*, ed. Hilde Sandvik, Kari Telste, and Gunnar Thorvaldsen (Oslo: Novus Forlag, 2002), 205–06.
80 Knutsen, *Servants of Satan*.
81 Henningsen, "The Database."
82 AHN, Inq, Lib 502, fols. 315r–316v.

2

A SYSTEM GEARED TOWARDS CONVICTION

The Inquisition's jurisdiction

The inquisitors of the Holy Office in Spain were formally papal heresy inquisitors, that is, they were (through the manoeuvres of the Spanish monarchy) appointed on apostolic authority to make Inquisition into heresy. However, their jurisdiction promptly expanded from heresy proper to a much wider range of offences. One of the reasons for this was the difficulty of pinpointing exactly who was a heretic, which we will discuss more extensively below. In addition to this, the jurisdiction of the Spanish Inquisition expanded in order to protect the Holy Office from outside influence.

The first development of this kind was to reserve all cases, both civil and criminal, for every type of personnel in any way affiliated with the Inquisition to the exclusive jurisdiction of the Holy Office. We have not included such cases in this study, and their inclusion would surely have increased the numbers of those acquitted substantially. The reason for giving the Holy Office exclusive jurisdiction over all offences and lawsuits involving its own personnel was to allow it freedom of action without countersuits or attempts at impeding its operation by initiating actions in other courts, the most common way of paralysing judicial operations in early modern Spain.[1] This jurisdiction certainly improved the Inquisition's efficacy, but it also caused great problems in enforcement, both since it was so violently disliked by other courts and because it was likewise exploited to the full by the officials of the Holy Office. It was therefore both a strength and a distraction since it was a source of constant strife and lawsuits as the Inquisition became an attractive patron for (presumably) God-fearing yet criminally inclined groups of men, in particular among the Inquisition's armed

DOI: 10.4324/9781003455691-2

branch, the familiars. Henry Charles Lea may have exaggerated when he stated of them that 'they were largely drawn from the turbulent element, seeking the position for the protection afforded against secular justice',[2] but the amount of mischief they were up to can scarcely be overstated. When one includes the trials of faith, the total number of trials against these men by the Inquisition could reach preposterous proportions: during a period of 40 years 1595–1634, the Holy Office in Sicily carried out trials against almost 500 familiars, one-third of its total personnel.[3] Of course, Sicily is an extreme case, due to the feuds among Sicilian nobility. However, the general point stands: the familiars were a constant source of embarrassment and conflict, yet necessary for the Inquisition.

Before we can get to the central issue of what heresy was and how it manifested itself, we must distinguish between two fundamental concepts that may be alien to modern readers, those of the internal and external forums.[4] These are the two jurisdictions which together make up Catholic ecclesiastical jurisdiction. The internal forum is the forum of conscience and deals with the individual Catholic's relationship to God. The external forum, on the other hand, is concerned with matters touching the public and the social good of the corporate body of Catholics. Thus, the forgiveness of sins is a matter for the internal forum, while redressing religious offences that had harmed the whole body of believers was dealt with in the external forum. Some offences would fall under both categories, and this was the case with most of those tried by the Spanish Inquisition. Each of the two forums was further divided into two, as shown in Figure 2.1.

The sacramental internal forum is the forum for sacramental confession and penitence and concerns the remittance of sins by God. It did not fall under the jurisdiction of the Inquisition, which reconciled repentant defendants to the Church but not to God: depending on the degree of heresy, a priest or bishop administered divine pardon once the penitent had been reconciled with the Church by way of the Inquisition's sentence and could again approach the sacrament. When it came to the internal forum, the Holy Office was only concerned with the non-sacramental branch, and even then, in relatively rare cases – for instance, when inquisitorial courts lifted the ecclesiastical penalties incurred for heresy by members of the clergy.

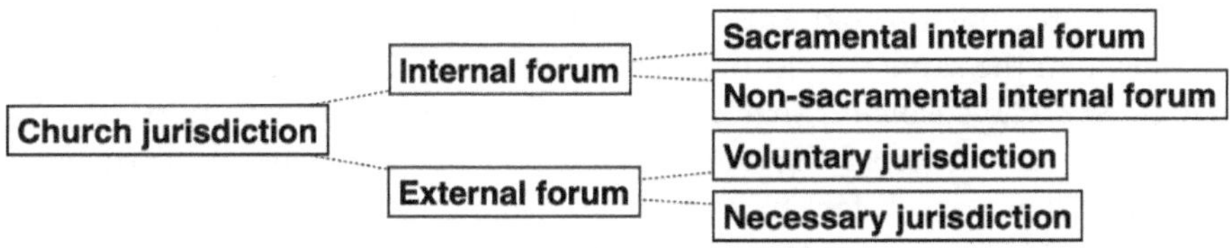

FIGURE 2.1 The internal and external forums.

Every offence that formed part of the judicial forum and the Inquisition's jurisdiction also incurred ecclesiastical penalties that could only be lifted after a sacramental confession. Thus, the two confessions were necessary for the salvation and the social reintegration of the defendant. Yet the influential Italian jurist Prospero Farinacci who was much referred to by Spanish inquisitors makes clear that the inquisitors do not absolve in the forum of conscience (i.e. the internal forum) but in the external forum and only those heretics that they try judicially and penance.[5] It is not infrequent to read that the inquisitors ordered the defendant at the end of the trial to go to a confessor and receive sacramental absolution in the case of a light sentence, just as every convict at an *auto da fe* (apart from the recalcitrant) was sacramentally absolved as part of the solemn ritual. A confession by the defendant would impact both forums, and one should think of an inquisitorial trial as following two parallel tracks at once: one concerning the defendant's alleged crimes and possible punishment by authorities, the other his alleged sins and possible mercy and forgiveness by the Church. Indeed, the *Repertorium inquisitorum* repeats and stresses that there is a difference between absolution of guilt and absolution of punishment.[6]

The non-sacramental internal forum was that of ecclesiastical censures which the defendants might have incurred, and the inquisitors had the power to lift these, at least temporarily, as we shall see when we come to the subject of absolution *ad cautelam*. This was also the case with a gradually increasing number of those convicted: in addition to receiving sacramental absolution after their conviction, a growing number were recorded as also being absolved *ad cautelam* of whatever ecclesiastical censures they might have incurred.

Heresy was the Spanish Inquisition's raison d'être and at the core of every offence that was tried by the Holy Office, although, strictly speaking, the vast majority of defendants were never in any real sense heretics – even in the eyes of the inquisitors. At its heart, heresy is a thought crime, and as such nearly impossible not just to prove, but also to actually identify with any certainty. Unlike ordinary crimes, it does not involve acts that take place at a particular place at a specific time, and it is therefore outside the scope of the ordinary system of proofs of the *ius commune* with its reliance on witness testimony detailing physical acts. Rather, heresy is a state, which may or may not be expressed in the exterior through speech and actions. These expressions are provable through the ordinary system of proof, and could therefore be judged in the same way as ordinary offences were. However, there always remained some suspicion that even those demonstrably not guilty of what they were accused of saying and doing, might in their heart of hearts entertain ideas that were in fact heretical.

In theory, heresy is easy to define: a heretic is a baptized Christian who willingly and knowingly holds other beliefs than those of the Catholic Church.

This apparently simple definition becomes unwieldy almost immediately when one tries to apply it to a person: the person must have had sufficient religious schooling to know what the Catholic church teaches and proscribes, must have the mental capacity to be able to make reasoned and deliberate choices, and must have expressed contradictory beliefs in words or acts that allows one to define his beliefs as contrary to Catholic doctrine.

'He who errs through simple-mindedness, believing that the Church holds forth what he believes does not commit heresy', writes Farinacci, 'because the simple-mindedness of the person destroys the presumption of evil intention'.[7] However, even this he subsequently moves to both extend by several amplifications and limit by limitations and sub-limitations, such as 'when persistence and impenitence coincide in a simpleminded, the simplicity does not free him from neither the sin nor the crime of heresy'.[8] And, 'all the sub-limitations above in which I said that simple-mindedness does not free one from heresy, do not change that in any case the punishment will be lesser'.[9] Moving on to ignorance, Farinacci states that, 'ignorance frees one from the crime of heresy', 'no crime sullies he who does not know', and 'one does not commit the crime of heresy without agreement and consent'.[10] To this also he applies a number of extensions and limitations, such as 'this [i.e. ignorance] is not valid in those matters where one is explicitly obliged to believe'.[11] Thus, even ignorance had its limits. Yet, 'it does nevertheless free one from heresy and the punishment derived from that'![12] At this point, it should be stressed that the Holy Office imposed both punishment (*pena*) and penance (*penitencia*), and that these sometimes overlapped. Thus, monetary exactions could be made as both punishment and penitence. While the difference was perfectly clear to early modern jurists and theologians, it may be presumed to be much less so to many of those tried by the Holy Office, and indeed to modern observers.

The Holy Office thus had to pass judgement based not only on the facts of the case in terms of what was actually said and done, as in an ordinary criminal court, but also on the qualities of the defendant along several axes. Instead of investigating an act at a specific time and place as in an ordinary criminal case, the inquisitors had to decipher the mental state of the accused, *in addition to* discovering whatever he had said and done and, finding out what those actions and statements signified.

A simpler situation was obtained with offences such as sodomy and bestiality, which were tried according to the procedure of local secular courts. The prosecution of sodomy (and later bestiality) by the Spanish Inquisition developed fitfully and somewhat fortuitously, starting with a single case against one of the Inquisition's enemies in Zaragoza and eventually becoming a recognized part of the jurisdiction of the Holy Office after a few decades of wrangling.[13] As William Monter notes, this broke the unity of the Spanish Inquisition in two ways, first geographically because this jurisdiction was limited to the tribunals of the Aragonese secretariat (Barcelona, Zaragoza, Valencia, Mallorca, Pamplona, Sicily, and Sardinia). Second, it ruptured the procedural unity of the Holy Office since the Pope demanded that such trials be conducted according to local secular trial procedures and not those of the Inquisition in heresy trials.[14] Furthermore, here the physical acts were in and of themselves the object of the investigation with the mental state of the defendant of limited interest apart from the question of whether he or she had been the victim of coercion in sodomy cases. In both sodomy and bestiality trials, the defendant was supposed to be given the name of his accuser and frequently they faced off physically with opportunity for cross-examination. However, the Holy Office never gained full an exclusive jurisdiction over these offences. As with bigamy and witchcraft and superstitions, these did not belong to Spanish Inquisition alone, but were subject to *fuero mixto*, which meant that the Holy Office had to share jurisdiction with other courts that never completely gave up their pursuit of such offenders.

While medieval inquisitors had punished sodomites, the Holy Office had no such precedent for assuming jurisdiction over bigamy. On the other hand, here there was the fig leaf of some pretended whiff of heresy in the alleged disregard for the sacrament of marriage. Nobody, of course, seriously entertained the idea that men and women who remarried while their first spouse was still alive were somehow real heretics who remarried because of a different theological standpoint than that held by the Catholic Church. Lea speculates that the initial impetus may have been that 'it obtained a foothold through the laxity of the marriage tie among Moors and Jews, so that bigamy, like abstinence from pork and wine and change of linen on Saturday, created suspicion of heresy'.[15] That certainly does not hold for the period after 1550 when the vast majority of those tried for bigamy were Old Christians. In any case, neither bishops nor secular authorities were ever willing to fully surrender their well-established jurisdiction over bigamy, and clashes were frequent.

A similar situation was obtained with witchcraft and other forms of magical crimes grouped under the heading of superstitions by the Inquisition: bishops and secular courts never surrendered their jurisdiction and continued to try such cases in parallel with the Holy Office.[16] The Inquisition appears to have been able to prevail in this as in so many other matters when it was determined to fight against the other courts for jurisdiction in individual cases, but it frequently chose not to do so.[17] Here its jurisdiction was clearer again: since magic did not work, magic and witchcraft could only produce results through the intervention of the Devil. The Devil never did anyone any favours, so if he or his demons intervened on somebody's behalf it was a clear indication that they had entered into some kind of arrangement, a pact, which could be either explicit or implicit. This pact could, according to theologians, only mean that the person in question had given the Devil the sole thing that he wanted: to be worshipped as a God. This was apostasy, formal heresy. Yet, again it was not possible for even the most hostile observer to believe that the abandoned Valencian wife who burned oranges on the fire and prayed to Saint Helena to bring her husband back home was in fact a devil-worshiping formal heretic who had forsaken God.[18]

The Inquisition also assumed the jurisdiction over certain aspects of clerical discipline, most notably that of marrying while in Holy Orders and soliciting sexual favours in the confessional. The latter somehow frequently gets confused with a general inquisitorial jurisdiction over the sex lives of priests. In fact, the Holy Office did not care about, nor have jurisdiction over priests who held mistresses and concubines; that was the bishop's business. It did, however, prosecute priests who abused the sacrament of confession to make sexual advances, frequently putting forth dubious theological claims to their victims about their own ability to erase the sin if only the lady in question would comply.[19] As with bigamy, the Inquisition's claim to jurisdiction rested on the assertion that the actions demonstrated a disregard for the teaching of the Catholic Church on the nature of the sacraments of marriage, and of confession in the case of soliciting priests. Again, nobody could seriously entertain the idea that these, admittedly, immoral men were moved by theology rather than biology in their search for sexual gratification.

While those who impersonated officers of the Inquisition were prosecuted for impeding the exercise of the Holy Office, those who impersonated clerics could be prosecuted for – again – heretically abusing or misconstruing a sacrament. Given that the priesthood was not a sacrament to Lutherans and Calvinists this was not quite as outlandish as it might sound. Yet those who did impersonate priests were more likely to be drunk or seeking sexual pleasure (for example by asking women to bare their breasts in order to place a crucifix over their hearts) than to be formal heretics demonstrating their disregard for Catholic doctrine.

Organization

The judicial practice of heresy Inquisition started in the Middle Ages with the naming of individual papal (apostolic) inquisitors and the endowing of the bishops with the ordinary right – and obligation – to perform *inquisitio* in their dioceses whenever there was suspicion of heresy, either themselves or by appointing episcopal inquisitors by virtue of their own authority.[20] The transition from inquisitors to Inquisitions has engendered some controversy[21] but need not occupy us here. What is not controversial is that the Spanish Inquisition was something new compared to its medieval predecessors: a permanent ecclesiastical court acting on papal authority and under royal control, with its own permanent buildings, staff, income, and possessions.

Like every other court of law, the Spanish Inquisition had been brought into existence to address a supposed problem and repress certain forms of socially circumscribed activities. Far from being an attempt to redress conflict by compromise settlement, it was designed to ensure compliance by punishment and publicity, breaking the offender's will to resist, if possible. The Medieval inquisitorial practice that the Spanish Holy Office built on had been developed after preaching and conversion failed to alone remove heresy. Inquisition in the Middle Ages was but one of several tools used to attempt to maintain unity within the Catholic church. It was meant for those heretics who could not be gently persuaded, yet whose capacity for physical resistance did not require an army to overcome.[22] It sat uneasily somewhere between preaching and crusade, encompassing elements of both attempts at persuasion and the forgiving of sins on the one hand and the physical destruction of the recalcitrant on the other.

Such a span of activities required a number of competent personnel, equipment, housing, and supplies. In short, it required organization, precisely what the Medieval antecedents took a long time to develop. At first, the Medieval inquisitors, frequently Dominican friars, lived in the houses of their order, while the men and means of physical constraint were supplied by secular authorities. This was in the long run insufficient, and in Bohemia by the 1330s, there had developed, based in Prague, 'one of the nearest things to a permanent office of the Inquisition in later medieval Europe, with its own building, its library, and a collection of registers'.[23]

This sort of infrastructure was what the new Spanish Inquisition was also provided with: buildings to house its activities and archives, and a substantial salaried staff. This created an institution which existed independently of the individual inquisitors, which outlived them and which did not cease to exist upon their death or the death of the inquisitors general who had named them, or even that of the pope who had named the inquisitor general who had named the inquisitors, a major concern in the first years of the Spanish Inquisition as it was making the transition from the medieval system to the early modern institution.[24] This, in turn, required an independent income, which then engendered its own necessity for bookkeeping and salaried officials to take care of finances when the Inquisition tribunals ceased to depend on the royal treasury.[25] The means of physical constraint continued to be supplied by the state: local executioners performed the torture and undertook the executions, but the torture chamber and the prisons now belonged to the Holy Office which no longer depended on secular authorities for these things. The prison wardens also were in the employ of the Inquisition, and the Holy Office had its own group of armed men to support it in the familiars. Yet the real muscle behind the institution continued to be the state which put its full machinery of violence, from executioners at work to soldiers on guard, at the disposal of the Holy Office.

To cover the territory of the Spanish mainland a number of tribunals were set up. After some variations in the early decades, a fixed number of peninsular tribunals were the end result.[26] Additional tribunals were set up in Majorca, the Canaries, Sicily, Sardinia, and in Mexico, Cartagena de Indias, and Lima in the Spanish Indies. These local tribunals were subject to a central council in Madrid, the *Suprema*,[27] led by the Inquisitor general.[28] There was thus a formal hierarchy, a permanent bureaucracy, and a territorial division which did not coincide with any other political or ecclesiastical division. This was done to reduce the influence of other political and religious institutions over the actions of the Holy Office.[29] Likewise, as mentioned earlier, those employed or in some other way affiliated with the Inquisition could be tried by no other court.[30] This was the cause of innumerable conflicts of jurisdiction, and perhaps the most legally controversial aspect of the Spanish Inquisition, attracting political opposition as early as the Cortes of Mozón in 1512. It was an important and attractive privilege, especially for the familiars who did not enjoy the ecclesiastical privileges that many other employees of the Inquisition did. However, the Inquisition was not the only court or institution in early modern Spain to enjoy such privileges. Apart from the *fuero militar* which reserved to military tribunals the right to try serving military personnel, the *cruzada* claimed the sole right to try its own personnel, as indeed did the Catholic Church more generally for its clergy in Spain right up to 1868.[31] If the personnel of the Spanish Inquisition enjoyed extraordinary freedom in the exercise of their functions, it was because the Holy Office was exceptionally successful in using traditional means and privileges in defending itself from outside interference.

Personnel

The Inquisition employed a significant number of men in various positions apart from the inquisitors themselves. In addition to the salaried staff and the familiars, the Inquisition had a corps of *commisarios* who took depositions and witness statements for the Holy Office in the districts when neither inquisitors nor witnesses could be expected to travel. The theologians employed as *calificadores* used the theological expertise that the inquisitors lacked to check if statements or acts should be considered heretical or not. Their statements were essential to the decision of whether the facts of the case had relevance for the Inquisition or not, in other words, if there was to be a trial or not.[32] Many other men in the Inquisition's Service, both salaried and unsalaried, are of no great importance to us since they to very little degree were in a position to directly impact the outcome of trials. In the following, we shall briefly meet the men who did systematically influence the trial outcomes, starting with the inquisitors themselves.

Inquisitors and fiscals

More than half a century ago, Julio Caro Baroja noted the paradox that while much had been written about the Holy Office, almost nobody had shown any interest in the figure of the inquisitor, as opposed to the inquisitor general. Neither detractors nor apologists, historians, nor critics had been much concerned with perhaps the most central person in the inquisitorial machinery.[33] His own study and the few pages by Bartholomé Bennassar 16 years later long formed the mainstay of our knowledge of the inquisitors. They emphasized the inquisitors' humanity, that they were not monsters. Frail, arrogant, ambitious, passionate, lecherous, and greedy, but also noble, generous, compassionate, competent, learned, and cultured men of letters.

In a fine modern study, Kimberly Lynn writes that the Spanish inquisitors were motivated by a potent combination of careerism and ideological commitment, a blend that varied from judge to judge in balance and content and that, for each individual was also liable to change over time and develop in a dynamic relationship to his acquired experience and to the particular situations in which he found himself.[34]

In short, they were representative of the group of men they sprang from; those lawyers educated at some of Spain's best universities, frequently belonging to the prestigious *collegios mayores*, and who came to rule Spain and her empire.

Despite the appearance of several prosopographical studies of the Roman inquisitors, we have no such large-scale studies on Spain.[35] The general lines of the inquisitors' identity are, however, agreed upon: They were, as a rule, members of the secular clergy, frequently from the gentry, educated in canon and ordinarily also Roman law (i.e., the *ius commune*) at some of the finest universities in Spain. They were generally not theologians and they frequently served as judges in a secular or church court before becoming inquisitors. Many served in more than one inquisitorial tribunal, and a number of them later became bishops. Yet this is not based on systematic study of the whole corps of inquisitors, but rather based on observations from a single tribunal in a number of different monographs,[36] or studies of a smaller group, such as those who became bishops or formed part of the Spanish Inquisition's highest leadership in Madrid.[37] This lack of studies of inquisitors is all the more striking given the much greater number of studies of the Inquisition's unsalaried officers, the familiars.[38] Contrary to Italy, we also know very little about how individual inquisitors affected the behaviour of the tribunals where they served. The inquisitors enjoyed great discretion in their decision-making. This was a feature of contemporary legal culture, and a consequence of the legal doctrine known as *arbitrium*, which we will discuss below.

The inquisitor was a functionary, a judicial bureaucrat following rules and well aware of his own rights as he ascended the professional and social ladder. Bennassar writes of the inquisitors' proclivity to end whatever business they attended to, even if it was the confession of a defendant that finally had started talking, when it was time for their midday break.[39] The office of the inquisitor was often simply one of several in a long career, which might have started out as cathedral canon and ended as viceroy or councillor on one of the royal councils in Madrid. The Holy Office was tightly woven into the fabric of Spanish legal and judicial systems, and the inquisitors were important royal servants.

The profile of the fiscal, the Inquisition's prosecutor, was similar to that of the inquisitor, and many fiscals did indeed later become inquisitors. As the lowest-ranking academically trained jurist on the tribunal, he was inevitably given some of the least desirable routine tasks of overseeing the compilation and production of many of the Inquisition's registries and indices which he later used to produce his accusations and appeals to the inquisitors.[40] As the one formally initiating prosecution, he also at times protested against acquittals and suspensions, although the state of the evidence precludes us from knowing how common this was. At times, the fiscal would also formally protest the inaction of the inquisitors, such as when the fiscal Paniagua in a series of letters in 1619 attempted to get the inquisitors in Barcelona to take action when alleged witches were prosecuted in secular courts.[41] The inquisitors favoured not getting involved, simply noting the lack of any evidence of crimes pertaining to the Holy Office.[42]

Perhaps one key to approaching the subject of acquittals in the Spanish Inquisition, then, is to consider that they were the result of trials presided over by career bureaucrats who were supposed to follow an entangled mass of rules and regulations regulating decision-making processes in cases dealing with matters whose theological technicalities often eluded them.

Local staff

While the inquisitors and fiscals moved from one tribunal to another during their careers, the rest of the staff comprised local men who normally remained in the service of a single tribunal their entire lives. Some came from families that served the same tribunal for generations, a practice implicitly encouraged by the Inquisition's habit of letting heirs inherit positions or allowing them to be passed on to the incumbent's son-in-law if he had no sons, and even selling them to other interested parties whose appointment was agreeable to the inquisitor general. For example, in 1750, Vicente Salvador y del Olmo informed the Suprema that the del Olmo family had served the tribunal in Valencia for 172 years.[43] This practice caused a great deal of continuity in how business was conducted within each tribunal, since jailors, doormen, scribes and so forth had frequently observed proceedings from the sidelines for years or even decades before assuming their posts. This served as a counterweight to the fact that the inquisitors had no local roots and were frequently moving between different courts and inquisitorial tribunals. This made them dependent on the local knowledge of the tribunal's other staff. As Lu Ann Homza has recently shown, this could have disastrous consequences when the inquisitors did not understand or even know what their employees were doing.[44]

The Holy Office made one significant invention which has received short shrift in the historiography of the institution, but frequent mention in more general legal history: that of the office of advocate for the defendant – a severely understudied character in the history of the Holy Office – who was also eventually made an employee of the Inquisition. These lawyers formed part of the tribunal's regular staff yet were tasked with representing the defendant's interests. Consequently, Starr-LeBeau finds that the advocate 'served as a mediator between the Holy Office, of which he was a part, and the defendant, whom he represented'.[45]

Most historians who have not worked on the original trials hold a rather dim view of the advocates and their functions. John Edwards, for example, thinks they were dissuaded from 'mounting an effective defence', and that it 'was evident that the career prospects of practitioners were unlikely to be enhanced by mounting an effective defence of such clients'.[46] However, those historians who have studied full trials in some detail have rendered a far more positive verdict on their efforts. Haim Beinart found that it 'can be fairly said that in almost every case the *procuradores* fulfilled their mission in defending their clients'.[47] Gretchen D. Starr-LeBeau also found attorneys to have diligently and sometimes effectively defended their clients within the limits imposed by the Inquisition's rules and regulations.[48] By closely following the development of the trials they studied, both Beinart and Starr-LeBeau were able to demonstrate that individual attorneys developed and deployed different strategies to defend their charges, sometimes vigorously and successfully, making the advocate an all the more intriguing figure. This is even more so when we consider that what little we know of the advocate is based on research on the Spanish Inquisition's first years, and nothing has so far been written on the advocate's role and impact in the following three centuries in a steadily more formalized and bureaucratic judicial system where Váldes' instructions of 1561 severely reduced their room for manoeuvre.

Finally, for our purposes, we must also mention the ordinary and the *consultores*. The first was the bishop's representative. His presence in the Holy Office thus formally maintained and yet usurped the bishops' right to hold Inquisitions within their dioceses,[49] while the latter were judges from the local chancery. These men passed sentence in every trial together with the inquisitors. They implicated the local elites both secular and religious in the operations of the Holy Office and their acquiescence was necessary for any legal sentence to be issued – unless the matter was decided centrally by the *suprema* in Madrid. These men were all drawn from the same group of *letrados* as the inquisitors (though the *consultores* were normally not men of the cloth) and shared their outlook and world view. They had studied at the same universities, read the same books, and their career paths were frequently similar, beginning their careers with postings to similar courts of first instance. The ordinary might deserve special mention since he represented the bishop and more than one hundred Spanish bishops had previously served as inquisitors before their elevation to a bishopric.

Operations

The inquisitorial trial in the early modern period followed a general pattern that had been established by medieval Inquisitions two centuries before the Spanish Inquisition was founded. It also closely resembled proceedings in Spanish secular courts, and both were based on the common European judicial tradition known as the *ius commune*, composed of Roman and canon law.[50] The inquisitors themselves were trained as lawyers in Spanish universities with the rest of the *letrado* elite that they formed part of, and there it was precisely the *ius commune* that they studied.

The way we think of trials is deeply influenced by our own times and the depiction of trials in contemporary culture, which again tends to be dominated by the contemporary judicial system of the United States, based on English common law. We thus tend of think of trials as public spectacles, and an adversarial process hinging on the two parties giving contradictory and diverging presentations and interpretations of evidence that has previously been produced, followed by a weighing and evaluation of that evidence by an independent third party in the form of judge and jury. A trial in the Holy Office was something very different, as the investigation and hence production of evidence was intertwined with the evaluation of evidence, all of it overseen in secret by the same individuals. Simply put, apart from an initial preliminary examination of evidence and questioning of witnesses that convinced the inquisitors that they had a case that was worth bringing to trial, the real investigation of the alleged crime was not to take place before the formal trial had been started.

The investigation and the trial were consequently inseparable parts of the same process, and the operations of the Holy Office cannot be conveniently divided into investigation and trial, or the production and evaluation of evidence. These operations were conducted in secrecy, at least ideally or in principle, as we shall have occasion to see, and they were handled according to the principle of *arbitrium*. Before we sketch the trial itself we shall have to examine these two principles. After that we can turn to the techniques the inquisitors used to put together evidence in their trials, before we finally look at sentencing.

Arbitrium

The discretion that inquisitors had is frequently referred to as a central characteristic of the Inquisition. In fact, it was the doctrine of *arbitrium*, which was a key feature of that contemporary legal culture. This was what allowed the inquisitors to significantly influence case selections and trial outcomes. *Arbitrium*, usually rendered in English as arbitrary justice, was an aspect of the *ius commune* that dominated the courts in large parts of Europe in the medieval and early modern periods. Essentially it meant that decisions were arbitrated by the judges, in the sense that they relatively freely decided trial outcomes and punishments according to the circumstances of individual cases, rather than follow detailed legislation, or indeed any legislation at all. Somewhat counterintuitively this arose from how tightly regulated punishment and evidence was in the *ius commune*, where ordinary punishments could only be inflicted where there was full evidence in the form of a confession or two perfect witnesses to the deed. Following this to the letter would have meant that many crimes would go unpunished, and it led to protracted discussions by medieval and early modern European jurists about how to balance the rights of the accused against society's need to also punish those many crimes to which there were not two perfect witnesses to the entire deed.

An obvious way out (apart from the unthinkable one of changing the law and its evidentiary rules) was to allow judges to inflict *extraordinary* punishments when the evidence convinced them of guilt without satisfying the legal requirements for *ordinary* punishment. The most common solution was therefore to accept that while the regular punishment could not be inflicted without full proof, various forms of circumstantial evidence could justify 'extraordinary' punishment.[51] This would then be much lighter than the 'ordinary' punishment prescribed by law, but allow crimes to be punished without formally disregarding the rules of evidence received through the *ius commune*. The alternative, as famously noted by John H. Langbein, was a complete dependence on torture to extract confessions in order to obtain full proof.[52] This is one part of what became known as the judge's *arbitrium*, and it was generally reserved for the higher end of the judicial hierarchy with well-educated judges – such as the inquisitors. Indeed, Pedro Ortego Gil argues that early modern lower-level judges in Spain were more likely to follow the law because of their lack of legal training had not exposed them to the ideas of the *ius commune*.[53] In a similar fashion, Giorgia Alessi Palazzolo found that lower-level judges were formally bound to follow the letter of the law, while higher and university-educated judges were not bound by the law and were allowed to exercise their *arbitrium*.

The *ius commune* and the doctrine of *arbitrium* was what the future inquisitors in the Holy Office in Spain studied in university before setting out on their legal carriers. This was not exceptional.[54] Manlio Bellomo makes the case that many trials in medieval and early modern Europe were decided based simply on the *ius commune* rather than statutory law, and that on much of the continent, jurists were in fact frequently trained in *ius commune* rather than what was nominally the law of the land.[55] The *ius commune* informed not so much their view of what was punishable and so forth, but much more profoundly they used its rules of evidence, its routines for evaluating testimony, and the very language of the *ius commune* shaped how they spoke of their cases.[56] *Arbitrium* therefore permitted the Spanish Inquisitors to impose punishments that had no explicit foundation in inquisitorial law, based on evidence that did not meet the full requirements for legal proof for offences that had not been detailed in legislation. Usually, this was less dramatic than it sounds, and solely meant the infliction of a lower punishment than that set by the law in cases where there was less evidence than that formally required for a conviction but where the sum of circumstantial evidence convinced the sentencing panel of the defendant's guilt. Nevertheless, the room for manoeuvre was enormous and afforded great possibilities for both abuses and generosity by the Inquisition, in particular when coupled with the notorious secrecy of the Holy Office. In the inquisitors' evaluation of the evidence produced for the defence of the accused, María del Pilar Rábade Obradó finds 'great disparities' between tribunals, 'caused by some particularly severe inquisitors'.[57]

The legislation of the Spanish Inquisition appears to reflect this liberty, and the instructions of the Spanish Inquisition make frequent and explicit references to the inquisitors' *arbitrium*. As we have seen earlier, this legislation was made up of a mass of instructions, regulations, and *cartas acordadas* so disparate that no single collection of all legislative documents ever existed. Hence the inquisitors often used their *arbitrium*, which, in turn, frequently meant that they instead of using inquisitorial legislation properly based their decisions on the *ius commune*, since it 'informed every act and every opinion of the agents of justice because it penetrated the jurists' reasoning mechanisms and because its language was the vehicle for all ideas', to quote Bellomo.[58] Farinacci writes that with 'a truly impenitent or relapsed heretic who confesses his heresy or has been proven to be [a heretic]' no-one can dispense or commute his sentence, but also that 'the punishment or penitence inflicted on penitent heretics is arbitrary: that the inquisitors can increase or decrease it depending on the quality of the facts and the persons'.[59] This is exactly the difference between ordinary and extraordinary punishment.

However, *arbitrium* was not without limits and in some cases, inquisitors may occasionally have exceeded their authority.[60] The *relaciones de causas* of the Spanish Inquisition from time to time contain marginal notes that were dictated by the members of the *Suprema*: 'Should have been given more punishment', 'appears to be excessive punishment', 'should have been flogged', and so on. These comments served only as guidelines for future conduct and not as orders to change the imposed sentences. As early as 1488 Torquemada called a meeting with all the inquisitors in Spain and tried to persuade them to unify proceedings in all the Inquisition's tribunals. Although agreement to do so was reached, it is clear that the inquisitors thought these variations were 'consistent with law', and 'tolerable'.[61] The preamble to Valdes' instructions from 1561 states that 'from now on there should be no deviation in the way of proceeding', clearly signalling that the previous 73 years had not produced the desired unification of procedure.[62] In the eighteenth century, the gradual centralization of the institution removed the variation of sentencing criteria through centralized decision making. However, this did not remove *arbitrium* from the Inquisition, even though its influence elsewhere was diminishing due to judicial modernization in much of Europe. Instead, arbitrium at sentencing was only exercised centrally, resulting in less variation than previously. Effectively, it was the end of judicial polycentrism in the Spanish Inquisition. Even so, local inquisitors continued to select which cases merited investigation and which were put forward to their superiors for trial. In short, the inquisitors continued to exercise *arbitrium* for as long as the Spanish Inquisition existed.

Secrecy

The inquisitors' *arbitrium* was – unlike in other courts – exercised in secrecy: absolute secrecy was a central principle for the operations of the Holy Office which drew on the experiences from Medieval Inquisitions. Secrecy pervades the very language of the Holy Office, sometimes verging on the parodical: interrogations were held in the Inquisition's secret chambers, prisoners were held in its secret prisons, and its papers never left the secret halls of its buildings.[63] All parties to a trial were sworn to secrecy, and anyone found to be revealing details of it were to be prosecuted. After arrest, the defendant, at least in theory, disappeared completely, only to reappear at an *auto de fe*, perhaps years later. Even the warrants were written to preserve secrecy, by producing separate documents for every person to be arrested: 'In an arrest warrant no more than one person should be named, because if it is necessary to communicate an arrest to somebody outside the [Holy] Office, the others remain secret'.[64] In the first years, this secrecy was enforced much less strictly, and repeated instructions had to stress that no outside person should see the defendant during the trial: in 1488, it was proclaimed that 'henceforth . . . no person from outside can see and talk to the aforementioned prisoners'.[65] Seventy-three years later, it was again ordered that 'no person can see him, nor talk to him, nor give him notice by writing or word'.[66]

Nevertheless, secrecy appears to have been frequently broken, something that we can see from prosecutions of witnesses who had talked, jailbreaks, complaints about buildings where outsiders could observe proceedings, jails that allowed communication with and between inmates, and reports of inquisitors who brought secret documents out of the buildings.[67] Furthermore, the *Suprema* had problems in the first decades when it lacked a permanent seat and many of its secretaries brought papers home to work on them, risking both secrecy and the loss of documents which the personnel often thought of as their own.[68] These sorts of breaches of inquisitorial secrecy fuelled the rampant rumours that naturally surrounded every observed denunciation or arrest. Nor was secrecy maintained within the so-called secret prison. When Jaime, the slave of Jaime Mas who was *alcaide* of the secret prison was prosecuted for having had a sexual relationship with Magdalena Gomila who was detained in the secret prison in Mallorca in 1689, there were no fewer than five witnesses testifying against him.[69]

Needless to say, the Holy Office did not manage to squash all talk and information about its ongoing trials – and it may not always have been interested in doing so. Rather, it ensured a lack of accurate information about what was going on, which fostered uncertainty, rumours, and perhaps fear, which may even have served the interests of the Inquisition by loosening tongues. Much of the Inquisition's activity was aimed at forcing people to utter words that they 'would rather have remained unsaid'.[70] Imperfect as it was, this secrecy nevertheless improved over time, generated an enduring mystique, and led to a number of misperceptions about the workings of the Holy Office, both of which survive to this day. The systematic use of secrecy was one of the ways in which the early modern Inquisitions developed and refined the methods of their medieval predecessors.

Secrecy served another purpose in that it allowed the Holy Office to conduct its trials with a minimum of outside pressure. The normal way of responding to a lawsuit in early modern Spain was to bring judicial proceedings to a halt by countersuing in one or more other courts, which depended on accurate information to be successful. With overlapping jurisdictions and courts actively seeking business and eager to expand their own competence this was easy to do – at least as long as one could pay the legal fees. As Jean Pierre Dedieu has shown, a number of trials in the Inquisition were also the results of such a series of suits in other courts.[71] However, once the case reached the Inquisition the rules changed, and the plaintiff lost control over events.[72] More to the point, the fact that the trial was conducted in secrecy and the defendant was held (at least ideally) in solitary confinement prevented countersuits and the interference from other courts. This is one of the differences between the Spanish Inquisition and contemporary Spanish secular courts. Unlike the latter, most trials in the Holy Office were brought to an end with a formal conclusion. In secular courts, they were not. The Inquisition was thus a court where social pressure could not force a suspension (or an acquittal) or simply the abandonment of the trial. Unlike judges in a secular court, the inquisitors were in no way appeasers trying to settle conflicts between two parties. Where other officials above all wanted peace in their districts and were more than willing to allow informal and private channels find settlements in parallel to the trial and eventually void it,[73] the inquisitors were supposed to pursue their cases as long as the evidence would sustain it. The inquisitors were quite definitely not peacemakers.

That secrecy was less than perfect and that this might influence and even encourage the Holy Office becomes apparent when we read the *relación* that Zaragoza sent of the cases it was preparing for its next auto da fe in 1639. In it, they eagerly report that Domingo Hernández who had still not confessed would 'play a very good part' in the auto 'accompanying the others because the public asks for it'.[74] Like good entertainers eager to please, the inquisitors promptly satisfied the crowd which had somehow gotten wind of Domingo Hernández' travails and wanted to see him flogged again after having been so twice by secular authorities.

The secrecy surrounding the Inquisition also allowed abuses to go unchecked, since normally the only persons outside the tribunal to knew its actions were the members of the *Suprema*. Inquisitors and their staff were rarely sacked or punished in other ways. However, it did happen, and they were not able to act with absolute impunity. We have already mentioned Lucero and the Cordoba trials. Another incident that caused consternation was inquisitor Sarmiento's burning of alleged witches in Barcelona in 1549 despite the *Suprema*'s explicit prohibition. He was called to court to explain himself, but procrastinated for years, so that in the end, he was simply side-lined by a new inquisitor who was sent to Barcelona, and then quietly offloaded to a Catalan bishopric when one became vacant.[75]

The system of visitations meant that an external inquisitor was brought in to investigate the running of a tribunal. He would then spend months poring over accounts and trial transcripts, asking witnesses if their testimony had been correctly written down, asking prisoners and convicts of their conditions in jail during their trial, and so forth. The result was a report sent to the *Suprema* which gave the visiting inquisitor the opportunity to gleefully expose whatever shortcomings in his colleagues that he might have discovered. This was more than simply a tool for control of the work the inquisitors did and to what degree rules and regulations were followed. It was also part of the process of gradual centralization whereby over time the *Suprema* enforced a greater uniformity in proceedings and reduced the number of abuses. Yet visitations were periodic affairs, and secrecy certainly facilitated abuses and corruption.

Trial procedures

The inquisitorial trial never ended. This is the essence of Torquemada's instruction that no sentence was ever final and that any trial could at any point in the future be reopened if new evidence appeared.[76] This means that an acquittal was never ever final – but neither was any conviction, which could similarly also always be changed for a more severe sentence if new evidence appeared. In practice, this appears never to have happened. Rather, in the case of a new evidence it was decided to initiate a new trial, charging the defendant with relapsing or making an incomplete confession in the first trial. Evidence produced in the first trial (including witness testimony) was then reused without treating it as a continuation of the earlier trial. The same holds true for those who had been relaxed in effigy in their absence, and who later were tried in person. A few of them were even sentenced to reconciliation instead of relaxation in person: Mari López, to take just one example, was burned in effigy as a Judaizer at an auto da fe in Llerena in 1569. Two years later, she was arrested by the Portuguese Inquisition and remitted to Llerena, where she appeared in person and was reconciled at a new auto da fe in the same city.[77] The reason for allowing cases to be forever reopened was not sheer malice on Torquemada's part. Instead, it followed logically from the definition of heresy and the impossibility of knowing what really went on in people's minds. The Inquisition's trials were centred on words that were spoken and actions that were taken and that were taken as representations of what was in the defendant's mind and belonged to the interior forum. While the Holy Office could produce legal evidence of what had been said and done, there would always remain some lingering doubt about what went on in the defendant's mind. For this reason, there could never be any final sentence, a case could always be reopened, and doubt could always be reduced, but never eliminated.

Before we delve into the details of how the Spanish Inquisition produced and judged evidence, it will be useful to give a brief outline of the inquisitorial trial. After a possible offence had come to the tribunal's attention, the summary phase, the *instrucción del summario*, aimed at ascertaining whether there was cause to proceed to a trial. The first step was to question all pertinent witnesses. This included all those mentioned in the denunciation, and all others who could bring relevant information about the case. After this followed the assessment by theological experts of whether the alleged facts were indeed heretical. This became a necessity as the Spanish Inquisition even in its first years and in contrast to medieval Inquisitions became staffed with jurists, rather than theologians. A careful summing up of the case, with anonymity assured for the accused and witnesses alike, was sent to the *calificadores* who determined if the matter at hand was a question of heresy or not.[78] If there seemed to be cause for suspicion of heresy, the tribunal would sometimes write the other tribunals and ask for any information they might have about the accused and his or her family. The extent of this practice is unknown, though it did become mandatory in the Inquisition's later years. Nevertheless, three preserved books from the tribunal in Valencia show that the other

Inquisitions asked the Valencia Inquisition for information on nearly two thousand defendants for a single offence, that of soliciting sexual favours in the confessional, in just the relatively brief period of 40 years from 1780 to 1820.[79] We have no way of knowing how many of these men were eventually tried, but this gives an indication of the number of such trials and the amount of correspondence undertaken in one of the Inquisition's most quiet periods. One caveat is that the high number of such consultations may in fact have been the result of a deliberate attempt to increase the number of such trials at a time when the tribunals were languishing under a lack of suitable targets. This correspondence could cause long delays as documents had to be transcribed and sent to the tribunal requesting information, yet at the same time, it was an important contributor to the Inquisition's efficacy and long reach. Instructions for fiscals stress the need for prompt replies to other tribunals' requests for information and underline that it was the obligation of the fiscal to ensure that this was done.[80] Patience and the strategic use of their archives meant that the inquisitors could track down perpetrators trying to get a fresh start and escape their past. An excellent example of this was the trial against a woman who called herself Ana Angela Mata and claimed to never have been in trouble with the Inquisition before when she was arrested for sorcery by the Holy Office in Zaragoza in August 1644.[81] There is a noticeable hardening in the inquisitors' attitude towards her visible in the trial summary after a letter from the tribunal in Valencia made clear that her name was Joana Angela Mata, and that she had in fact been convicted by the Inquisition in Valencia no less than three times, in 1615, 1638, and 1640.[82] Even so, this multiple offender escaped a fourth conviction by the Holy Office, as she died 62 years old in the hospital of Our Lady of Mercy in Zaragoza on 15 October 1644 before her sentence could be read to her.

The probatory phase began with the *Informe del fiscal*. This was the prosecutor's summing up of the evidence and ended with a recommendation on whether to continue the proceedings and formally prosecute the accused, or to abandon the case. This was immediately followed by the *acuerdo de los inquisidores*, which was the inquisitors' formal decision on whether to proceed or not. This was one of the key points along the way from a denunciation to a trial, as only one in 20 denunciations appear to have passed this juncture and resulted in a formal trial. At this point, the inquisitors selected those cases that they would bring to trial, and they did so by criteria we can only guess at. Most likely they chose cases by applying the same logic as modern-day prosecutors, choosing cases by favouring the most serious offences and those having potential for exemplary punishment, as well as following policies from central authorities and pleasing their superiors who could influence their future careers. In the case of the Spanish Inquisition, this meant the instructions sent by the *Suprema* ordering shifts in policy or posture, either as a result of internal deliberations within the Inquisition's leadership or reflecting political priorities that the Holy Office had to follow up. Examples of this are numerous, and it should not be necessary to mention more than a few. The discovery of alleged protestant cells in Seville and Valladolid in 1557 caused a full-blown panic and sent the inquisitors on a much more active hunt for Protestants in Spain. A few decades later, the peace (and later trade) treaties that the Spanish monarchy signed with Protestant powers included limited religious toleration which forced the Holy Office to stop actively prosecuting subjects of those nations as heretics.[83] This had immediate and long-term consequences for the Inquisition's trial patterns.[84] So too did the so-called edict of silence issued at the end of the Zugarramurdi witchcraft trials in 1614. These new instructions from the *Suprema* made it to all intents and purposes impossible for the Holy Office to successfully prosecute cases for diabolical witchcraft, and such cases virtually disappeared from the Inquisition's activity after that date.[85]

Of almost equal importance must have been another consideration that also weighs upon modern-day prosecutors, which is the deliberate selection of winnable cases to the detriment of those were the evidence looked less convincing. At first glance, this may seem an improbable concern for the inquisitors: they held all the cards, as it were, collecting the evidence and being able to bring great pressure on the defendant. The inquisitors could even torture the accused to force a confession. An amusing example – for us, at least – of how they could produce something from nothing is that of the shoemaker Diego Diaz who was arrested by mistake by the Spanish Inquisition's tribunal in Llerena because 'he had the same name and profession' as a wanted man. Eventually, the inquisitors became aware that they were looking for another Diego Diaz, but by that time 'his genealogy was checked, and he started confessing'. The two Diegos were reconciled together for Judaizing at an auto da fe in Llerena in 1573.[86] In fact, things were as a rule not quite so simple, and the inquisitors do appear to have followed and respected the procedural rules to a considerable degree. They were, in any case not allowed to sentence the cases alone and were therefore obliged to produce evidence that would be convincing to the other members of the sentencing panel. Given that the Inquisition tribunals had a limited capacity and could only prosecute a fraction of the cases that came to their attention, choosing the winnable ones was a way of ensuring their own success but also the finances of the Holy Office which, for long, depended to a great degree on convictions. Trials could be costly, so expensive that some tribunals requested extra funds to prosecute more of those that came to their attention, as recently shown by Homza in her study of the Navarrese witchcraft trials of 1609–1614.[87]

Here we find another two possible motivations affecting cases selection: the oft-claimed tendency to primarily prosecute wealthy men of converso origin, and the prosecution of entire families for Judaic or Muslim practices. The first was simply not true for the first years of the history of the tribunal.[88] Later, there was much political intervention behind these trials against wealthy conversos, with many of the defendants related to the contractors' network.[89] Furthermore, the pyramidal organization of converso society made the wealthy the protectors of poorer ones. The prosecution of entire families carried with it the two great advantages of facilitating the confiscation of property when it did not have to be purged of dotal assets, if only one of the spouses was convicted, and that evidence against one of them often implicated the other as well since illicit religious practices frequently took place in the home.

A related consideration must have been flight risk: whether the investigation could proceed to gather more evidence without risking to lose the opportunity to arrest the suspect or whether he was likely to leave as transients were wont to do. To these factors was added a final one when the inquisitors chose whether to prosecute or not, and this one is of particular interest to us. That is, again, given that the tribunal could prosecute yearly only a limited number of cases, they were most likely inclined to select for bringing to trial only those cases where they believed that guilt could be legally proven. One of the keys to the acquittal rate is quite simply the selection done here, by choosing not to prosecute cases that had weak evidence, taking extra care when the defendant had more extensive legal protections – principally women and children, and perhaps rushing to arrest those that might be on the point of leaving forever – foreigners and the internally banished. Thus, the decisions taken at this point, to abandon the case, to investigate further, or to formally prosecute are essential to understand and interpret the final sentences of those cases brought to trial.

Even if abandoned at this point, the case could be reopened and a full trial initiated at any time if further information was forthcoming, which is a practice we have evidence of in our records. If the decision was made that the case was to continue with a formal prosecution, the accused would normally be arrested and then charged. It is important to remember that this was the beginning of the trial proper, and also that this would only occur if the assembled preliminary information was sufficient for the inquisitors to decide that the accused could be presumed to be guilty and that this guilt could be legally proven as the inquisitors applied their *arbitrium*.

The *accusación del fiscal* should be formulated within ten days of the arrest of the accused. It should be made even if the defendant had confessed during the first three *audiencias*, because the accusation was formally consubstantial to the trial: no trial without an accusation.[90] The charges should include all heresies mentioned by witnesses and confessed by the defendant, as well as all other crimes not part of the Inquisition's jurisdiction that might be relevant to proving him a bad Christian. If the alleged offences were not sufficiently proven, the accusation should also include a petition for submitting the accused to torture. The accusation was then read to the defendant who had to respond immediately to all the charges, which were made in an anonymous and sometimes almost generic form to prevent the defendant from knowing or guessing who the witnesses were. Afterwards, he was given a copy of the accusation so that he could state if the witnesses had spoken correctly or should be questioned again, and so that he could prepare an answer to all the articles it contained. To help him with this he was given an advocate.

History, or at least historians, have not been kind to the advocates who defended the accused in the Holy Office. However, those few historians who have studied full trials in some detail have rendered a far more positive verdict on their efforts than those who have based their research on *relaciones de causas* where the advocates are practically invisible. As we have alluded to earlier, by closely following the development of the trials they studied, both Haim Beinart and Gretchen Starr-LeBeau were able to demonstrate that individual attorneys had a clear impact on the trials. Again, however, both of these researchers worked on early trials, and we have no real knowledge of how the advocates functioned later after they had become permanent employees of the tribunals and the instructions of 1561 reduced their freedom of action.

In any case, the advocate's first task was the same as the inquisitor's: To find out if the accused confessed if he was guilty. Concretely, he should not knowingly help the defendant to hide his guilt or plead not guilty when he knew him to be guilty. Furthermore, he should stress that making a full confession was the best strategy for the defendant in case of pleading guilty. If he was innocent, the advocate should try to prove so by all legal means. If the defendant was guilty, he should do everything in his power to bring forth a confession. Bringing the defendant to confess might be in his own interest and a sincere confession might result in a more lenient sentence than a spirited defence. Yet, this was not always so since there might not be sufficient evidence to secure a conviction without a confession. In this case, pressuring the accused to confess did not serve his best interests, at least legally. It might, of course, be argued that a confession was necessary for his salvation as a Catholic, and since an inquisitorial trial had a religious as well as a judicial aspect where the defendant's interests might not be aligned in the two different aspects of the trial – at least if he really wasn't a Catholic.[91] The advocate could only meet the defendant in the presence of an inquisitor.[92] The advocate could make them read out the testimony of the witnesses and the confession of the defendant, but if the accused wished to continue his confession the advocate had to leave the room.[93] The *relación* of the second trial of the Sicilian Juan Russo on Mallorca in 1614 spotlights the role of the normally shadowy advocate and the limits of his intervention:

> [H]e was negative [i.e. refused to confess] until his advocate persuaded him and he said he wanted to talk to him in secret. When told that he could

> not, but rather that the advocate had to go outside if he wanted to confess anything, he said yes. And after having ordered the advocate to leave and admonished [the defendant] he said that . . . everything was true.[94]

The advocate was the one who managed to get him talking but could not even be present when he did! After reading such a scene one might well wonder if the advocate wasn't really working for the prosecution, and in a way, he certainly was. Though it might be argued that bringing the defendant to confess would be to his benefit since it lowered the punishment in the final sentence, that was not the case here: there was only a single witness against Juan Russo and without his confession, the Holy Office could not have convicted him. By his confession, he also allowed for his reintegration as a member of the Catholic church in full compliance with the church, no longer bound by any of the ecclesiastical censures he had incurred, and his salvation was no longer in question.[95] We will not go further into the defence mechanisms available to the defendant and his advocate in this chapter. Instead, we will study those in the context of the acquittals, which ones seem to have been used successfully.

After the trial, the advocate had to maintain secrecy of the proceedings, and hand over all documentation to the inquisitors. This, of course, had the useful side effect for the Inquisition of preventing conscientious advocates from building libraries of proceedings and effective defences to be used in future trials.

Presumption of guilt was not sufficient to convict the accused as a heretic, it was however sufficient to convict him as suspected of heresy. This could be based on affinity with heretics, education and conversation, way of life, bad deeds and ambiguous propositions, and so on. The suspicion could be *vehemente* or *levi*, according to gravity. Full proof of guilt of heresy demanded at least two perfect eyewitnesses to the offence who had ratified their testimonies, preferably in the instructory phase. Their testimonies were to be ratified in the presence of the fiscal, notary, inquisitor and two honest persons. If necessary, the witnesses were recalled for further questioning, also at the defendant's behest.

After being ratified, the testimonies, after anonymization, were 'published', which meant that they were given to the defendant to help him prepare his defence with the help of his advocate. The main ways of defence for the accused were derived from the general principles of the *ius commune* (to deny the factual allegations of the charges, to claim that the prosecution's witnesses were his mortal enemies) or derived from specific characters of heresy (claim mitigating circumstances such as love, passion, drunkenness, just fury, ignorance, or being a woman or a rustic). After having received the advocate's brief, the probatory phase could be closed, or the accused could be submitted to torture to attempt to obtain a confession. After this, the trial went to sentencing, which we will deal with in a later chapter. Before going there, however, we shall study the techniques the Inquisition used during the course of the trial to produce the evidence that was used for the sentence.

Techniques

The foregoing brief description of the inquisitorial trial makes clear that the Holy Office used a number of techniques to investigate and prosecute offences, many of which were originally developed by the Medieval Inquisitions and subsequently adapted and further refined by the Spanish Inquisition. Central were both the extensive use of archives and the search for a confession from the defendant. Yet, in an age of scant forensic evidence, witness testimony was the most important form of proof besides confession, itself a form of testimony (though contemporary jurists disagreed on whether a confession really was evidence or something that obviated evidence).[96] A great deal of the sophistication of the Holy Office therefore consisted of the ways in which it managed witnesses, confessing defendants, and the archives produced by these confessions and testimony. As Beinart writes, testimony in the Spanish Inquisition 'was the central pillar upon which that institution's action rested'.[97] The main form of investigation was therefore the questioning of witnesses and the repeated questioning of the accused in increasingly unpleasant circumstances. Torture played a small, if important part in this. However, the main way of breaking the defendants' will to resist was the application of long-term jail, usually in isolation, with uncertainty about the trial's cause, purpose and end.[98] Sophisticated questioning was brought to bear on the defendant, usually based on the evidence from witnesses as stored in the Inquisition's archive.

Archives

The Spanish Inquisition was among many other things a formidable bureaucracy, producing and storing prodigious amounts of information. This was one of the keys to its power, in that it was able to accumulate and use massive amounts of information about individuals and their families over not just years, but decades and generations. We have already alluded to the use of its archives when retelling the story of Juana Ana Mata above. It was the existence of large archives with alphabetical indexes which underpinned the correspondence that revealed her earlier convictions in another tribunal.

The systematic assembly of collections of large amounts of information was established already by the medieval Inquisitions in Languedoc in the thirteenth century,[99] in marked contrast to contemporary French secular courts which frequently 'did not consider themselves responsible for keeping archives and instead relied on private citizens to archive their own acts'.[100] For the French inquisitors in contrast, 'the preservation and protection of their records was a major concern'.[101] This led to a long-term build-up of comprehensive archives that outlasted the term of office of any single inquisitor – perhaps the first step to a permanent Inquisition.

For early modern Italy, Jeremy Black stresses that the Roman Inquisition 'had a long memory and good records'.[102] This was also part of a deliberate policy, with a central archive established in Rome in 1593, and 'campaigns to ensure local Inquisitional archives were created (if not already in place), and properly maintained'.[103]

The importance of the archives to the inquisitors' work was recognized by those targeted by the Holy Office. Famously, Cathars planned to attack the inquisitorial archive in Languedoc.[104] Attacks and thefts aimed at trial documents from the tribunals of the Roman Inquisition in the sixteenth century have been documented in Bologna and Rovigo.[105] In Valencia in 1555, documents from a secular court disappeared when a number of men in the service of don Guillem Rocafull, governor of Orihuela, 'entered the archive of the court' and 'took from the archive all the trials and acts that they wanted and hid all those that don Guillem wanted'.[106] In another incident, the court of criminal justice in Valencia discovered in 1548 that it had lost part of its archive because one of the notaries was selling paper from the archive to local merchants.[107] However, while we have such stories from various Inquisition. in the middle ages and early modern Spanish secular courts, physical attacks on the archives of the Spanish Inquisition have left no trace in the sources used for this study. Nonetheless, we find numerous other attempts at preventing correct information from reaching the Inquisition's archives or at injecting false information by threatening potential witnesses or by giving false testimony. For example, María Reoli appeared at an *auto da fe* in Valencia in 1573 after having been convicted of falsely accusing another person of having said that one did not need to confess to a priest, only to God, in other words of Lutheranism. The falsely accused was acquitted and María was whipped a hundred strokes before being banished perpetually from the district of the Holy Office in Valencia.[108] This was a harsh punishment, publicly meted out to someone who tried to kill or at least destroy another Old Christian by judicial means.

It was an inflexible principle that the Inquisition should write down all testimony, denunciations and other relevant pieces of information and enter it in registers put in alphabetical order after the relevant person's name. Though, of course, some scribes were less than perfectly diligent in the execution of their duties, as evinced by the warning to secretaries not to leave part of interrogation transcripts blank in order to fill them out later, because it was not according to the rules 'and the secretary may forget and [the pages] remain blank'.[109] Keeping up with oral proceedings, writing them down as they progressed, was hard secretarial work, and it is no surprise that some notaries may have had difficulty writing down everything as it was said.

Furthermore, the wording of the testimonies, questions and answers in the sources raises serious questions as to well they reproduce what was really said. An often-reprinted manual for scribes states:

> The scribe must transcribe the statements verbatim, and not in shorthand, or in very tiny letters, without changing a word, or clarifying it, but as it is said, for this is what the law commands. However, despite this legal precept, it is allowed and common practice to express them in clear, understandable, and well-sounding words that do not change the substance, and rather make the facts more perceivable because otherwise, if the witness is unsophisticated, their testimony serves not as a declaration but as confusion. It's quite laborious to understand some people, and it almost requires guessing, and repeatedly clarifying what they say so that they understand it and see that they are being understood.[110]

Add to this that many defendants outside of Castile had their words taken down in a language different from that which they spoke, and it should be clear that our sources may give us the meaning of what was said, but they very rarely constitute verbatim transcriptions.

Furthermore, what was taken down during interrogations should later be copied into other files, which was similarly demanding and time-consuming work. Beinart goes so far as to speculate that the cases against the deceased in Ciudad Real may not even have been put to paper 'because of the mass of work with which the Ciudad Real court was burdened', noting that this would constitute 'a serious defect in the meticulous method of the Inquisition'.[111] His argument is that some cases may never have been put to paper, not because the Holy Office kept things off the books, but because it wrote so much that it just didn't have time for the least important documents in time of great work pressure.

In any case, the volume of documents produced was enormous, forcing the production of yet more paperwork in the form of alphabetical indexes. Information about every defendant was spread out over a large number of volumes, such as the books of denunciations, books of testimony, prisoner registers, registers of the inquisitors' routine visits to the prisons, various votation registers, and so forth, in addition to the trial manuscript which was being assembled as the trial progressed. Information was supposed to be entered into these registers as it was being received or produced, but as the warning quoted earlier shows, this was not always observed. Part of the challenge of running a tribunal was to manage this flow of information to ensure that the information was not simply entered but also later retrieved when needed.[112] The person entrusted with managing this flow was the fiscal, as several manuscript instructions for the office of fiscal make clear.[113]

In some ways, the archive was the axis on which the wheels of the Inquisition's activities turned, and it was both the end and the beginning of a trial. Even before the defendant was brought to the tribunal for the first time a file would have been created with his or her name, and an entry made both in a book of denunciations and the alphabetical index to that book. Whenever information about someone was received, the name was looked up to see if there was previous information that would lend weight to what was now being claimed. At the other end of the trial was the information that it had produced against the defendant and others that had been named as possible offenders during the course of the investigations. This now remained recorded in both the written trial file, the books of interrogations, the books of denunciations, and their alphabetical registers. These again could then form the basis for future trials. As James Given writes of the inquisitors of Medieval Languedoc:

> Effective record keeping, in addition to making it possible to discover individual lies, allowed the inquisitors to search for and collate material with which they could build a case against a suspect. The original manuscripts from the thirteenth and fourteenth centuries contain indications that inquisitors or their agents have carefully searched them, looking for and marking evidence that could be used against particular individuals . . . To indicate depositions containing information against individuals in whom the inquisitors were particularly interested, notes were made in the margin, taking the form, for example, of Contra Willelmum de Rocovila.[114]

This description could equally well have been of the sources of the early modern Spanish Inquisition, where such marginal notes frequently marked information to be extracted and put in alphabetical registers or copied to other trial files, or references to other trials containing information relevant to the one at hand. Thus, there was a system of cross-references within the archive.

The archives constituted a clear danger for medieval Cathars and Waldenses, and for early modern *conversos* and Moriscos since they performed or were believed to perform non-Catholic religious rituals in groups, customarily centred on the family. The inquisitors aimed to, and frequently succeeded in, implicating a large group of people when a person from such a religious minority was tried. Yet we know of no attempts at destroying the archives of the Holy Office in Spain in peace time such as we know from Medieval France, while they did suffer significant damage whenever public order broke down as a result of French invasions from as early as 1522 right up to 1808 and the first abolition of the institution.[115] Curiously, we know of several attempts to break into the archives of the Spanish Inquisition to extract information rather than to destroy it. The Seville 'Lutherans' contrived to extract Protestant writings from the Seville tribunal in the 1550s, as 'the Inquisition under Valdés probably had the best "Protestant" library in Spain'.[116] Mosén Francisco Montañaner – an inveterate and unsuccessful magician who was tried by the Holy Office in Valencia for magical offences on at least three occasions – was penanced there in 1682 for copying the keys to the Inquisition's secret chambers to steal books on magic.[117]

As should be clear by now, the amount of writing that took place in a tribunal was significant and took tremendous time and effort. Thus, this was one of the constraints on the number of trials that a tribunal could hold in a year, besides the actual interrogations, witness depositions, and so on. It simply took too much time to produce and maintain the prodigious archives of the Holy Office. The time needed for this only increased during the existence of the Holy Office, not just because the Inquisition was increasingly bureaucratic and insisted on keeping ever more comprehensive and detailed records of each trial conducted, but also because the genealogical archives over *conversos* and their descendants (real and alleged) were continuously updated and grew with each generation. These were not the only papers written: the inquisitors and their staff were also diligent letter writers, and because of its extensive archives, the Holy Office became the most desired issuer of certificates of *limpieza de sangre*. Officially, the Spanish Inquisition only issued such certificates for those who sought positions with the Holy Office. In reality, these became an important source of income for the Inquisition's scribes. Jean-Pierre Dedieu has shown how the sheer weight of this work brought the actual work of trying cases to a virtual standstill in Toledo in the middle of the seventeenth century, while Homza has recently demonstrated that the witch trials in Logroño in 1609–1614 were obstructed by the prolonged absences of notaries who preferred to work on the certificates.[118]

Given the significance of the archives to the Holy Office, an important part of the work of the inquisitors was to generate the information that could fill the archives and hence serve to produce future trials. The trials themselves were important in this regard since they often furnished incriminating evidence against other than the person initially being prosecuted. When *Conversos* and Moriscos were prosecuted for performing religious ceremonies and rites within the confines of the family, the evidence against one person would nearly always implicate others: spouse, parents, siblings, and children. However, denunciations were fundamental both to set the ball rolling by causing the first trials that could then generate further denunciations and because, contrary to a well-entrenched misconception, the Spanish Inquisition did not possess a corps of professional spies. It depended instead on denunciations and self-denunciations from ordinary people. In the rather hyperbolic words of Henry Charles Lea, it 'rendered every individual an agent of the Inquisition'.[119] This was in fact not peculiar or unique to the Spanish Inquisition. Rather, as Robert Gellately remarks, the participation of the population is typical of how repressive systems work: 'it is not 'big brother' alone, nor the 'police state' for that matter, but the participation of fellow citizens who make the 'all-seeing' and 'all-knowing' system come to life'.[120] To which degree, the Inquisition really was 'all-seeing' or 'all-knowing' is debatable, and to what degree the Holy Office really had access to local information has been little studied.[121]

Denunciations and testimony

A denunciation was the most common beginning of a trial in the Holy Office in Spain. In theory, this was a formalized process performed in the presence of a notary and two witnesses in front of an inquisitor who asked any questions he felt to be relevant. Afterwards, the informer swore on the Holy Bible that she or he had told the truth. Because heresy was a *crimen excemptum*, the Inquisition allowed informers and witnesses that would be inadmissible in other courts. The prominent Italian jurist Tiberio Deciani is explicit: 'Even those persons who are normally forbidden from accusing can accuse in this crime', and 'witnesses who are invalid in other lawsuits are admitted for this crime'.[122] He even suggested that delations could be anonymous and need not be identified.[123] In theory, the Spanish Inquisition was stricter on this count, and Inquisitor General Torquemada's instructions from 1498 prohibit the acceptance of anonymous denunciation. However, the Spanish Inquisition sometimes did accept unsigned delations, such as small paper slips stuck under the doors of inquisitors or familiars.[124]

This acceptance of anonymous denunciation did, of course, much to facilitate the Inquisition's work. It also made it very easy to initiate an inquisitorial process against someone, whether out of spite or genuine concern for the purity of the Catholic faith. However, this should not be overstated, because since such an unsigned slip of paper could not be used as evidence it was only useful insofar as it was detailed enough to allow the Inquisition to call in witnesses who could confirm its contents and who could later ratify their testimony. It did allow the delator to partake in the fiction that he or she was just a witness who had been called to testify like everyone else, and this may have been important: one of Dedieu's findings in Toledo was that 26 per cent of all denouncers made some sort of reference to the edict of the faith during their denunciation.[125] This mention of the edict and the way in which its reading stated the personal obligation that they had to denounce any offence that they knew of, served to a certain extent to relieve the delator of the onerous title of 'denouncer' in favour of a 'good Catholic', just as the anonymous denouncer could be transformed into a simple witness.

'The denouncer does not like to travel', Dedieu wrote.[126] In Spain as in Italy, 'many delators were neighbours, who denounced in vengeance',[127] something frequently noted by the inquisitors. This did not by necessity mean that such denunciations were untruthful (though many undoubtedly were), as delations based at least partially in truth were much more damaging and more likely to lead to a conviction than those which were simply made up. Like other medieval and early modern systems of justice, the Spanish Inquisition relied on the local population to provide it with the information needed to initiate proceedings. Those denunciations had by necessity to spring from local events and local knowledge, and they were equally inescapably entangled in local sympathies, antipathies, and enmities. The Holy Office was only one of the judicial systems available to the inhabitants of early modern Spain, and some of the denunciations made before the inquisitors formed part of a larger web of lawsuits and countersuits between litigants.[128]

With its secret proceedings and acceptance of anonymous delations, the Holy Office was an exceptionally convenient channel for 'transactions of enmity', to use Daniel Lord Smail's felicitous phrase.[129] In terms of 'investment' in 'the market in retribution', to follow Smail, the Inquisition was cheap compared to civil litigation or criminal accusations in secular courts. Indeed, it was free, probably the only free system of justice in early modern Spain, and as such, it also became one of the few options for the poor and powerless to attack their superiors. By means of delations 'socially or politically powerless people can find ways to be taken seriously. Their words are followed up relentlessly, and their opinions are given more meaning than ever'.[130] Looking at personal motives for denouncing others to the Inquisition, Homza found that in witchcraft trials, one 'such motive in early modern Navarre was loaned and borrowed money', while illegitimate children and sex out of wedlock were others.[131] As tempting as denouncing for personal reasons might be, there was also religious pressure to do so. Every Catholic was obliged to go to confession at least once a year, and every confession to a priest started with a question of knowledge of heresy: had he or she committed, or know of offences committed that fell under the jurisdiction of the Inquisition? If the answer was affirmative the confession ended and the confessant was obliged to seek out the Holy Office to make a denunciation or self-denunciation, there before the confession before the priest could be resumed and his or her sins pardoned.[132] Failure to comply entailed excommunication. This provision also made it into the edicts of faith, and it created an extraordinary psychological pressure to denounce: failure to do so condemned you to eternal damnation. Dividing the task of eliciting denunciations and withholding pardons between several clerical actors raised fierce controversies between the secular parish clergy (in charge of confessing) and the Inquisition, in both Italy and Spain.[133]

Denunciation was almost without risk as well, although the defendant might be able to guess the identity of his delator and witnesses, and as we have seen, the Holy Office could be fierce against false witnesses. That ferocity was tempered by the low number of trials – only 397 among 67,201 trials in EMID have been identified as containing this charge. Indeed, a number of those prosecuted for this charge were acquitted. It turned out to be virtually impossible for the Holy Office to prove that they had deliberately lied as long as they simply insisted that they had told what they had seen and heard without claiming any other knowledge of their target's guilt or innocence.

A trial could only start when denunciation had been followed up and had resulted in sufficient evidence to establish the presumption of guilt. This normally involved questioning other witnesses mentioned by the original delator who could confirm the content of the denunciation. It was this preliminary collection of evidence that enabled the inquisitors to select those cases they believed that they could prove legally from the many denunciations before moving to a trial. Yet, the control of this first phase was firmly in the delator's hands. He or she decided what to denounce and which corroborating witnesses to name. As Cristian Berco writes:

> The built-in separation of the process into denunciation and trial shows both the strengths and the weaknesses of this early modern system of control. Without denunciations, the process would have been stillborn. It was only the cooperation of the local populace that fuelled the judicial machinery. On the other hand, this separation spread the control of the process between local society and magistrates.[134]

There is a similarity to more modern repressive systems here, for example, the German Gestapo, which also had a relatively small staff and was completely dependent on denunciations from ordinary Germans in order to actively repress the German population.[135] The fact that many denunciations were and continue to be made because of personal motives has historically done very little to dampen authorities' enthusiasm for exploiting them. The Inquisition's measured nod to the danger that this entailed was to allow the defendant to name his mortal enemies and thus invalidate or at least weaken their testimony.

Since the Holy Office sought trials, it actively sought denunciations. Edicts of faith were read yearly in order to remind every Christian of his or her personal obligations to make such denunciations, on pain of excommunication in case of failure to so, a yearly reminder to come forward to ensure one's eternal salvation.[136] The edict of faith enumerated the possible heresies, and most importantly, their external signs, that a Christian was required to avoid and denounce, under threat of prosecution for harbouring heretics if he did not.[137] Its reading was tremendously effective: as noted before, Dedieu states that 26 per cent of all delators made some allusion to it in their denunciations, yet he also states that it was closely tied to the practice of visitations of the district, when it was read publicly and an agent of the Inquisition, external to local society, was immediately available to receive the denunciation. Outside of the visitations of the district, its impact was negligible.[138] Since these visitations were unpopular with the inquisitors and fell out of use as soon as the inquisitors could get away with it, the reading of the edict of faith lost its significance in the seventeenth century.

The edict of grace was similar to the edict of faith, being read aloud to the assembled populace. In the seventeenth century, it fell out of use after having been converted into an innocuous way of closing up an embarrassing 'complicidad', but it was instrumental in bringing out denunciations when the Inquisition was being established.[139] It declared a period of grace of 30 or 40 days for all those guilty of heresy. The period of grace permitted anyone to come forward and voluntarily confess without being punished by death, prison, or confiscation of property. Such confessions had to be absolutely complete in laying out the heretical acts committed, and in naming all those taking part. If the confession later was found to be incomplete it was considered to be insincere, and the person making it impenitent. Confessions made in the time of grace formed the core of the Inquisition's archive in its first years of existence and were important tools in the repression of the alleged Judaizers in the first decades of the Holy Office's existence. It was also the use of an Edict of Grace that made almost 2,000 persons come forward and confess that they were Satan-worshipping witches in 1614, thus pre-empting any accusation that might fall on them from their neighbours during the great Basque witch craze.[140]

All testimony, including that made as part of a denunciation, had to be ratified before it could be used in court. This rule was strictly enforced and did cause trouble as witnesses could not always be found again. Joan de Tarazona was acquitted of sodomy in Barcelona in 1575 because none of the five witnesses could not be found in time to have their testimony ratified.[141] When their testimony could not be ratified, there was no legal evidence at all against Joan de Tarazona, who for good measure was able to prove both that the witnesses were his enemies and that he regularly shared bed with men and boys without engaging in illicit sexuality. For this reason, manuals for fiscals recommending that the testimony of witnesses should be ratified immediately, *and* also at the proper point in the course of the trial. This was to ensure that ordinary procedure could be followed, but that evidence would not be voided in the middle of the trial if the witnesses could not be located again, as was the case with Joan Tarazona. Despite such admonitions and suggestions, a number of trials ended with an acquittal or a suspension precisely because the Holy Office was incapable of locating the witnesses to have their testimony ratified.

Every witness thus passed through the Holy Office at least twice and was on every occasion encouraged to tell everything they knew that might be of relevance. In theory, witnesses were not to be informed of the reason why they were called to appear before the tribunal. The questions put to them should not be formulated in such a way as to suggest the answer, and the name of the suspect and the place of the supposed offence should not be revealed. Before being questioned, the witnesses had to swear to tell the truth and maintain secrecy about their testimony. In practice, it often shines through that they had been approached and even coached as to what testimony was expected from them, whether they testified for the prosecution or the defence. After testifying they were again admonished to maintain secrecy about the proceedings – the Inquisition's eternal obsession. The inquisitors used these testimonies and the archives they produced very skilfully, building new cases with evidence from old ones, forcing both witnesses and defendants to respond to anonymous claims, and pressuring, luring, and cajoling them to give more evidence and implicate more people.

The decision to allow, in matters of heresy, testimony from witnesses that would ordinarily be unacceptable had important ramifications for the trials of faith conducted by the Holy Office. Not only did this mean that convicted criminals (including heretics), children, and the mentally infirm could testify, but it also authorized the use of testimony by close family members. This, in turn, meant that every confession of a proscribed action or utterance within the confines of the home would become evidence against other family members, thus enabling the same sort of chain-trials normally associated with witchcraft trials. This in combination with the Inquisition's procedure of burning those who maintained their innocence in the face of sufficient evidence to convict them, while reconciling those who confessed (at least once, while the relapsed were, in principle, to be burned even if they confessed) created very large chains of trials where members of the same family or clan denounced each other in order to make full and satisfactory confessions, what the inquisitors called complicities. This is the reason for many of the trials against women and children for Judaism and Islamic practices: there was already evidence against them from the confessions of others in their families, and this allowed the Holy Office to proceed against them with ease and little expense, facilitating the confiscation of a family's entire estate and thus avoiding future lawsuits over its division. This, of course, also impacted their conviction rates. Yet, even so, the majority of the defendants for these offences were male, though the gender disparity was greater among Moriscos than among Judaizers.

Prisons

While witnesses were being questioned, the defendants were normally placed under arrest, without being told why. An arrest could by law be made only if there was reason to fear an escape, or there existed sufficient circumstantial evidence to warrant the application of torture. As the fiscal always requested the accused to be arrested when he recommended going to trial, arrest was the rule rather than the exception. In some cases, arrest preceded the examination by *calificadores*, and some unfortunate persons even sat in prison without any charge ever being produced against them.[142] With the arrest followed the sequestration of the defendant's property. The defendant had to pay for his stay in the Inquisition's jail even if he was acquitted. As soon as whatever he had in ready money had been used up, the tribunal would gradually sell off his belongings and property to pay for the cost of his imprisonment. These auctions were vulnerable to corruption and the defendants' belongings may often have been sold for much less than they were worth.[143] The sequestration of property also served to ensure that it could actually be confiscated if the defendant was convicted and sentenced to a loss of property.[144] The cost of months or years in jail could in itself be crippling and must have been a powerful incentive to confess quickly and thus end the trial swiftly for those who knew what they were accused of and who faced less severe punishment if convicted. With the sequestration of property, the family of the accused was reduced to poverty or even hunger, since the Inquisition made no provision at all for providing for the defendant's relatives until 1561.[145] This was of some importance since the majority (almost 75 per cent) of those tried by the Spanish Inquisition were males, and thus responsible for providing for their families if they were married, which many Spanish adult males outside the clergy were.

The Inquisition had various grades of prison, the 'secret prison' being the harshest. This was where most defendants awaited their fates during the increasingly lengthy trials of the Inquisition. Though meant only as a temporary means, and not a punishment in itself, some remained in this jail for months or years as their trials dragged on. Because of the relatively good state of these cells, the Inquisition's prison was considered better than royal or ordinary ecclesiastical gaols, as is testified by a letter from the Inquisition in Barcelona which refused to move its prisoners to the unhealthy city jail in 1624.[146] Nevertheless, the conditions were sufficiently unhealthy to cost a number of defendants their lives during the course of their trials.[147] Valdés' instructions from 1561 orders that 'the inquisitors shall treat the prisoners humanely, treating them according to the quality of their persons'.[148] The inquisitors recognized that long-term imprisonment, while an investigatory tool, felt as a form of punishment to those subjected to it. Thus, when Ana Suárez was acquitted for superstitions in Cartagena de Indias in 1650, the inquisitors wrote that they considered 'her long imprisonment' as 'punishment'.[149] We see that same in the case of the cleric Juan Angulo de Cabrera, accused of impeding the operations of the Holy Office in Lima in 1583. He was let off with a reprimand and saying mass and singing penitential psalms on an empty stomach four Fridays, and 'that his incarceration [during the trial] should be given him as punishment'.[150] There are others. The message is clear: the inquisitors recognized that imprisonment was sufficiently onerous to be a real punishment, inflicted on those who were being prosecuted and not yet been found guilty.

As well as the secret prison, the Inquisition maintained a jail for familiars who were arrested for criminal matters. This was occasionally also used for defendants who were being tried for crimes against the faith if their cases were not considered very serious, or if they were of high social status or in delicate health. The latter could also be taken in by the Inquisition's staff, some of whom lived in the tribunal's buildings with their families. Thus, the widow Jusepa Vendrell was incarcerated in a room in the *alcaide*'s house because she was pregnant when she was being tried for superstitions in Valencia in 1656. There she gave birth to a stillborn son before she herself expired six days later. She died on 13 April 'with all the sacraments', the inquisitors in Valencia informed the *Suprema* by letter at the end of May.[151]

In addition to those forms of prison outlined earlier, the Holy Office made use of so-called perpetual prisons, which were used for punishment. They were meant to hold those sentenced to perpetual prison. 'Perpetual' prison was never in reality perpetual, and by the seventeenth century generally meant a few months for a repentant prisoner, while 'lifetime' prison meant a term of about ten years.

Prison was used to break the defendant's resistance to tell the inquisitors what they wanted to hear. In the secret prisons, ideally, the defendant was completely isolated for the entire duration of the trial. In reality, lack of space frequently forced the inquisitors to place two inmates in the same cell. Isolation took its toll and appears to have been more effective than torture in bringing forth confessions. The most vivid description of the effect of isolation in inquisitorial jail comes from the autobiographical account Charles Dellon wrote of his travails in the Portuguese Inquisition in Goa.[152] A best seller that has been translated into numerous languages and has remained in print continuously for more than three centuries, it details his mounting despair and attempted suicide as he awaited his fate and unsuccessfully attempted to bring his trial to an end by confessing what he had been accused of – a difficult task since the inquisitors followed the procedural rules and, at that early stage of the trial, never told him the charges against him.

Interrogations

Confession was the aim of the interrogations of defendants. Since the trial started with the supposition that the defendant was guilty as indicated by the preliminary evidence, the goal was to elicit a confession that would confirm the claims made against him. Here also the Inquisition's obsession with secrecy pervaded the proceedings, and what the defendant was accused of was kept secret almost until the very end of the trial. The identity of the witnesses was never revealed. This secrecy served several purposes. In theory, it made it difficult for the defendant to know exactly who his accusers were, and hence to seek revenge after the trial; it made it more likely that the defendant confess things that he had not been accused of; it made it impossible for the defendant to end the trial quickly by simply confessing whatever was alleged, as Dellon discovered to his cost; and finally it made false confessions less likely since innocent defendants would not know what to confess.[153] In practice, many were able to guess who their accusers were, and since the full contents of the accusations were eventually revealed in the publication of testimony, the defendants would almost always be able to make a satisfactory (even if false) confession in the end. In an extraordinary case, the inquisitor Estrada y Escobedo in Mexico was accused in 1642 of secretly giving the very attractive Margarita de Moreira a small piece of paper with instructions on what she should confess in order to escape her trial for Judaizing without heavy punishment.[154] Yet, such anecdotes aside, we see here some possibility for innocent defendants to convince the inquisitors of their innocence by their sheer inability through much of the trial to confess of what they had been accused of if they could not guess what it was, or by naming their accusers as mortal enemies if they in fact could guess who and what had caused their trial.

As soon as possible, and no later than three days after his arrest, the defendant was supposed to be called in for the first of his three *audiencias* with an inquisitor.[155] Each *audiencia* was to be held on a separate day, but a single *audiencia* could also last for several days. During these questionings, the inquisitor admonished the accused to tell the truth and confess his crimes. If the defendant confessed 'spontaneously', he was received in confession. Thereafter the trial went to the next stage: the fiscal's formal accusation. Only then would the defendant be told what he was being accused of.

The actual conduct of these interrogations was left to a large degree to the inquisitor's *arbitrium*. The first *audiencia* was legally obliged to be dedicated to general questions: If the defendant knew or guessed the reason for his arrest, his genealogy, place of origin, profession, if he had travelled to foreign countries, and so forth. Eventually, the various tribunals developed their own lists of questions to be directed at the defendants during the first *audiencia*. While developed separately, they generally contained the same questions. These lists were to ensure that everyone was asked all relevant questions, and they enabled the Spanish Inquisition to write short biographies of all its prisoners, as it started to do by the eighteenth century. After gathering this preliminary background information, the defendant was asked if he knew or presumed the reason for his arrest. In case of a negative reply, the inquisitors would sternly warn him that they did not prosecute people without good reason, and then admonish him to search his memory. Thereafter the defendant was returned to his cell, leaving him to reflect in solitary confinement until he either requested to see an inquisitor or was called for his second *audiencia* some days later.

This set the pattern for all the *audiencias* that a defendant went through. Lengthy solitary confinement combined with a total lack of information was punctuated only by the inquisitors' insistence that the accused was known to be guilty and their vague but increasingly suggestive questions. The psychological pressure created by this procedure was significant and it had great effect on the human beings subjected to it. Dellon claims in his autobiography that he would happily have confessed whatever he was accused of if the inquisitors would only have told him what he had done wrong. That way out, however, was denied him, as they followed procedural rules and never told him what he was accused of.[156]

Arguably, this form of interrogation was more effective, if slower, than torture. Torture should in any case not be used until all evidence had been gathered and evaluated. Contrary to general opinion, torture was only used in a minority of cases, and it was only used as an instrument of procedure, never as a punishment.[157] During the eighteenth century, torture fell out of general use, and was finally banned by the pope in 1816.[158] A confession made during torture was not immediately accepted as proof. It had to be ratified the next day in order to be used as evidence. If the defendant refused to ratify his confession, torture was normally resumed. The aim of the torture was to bring forth a confession without physically damaging the prisoner, and the number of methods used by the Inquisition was therefore limited. Legally, the defendant could only be tortured once during a trial unless new evidence resulted in further charges, or he refused to ratify his confession. This could be overcome by suspending rather than ending the torture session. Thus, he was formally tortured only once – but over the space of two or more days. The Inquisition knew that torture was a double-edged sword, and all its instructions on torture make this abundantly plain: torture could force a defendant to reveal the truth that he wanted to conceal but could also make him confess a crime he did not commit, simply to escape the pain. The manuals urged caution on this point, and therefore it should not be any surprise that a number of defendants overcame their torture without confessing. To give an example, Garcia Lopez did so not once, but twice, being acquitted of Judaizing in Llerena in both 1575 and 1579 after successfully resisting torture.[159]

Sentencing and punishment

Prospero Farinacci writes that 'he who utters heretical words in jest by misspeaking or in anger, is not set free without some penitence even if he goes free of the punishment of the heretic'.[160] Somewhat later comes the very enlightening statement that 'even if the penitent is admitted to mercy and absolved it does not mean that he is released without punishment'. Going on he quotes Decian who said that 'the specificity of heresy is that one gives sentences that are neither condemnations nor acquittals but purging, which consist of a penance'.[161] It is this unique quality – that even the death sentence could be accompanied by an absolution – that makes the inquisitorial trial so alien to us.

The single most important influence on the outcome of an inquisitorial trial was whether the defendant confessed or not. Confession would, of course, almost automatically lead to conviction; confession would also lead to a reduction of the punishment that accompanied a guilty verdict. Any trial has elements of negotiations, and in the Holy Office, an admission of guilt could be traded for a more lenient sentence, just as with a modern plea-bargain. Yet, it was not with the prosecutor the defendant could strike such a deal, but rather with the inquisitors. Hence, the extent of the reduction of punishment depended on when and how the confession was made. We should also remember that in theory, a trial in the Inquisition was not just a trial for law-breaking but also an attempt at saving the defendant's soul. Confession affected both the internal and external forums and was essential to both convict and convert and reintegrate the heretic so that he could be saved from eternal damnation.

A general outline of the effects of a confession in cases of formal heresy carrying the death penalty is the following. If the confession was made during a period of grace, the defendant would not suffer the death penalty, imprisonment, or confiscation of property. Outside of the period of grace, a voluntary confession made before he was arrested would lead to reconciliation with confiscation of property. If he confessed after witnesses had been questioned, or after having been cited to appear before the tribunal, he could likewise be reconciled and sentenced to perpetual imprisonment with loss of property. In a similar fashion, if the defendant confessed after having been sentenced to death, the inquisitors had the option of converting the sentence to reconciliation with perpetual prison and confiscation of property. As an example, Cándida Compañero had been reconciled for Islamic practices in Zaragoza in 1587. In 1609, she was sentenced to be relaxed for the same offence, but on the morning of 16 November 1609 – the day of the auto da fe in which she would be burned – 'she asked for an *audiencia*, confessed and asked to be absolved and reconciled'. Even though she had been reconciled once, the Inquisition agreed to spare her life and reconcile her a second time, this time with perpetual jail and *sambenito*.[162] Even more dramatically, at the auto da fe in Llerena in 1570, two women, doña Beatriz Rol and doña Catalina de Torres, who both had refused to confess during their trials did so on the stage during the auto da fe itself in front of the suitably awed crowd who saw them taken back to the Inquisition's jail to have their cases reopened. Both were reconciled in an auto da fe the year after, on 23 July 1571, and doña Beatriz was penanced again six years later.[163] Such last-moment confessions were considered so important events by the inquisitors that they made it the subject of the famous painting 'Saint Dominic presiding an auto', by

Berruguete, (today on display at the Prado Museum), and painted on Torquemada's direct order.

If the defendants cried, begged for forgiveness, and expressed great remorse at their previous actions and a great desire to live as good Catholics in the future, that could make the sentence much lighter than if the confession appeared strategic and insincere. A tearful confession on the threshold of death and a claim to suddenly have become a sincere Catholic might certainly appear less than heartfelt to a cynical spectator (and we know that there were some), but its dramatic effect on the electrified crowd who witnessed it would compensate for this. It certainly paid to be charismatic and a good actor when on trial. The principle of *arbitrium* left the inquisitors – and the Inquisition as an institution – enormous discretion in deciding their sentences, though the general principle was that it was to be lighter the earlier a confession was obtained, and suitably heavier when the guilty stubbornly refused to repent and confess.

The decisory phase of the trial started with the *consulta de fe*, which later was abandoned, in the late seventeenth century, when the *Suprema* made all final judgements. During this votation, held in the fiscal's absence, the opinions on the case were first set out by the *consultores* (judges from the local chancery), then by the ordinary (the bishop or his representative), and finally by the inquisitors with the senior one speaking last. The fact that inquisitors sometimes had been bishop's vicars and later in their careers many became bishops or chancery judges, meant that the two groups of men who voted with the inquisitors in sentencing inquisitorial trials normally came from the same social group and shared a common outlook, education and career path. The inclusion of these men did not so much give the sentencing panels different cultural and intellectual influences as ensure the integration of the Inquisition in the local power matrix and commit other local authorities to the decisions reached by the Holy Office. Being part of the decision-making process, the bishop and chancery could hardly complain too loudly of the Inquisition's actions afterwards.

Following the vote came the promulgation of the sentence. In case of a conviction, the written sentence should contain all the errors the convict had confessed or had been found guilty of. It should not contain the names of the witnesses, or circumstances that would enable the convict to identify them. If on the other hand it ended with an acquittal, the verdict frequently did not name the crime the defendant was acquitted of. Another possibility was sentencing to torture if there was insufficient evidence for a conviction, but too much for an acquittal, and so the trial would resume again. The final sentence should then be read to the defendant by an inquisitor.

If the defendant was not acquitted, and the trial was not suspended or simply dropped, the sentence would end with one of three types of conviction. By far the most common one in our period was that the convict was 'penanced', which meant that he or she had committed some minor offence or was suspected of some lesser form of heresy. Punishing those merely suspect had Medieval roots. The council of Tarragona in 1242 had decided that suspicion of heresy in itself was punishable, and not simply grounds for an investigation and trial.[164] This, of course, was also in line with the development of the doctrine of *arbitrium* outlined earlier, which aimed precisely at avoiding situations where serious offences went unpunished because of strict evidentiary rules. The convicted person usually appeared in a public *auto da fe* dressed in a *sambenito* (penitentiary garb), and heard the sentence read aloud. Normally, the convict was required to abjure the heresy he or she had been accused of, either *de levi* or *de vehementi*, depending on the seriousness of the offence and the implied degree of suspected heresy. This was followed by whatever punishment the tribunal decided to inflict.

The second type of conviction was that the accused was sentenced to be reconciled, signifying that he or she was found to have been a heretic formally outside the community of Catholic believers and would now be readmitted. As with the penanced, the reconciled were ordinarily presented at an *auto da fe* where their sentence and punishment was read out. Their punishment was not necessarily any harsher, since both the penanced and the reconciled where subjected to pecuniary and corporeal punishments which varied much over time, being much harsher in the late fifteenth and sixteenth centuries than in the second half of the seventeenth century and later.

The Spanish Inquisition never used the word execution about those killed on its orders, preferring the euphemism 'relaxation to the secular branch' to describe the burning of those sentenced to death, the third type of conviction. This could be in person or in effigy, as could any other sentence, at least in theory. Relaxation in effigy was quite common. It was necessary for the successful confiscation of the convict's property, in addition to sending a clear message of the reach of the Holy Office which could even pretend to judge and convict the dead. In fact, relaxation in effigy is more frequent than that in person according to the data currently in EMID. This may possibly be due to the relative weight of later trials among those registered, yet the Holy Office was always eager for the prosecution of the deceased and the subsequent confiscation of their property, even in its early period when many converso families and clans were being convicted wholesale with testimony and confessions that implicated the dead as well as the living. Furthermore, like every other early modern judicial system, the Spanish Inquisition considered flight to be an open admission of guilt, and therefore systematically convicted the absent to be relaxed in effigy. Some of those burned in effigy were later tried in person. Not all died: As an example, Guiomar de Alvarado was burned in effigy as a fugitive Judaizer in Llerena at an auto da fe on 12 June 1569. She was thereafter arrested by the Portuguese Inquisition in Evora and remitted to Llerena where she was reconciled at an auto da fe on 29 July 1571. Her travails did not end there; she was convicted a third time and penanced in Llerena in 1577 or 1578.[165] Mari López, who we have already met, Catalina Pérez, and Joana López were – as far as we know – spared a third trial, but they all appeared at the same first two auto da fe as Guiomar de Alvarado, convicted of exactly the same offences and they were condemned in the same way: first relaxation in effigy and then two years later reconciliation in person. These were not the only ones, we have other examples spanning at least a century over various tribunals, that show that the Holy Office was willing to reconcile someone who had already been sentenced to die in absentia and let them be reincorporated into the Catholic Church. It was not, however, willing to restitute their confiscated property when it did so, confiscating rather whatever new belongings the defendants had brought with them.

Other sentences in effigy were relatively rare: Only 233 other sentences were declared in effigy in our material, 217 of them reconciliations and the other 16 penanced in effigy, typically, but not always, when the defendant had died after sentencing and before the *auto de fe*. Yet they never seem to have stopped being attractive to the Holy Office. The earliest records in EMID are from 1493 when no fewer than 30 such cases are registered from the tribunals in Valladolid and Toledo,[166] and as late as 7 July 1754, Manuela Fernanda was reconciled in effigy as a Judaizer in an *auto particular* in the convent of the Poor Clares in Llerena after perishing in jail during the course of her trial.[167]

Every inquisitorial conviction carried a sentence which had a spiritual, corporal and pecuniary component. The spiritual component was in part made up of the decision to penance, reconcile, or execute the convicted. Relaxation was, of course, a physical as well as a spiritual punishment, and even in effigy, it always implied confiscation of all the convicted person's property.[168] Sentences of reconciliation normally entailed confiscation of all property. Since the very beginning and throughout the Inquisition's existence, such confiscations were in fact not usually executed. The assets were restored to their owner when returning home against a yearly rent paid to the tribunal, sometimes on a collective basis when various members of the same complicity had been dispatched together.[169] Penitence rarely includes full or partial confiscation of property, but usually simply a fine as pecuniary punishment. Alternatively, the defendant might be ordered to pay a sum of money to cover 'the extraordinary expenses of the Holy Office' – even if acquitted, since this was disingenuously claimed by the inquisitors not to be punishment. The corporeal part of the punishment could be anything from isolation in a monastery to service as a galley slave or burning alive, with banishment in combination with flogging a very common one.

The pecuniary, corporeal, and spiritual components of the inquisitorial sentence could be combined in myriad ways, depending on the offence, recent instructions, the physical and financial state of the convict, and so on. For example, Francisco de Reina was one of a number of convicts who escaped the galleys because he lacked an arm, and thus was useless as a rower.[170] As a result of the many ways a sentence could be combined, somebody sentenced to be penanced could well have a harsher physical punishment than someone who was reconciled. For example, in 1724, Andrés García de Soria, alias don Manuel López de Toro, was convicted of bigamy in Murcia and sentenced to abjure *de levi*, two hundred strokes of the whip, and eight years of banishment, the first five of which was to be served as a galley slave.[171] In contrast, the Frenchman Fabian Dalvi was denounced, convicted, and reconciled as a Protestant in the same tribunal in 1688. His punishment consisted of reconciliation with *sambenito*, which he had to wear for one year while he was imprisoned and received religious instruction as a Catholic.[172]

Sentences changed over time, gradually growing lighter in terms of the punishment inflicted, and they were to a great degree left to the *arbitrium* of the local Inquisition tribunals with limited concrete guidance in laws and instructions. Sometimes political considerations came into play, such as when the crown's need for galley rowers led to the introduction of 'unpaid penance at the oars' as a new form of physical punishment in the sixteenth century.[173] Furthermore, the Inquisition was economically totally dependent on confiscations and fines up to the mid-sixteenth century. It has been convincingly demonstrated that the start of the persecution Moriscos around 1540 was due to the necessity of tapping a new source of income.[174] The Inquisition's permanent need for money undoubtedly influenced the pecuniary aspects of the sentences,[175] while trade and peace treaties and propaganda needs also influenced how harshly some groups of convicts were treated at various times.[176] In addition to these forms of convictions, the Inquisition used a number of devices to end a trial without conviction, or even a final sentence.

Acquittals in law

The instructions of the Inquisition do not have a great deal to say on the issue of acquittals. Clearly, the demonstrated innocence of the accused was not considered an important matter or a real problem. Contemporary manuals on canon and secular law also make few references to acquittals and are not very loquacious when they do. For example, fray Pedro de los Angeles writes that a definite sentence can be only a conviction or an acquittal. The only discussion he makes of acquittals in the chapter on sentencing is the rather improbable conundrum of whether or not a judge should convict a man he secretly knows to be innocent even though the crime has been legally proven.[177]

Since formal prosecution in the Spanish Inquisition was to start only on the basis of evidence of guilt the whole system of trial was directed towards a conviction. The instructions state that where the prosecution did fail to prove the accusation, the defendant was to be acquitted using the form of acquittal known as *absolución de la instancia*, which was, in fact, the form used in almost all the acquittals under study here. If at the end of the summary phase, there was suspicion of guilt but insufficient evidence to convict, the defendant could be tortured. The instructions issued in Toledo in 1565 by inquisitor general Valdés state that if the crime is 'half proven', so that the defendant cannot be acquitted, there are three options; he may be sentenced to swear off the heresy which he is suspected of, he may be ordered to swear an oath of compurgation with a number of others who swear to his innocence, or he may be tortured.[178] In practice, the Inquisition, like Spanish secular justice in this era,[179] did not use the medieval oath of compurgation,[180] so the real choice was between torture or a sentence of penance with abjuration of heresy and other, frequently harsh, 'extraordinary' punishments instead of the law-prescribed 'ordinary' punishments. As time wore on and the use of torture declined, so did the harshness of those extraordinary punishments. A decision to torture raised the stakes for both the defendant and the Inquisition: the defendant received a much more severe punishment if he confessed, but it also meant that he could be acquitted, since resistance to torture was considered to purge the 'half-proof' evidence against the defendant.[181] The Toledo instructions order that

> if the defendant resists the torture without confessing, the inquisitors shall consider the quality of the evidence, the form and quantity of the torture, the age and disposition of the defendant. And, when everything considered, it appears that the defendant has sufficiently purged the evidence, the inquisitors shall acquit him *de la instancia*.[182]

This, then, was the form for acquittals to be used when the prosecution failed to prove its case, and the defendant did not confess under torture. In practice, it was also used without torturing the defendant when it became obvious that there was not even circumstantial evidence against him.

There are more frequent mentions of acquittals in the *cartas acordadas* than in the instructions, usually in the context of specific types of trials or cases. Given the nature of the *cartas acordadas* and the vast number of them that have survived, it is impractical to attempt to give a full account of their content in its entirety, in particular when we take into consideration that so many of them have been lost and that they frequently only applied to a single tribunal.[183] What follows is a sample of such letters, showing how the issues of absolution and acquittal occasionally turn up in the preserved *cartas acordadas*.

One context was the attempts of some confessors to absolve confessed heretics without informing the Inquisition. The formal procedure was to allow sacramental absolution only after the completion of an inquisitorial trial, and all confessors had strict orders to send all confessants who admitted heresy or other offences under the Inquisition's jurisdiction to the Holy Office without giving them absolution until they had been judged by the inquisitors.[184] This could be challenged during papal Jubilees and under the Crusade Bull. The Crusade Bull was a papal bull issued to the Spanish monarchy to help finance the wars against Muslims.[185] It was instrumental in helping finance the conquest of Granada, and it was reissued and extended a number of times over the next centuries to help pay for new wars against enemies of the faith. In reality, the money was frequently spent for other purposes. The Crusade Bull granted a number of indulgences, absolutions, and privileges to those who made economical contributions to the Holy War as a substitute for other penance for their sins. Jubilees could also carry promises of absolution, and hence be seen as a threat to the Inquisition's position. According to a recent study, the Crusade Bull 'gave confessors the power to absolve penitents of nearly all sins, even those reserved sins that would otherwise have fallen under episcopal, papal, or inquisitorial jurisdiction'.[186] The *Suprema* most certainly did not see it this way.

Thus, Granada received a *carta acordada* in October 1628 ordering the tribunal to inform all priests and prelates that they were not allowed to absolve heresy during the Jubilees, despite the fact that the papal bull did not say so explicitly. Reference was made to an earlier letter dated 30 May 1572, stating that under no circumstance could confessors absolve heresy.[187] This was probably a reference to the *carta acordada* originally sent on that day to the tribunals of Cuenca and Toledo, informing those tribunals that the *cruzada* did not allow the absolution of heresy and that they should make this information public.[188] In October, the same year, both these tribunals were instructed to inform the prelates in their districts of the papal brief. Four years later, the same two tribunals received a new letter on the same subject, stating that any absolution for heresy received through the Crusade Bull would be invalid because it was never the intention of Pius III or Gregor XV that the bull should absolve heresy. The next year, in 1577, both Cuenca and Toledo were once more instructed to have this papal brief read from the pulpits.[189] Again in 1578, Toledo was instructed to declare publicly that a Jubilee did not affect matters belonging to the Inquisition, according to a papal brief from Gregor XV. Thus, a century and a half after its introduction, the Spanish Inquisition was still having to defend its monopoly on dealing with heresy from confessors eager to expand their own powers of absolution.

So far we have seen how the Inquisition operated, the legal framework it was based on, and what the legislation had to say about acquittals. However, acquittals were not the only way a trial could end without a conviction. Some of these other ways of ending the trial, most notably the suspension of the trial, are very similar and have to be considered alongside acquittals. This we will do in the following chapter.

Notes

1 See, for example, the classic study by Kagan: Richard Kagan, *Lawsuits and Litigants in Castille 1500–1700* (Chapel Hill: University of North Carolina Press, 1981). See also Pablo Pérez García, *la comparsa de los malhechores: Valencia 1479–1518* (Valencia: Diputació de València, Centre d'Estudis d'Història Local, 1990).
2 Lea, *A History*, vol. 3, 273.
3 Monter, *Frontiers of Heresy*, 63–64.
4 See, Jean Pierre Dedieu and Gunnar W. Knutsen, "la cause de foi dans l'Inquisition espagnole," *Annales*, no. 1 (2023).
5 Prospero Farinacci, *Prosperi Farinacii jurisconsulti romani Tractatus de haeresi, in quo per questiones, regulas, ampliationes, limitationes quidquid jure civili et canonico, quidquid Sacris Consiliis, Summorumque Pontificum constitutionibus sancitum et communiter in ea materia receptum, quidquid denique in praxi servandum, brevi methodo illustratur, cum argumentis, summariis et indice locupletissimo* (Antwerp, 1616). Quaestio CXCII §52.
6 Quintiliano Mandosio, Pietro Vendramini, and Damiano Zenaro, *Repertorium Inquisitorum prauitatis haereticae: in quo omnia, quae ad haeresum cognitionem ac S. Inquisitionis forum pertinent, continentur* (Venice, 1575), 10.
7 Farinacci, *Tractatus de haeresi,* CLXXIX §8.
8 Farinacci, *Tractatus de haeresi,* CLXXIX §20.
9 Farinacci, *Tractatus de haeresi,* CLXXIX §22.
10 Farinacci, *Tractatus de haeresi,* CLXXIX §23.
11 Farinacci, *Tractatus de haeresi,* CLXXIX §33.
12 Farinacci, *Tractatus de haeresi,* CLXXIX §35.
13 For these trials, see Monter, *Frontiers of Heresy*; Rafael Carrasco, *Inquisición y represión sexual en Valencia. Historia de los sodomitas, 1565–1785* (Barcelona: Laertes, 1985); Berco, *Sexual Hierarchies*.
14 Monter, *Frontiers of Heresy*, 279.
15 Henry Charles Lea, *A History*, vol. 4, 316.
16 The only study of all such trials in all three jurisdictions in parallel in a given area remains María Tausiet, *Ponzoña en los ojos. Brujería y superstición en Aragón en el siglo XVI* (Zaragoza: Institución Fernando el Católico, 2000).
17 Knutsen, *Servants of Satan*, 100–115.
18 This was a variation of the love magic that was so prevalent in Valencia. See, Knutsen, *Servants of Satan*.
19 Adelina Sarrión Mora, "Clérigos torpes y mujeres solicitadas en los procesos de la Inquisición española," *Arbor: Ciencia, pensamiento y cultura*, no. 611 (1996); Juan Antonio Alejandre, *El veneno de Dios. la Inquisición de Sevilla ante el delito de solicitación en confesión* (Madrid: Siglo Veintiuno, 1994); Stephen Haliczer, *Sexuality in the Confessional. A Sacrament Profaned*, Studies in the History of Sexuality (New York: Oxford University Press, 1996).
20 Winfried Trusen, "Der Inquisitionsprozeß: Seine historischen Grundlagen und frühen Formen," *Zeitschrift der Savigny-Stiftung für Rechtsgeschichte. Kanonistische Abteilung* 74, no. 1 (1988), https://doi.org/10.7767/zrgka.1988.74.1.168.
21 The question of whether it is meaningful to speak of a Medieval Inquisition or simply Medieval inquisitors hinges on whether there was an institution that existed independently of the men who at any given time exercised the function of inquisitor. The negation of this has been most forcefully stated by Richard Kieckhefer and Henry Ansgar Kelly. Richard Kieckhefer, "The Office of Inquisition and Medieval Heresy: The Transaction from Personal to Institutional Jurisdiction," *The Journal of Ecclesiastical History* 46, no. 1 (1995), https://doi.org/10.1017/

S0022046900012537; Henry Ansgar Kelly, "Inquisition and the Prosecution of Heresy: Misconceptions and Abuses,"' *Church History* 58, no. 4 (1989). The contrary view has been defended by Euan Cameron and Alan Friedlander, while Bernard Hamilton explicitly rejects Kieckhefer's views. Bernard Hamilton, *The Medieval Inquisition* (London: Edward Arnold, 1981), 9. Alan Friedlander found that by the early fourteenth century, contemporaries saw the office of Inquisition as having an existence independent of the individual inquisitors. Alan Friedlander, *The Hammer of the Inquisitors: Brother Bernard Délicieux and the Struggle Against the Inquisition in Fourteenth-Century France, Cultures, Beliefs and Traditions Medieval and Early Modern Peoples* (Leiden, Boston, MA and Köln: Brill, 2000), 270–72. In the same vein, Euan Cameron writes that in Prague, one came very close to having a permanent office of the Inquisition in the late Middle Ages. Euan Cameron, *Waldenses: Rejections of Holy Church in Medieval Europe* (Wiley, 2001). More frequently, perhaps, the phrase 'Medieval Inquisition' has been used as a convenient designation without considering the question of whether it actually existed as an institution.

22 A dated, but useful survey is Walter L. Wakefield, *Heresy, Crusade and Inquisition in Southern France 1100–1250* (G. Allen & Unwin, 1974).

23 Cameron, *Waldenses: Rejections of Holy Church in Medieval Europe*, 110.

24 Lea, *A History*, vol. 1, 176.

25 For the finances of the Spanish Inquisition in its first decades, see the painstaking reconstruction undertaken by José María Cruselles and his team: Cruselles Gómez, "la primera contabilidad inquisitorial."

26 Jaime Contreras and Jean-Pierre Dedieu, "Estructuras geograficas del Santo Oficio en España," in *Las estructuras del Santo Oficio, Historia de la Inquisición en España y America*, ed. Joaquin Pérez Villanueva and Bartolomé Escandell Bonet (Madrid: Biblioteca de Autores Cristianos, 1993); Jaime Contreras and Jean Pierre Dedieu, "Geografia de la Inquisición española: la formación de los distritos, 1470–1820," *Hispania* 40, no. 144 (1980).

27 José Ramón Rodríguez Besné, *El Consejo de la Suprema Inquisición* (Madrid: Editorial Complutense, 2000); Teresa Sánchez Rivilla, "Biografía de la cúpula del Santo Oficio: inquisidores generales y consejeros de la suprema: documentación biográfica," in *Historia de la Inquisición en España y América*, ed. Bartolomé Escandell Bonet and Joaquín Pérez Villanueva (Madrid: BAC, 2000).

28 The literature on the figure of the Inquisitor general is not as extensive as one might think, all though there are biographies of some of the most important ones. The most important works are Luis González Novalín José, *El Inquisidor general Fernando de Valdes (1483–1568). 1. su vida y su obra* (Oviedo: Universidad de Oviedo, 1968); Luis González Novalín José, *El Inquisidor general Fernando de Valdes (1483–1568). 2. cartas y documentos* (Oviedo: Universidad de Oviedo, 1971); Eduardo Galván Rodriguez, *El Inquisidor General* (Madrid: Dykinson, 2010); Isabel Mendoza García, "El Inquisidor General Don Diego de Arce y Reynoso," Unpublished doctoral diss., Universidad Autónoma de Madrid, 1993.

29 For the evolution of the geography of the Spanish Inquisition, see Contreras and Dedieu, "Geografia de la Inquisición española: la formación de los distritos, 1470–1820." Bartolomé Bennassar, "Aux origines du caciquisme: les familiers de l'Inquisition en Andalousie au XVIIe siècle?," *Cahiers du monde hispanique et luso-brésilien*, no. 27 (1976).

30 Some of the most biting indictments of the character of the familiars and accusations against the Inquisition for tolerating their excesses come from Lea and Monter: Lea, *A History* 2, 2, 272–82; Monter, *Frontiers of Heresy*.

31 José M. González del Valle, *Derecho eclesiástico español*, 4th ed. (Oviedo: Universidad de Oviedo, 1997), 266–68.

32 See, for example, Pedro M. Guibovich Pérez, "Custodios de la ortodoxia: los calificadores de la Inquisición de Lima, 1570–1754," *Revista de la Inquisición: (intolerancia y derechos humanos)*, no. 10 (2001); Manuel Peña Díaz, "Sobre expurgos y calificadores. Debates en torno a la censura inquisitorial (siglos XVI–XVII)," in *Edición y literatura en España (Siglos XVI y XVII)* (Zaragoza: Universidad de Zaragoza, 2012); Marina Torres Arce, "Comisarios, familiares y calificadores en el distrito del tribunal inquisitorial de Logroño (1690–1705)," in *Política, religión e inquisición en la España moderna: homenaje a Joaquín Pérez Villanueva* (Madrid: Universidad Autónoma de Madrid, 1996); Contreras, *El Santo Oficio de la Inquisición en Galicia, 1560–1700.* Poder, *Sociedad y cultura.*
33 Julio Caro Baroja, *El señor inquisidor, y otras vidas por oficio* (Madrid: Alianza Editorial, 1968), 17–18.
34 Kimberly Lynn, *Between Court and Confessional: The Politics of Spanish Inquisitors* (Cambridge: Cambridge University Press, 2013), 3.
35 Herman H. Schwedt, *Die Anfänge der römischen Inquisition: Kardinäle und Konsultoren 1542 bis 1600, Römische Quartalschrift für christliche Altertumskunde und Kirchengeschichte* (Freiburg: Herder, 2013); Herman H. Schwedt et al., *Prosopographie von Römischer Inquisition und Indexkongregation 1701–1813*, 2 vols., Römische Inquisition und Indexkongregation Grundlagenforschung 1701–1813 (Paderborn: Ferdinand Schöningh, 2010).
36 See the relevant sections in, for example, Contreras, *El Santo Oficio de la Inquisición en Galicia, 1560–1700.* Poder, *Sociedad y cultura*; Dedieu, *L'Administration de la foi*; Haliczer, *Inquisition and Society*; Solange Alberro, *Inquisition et societe au Mexique: 1571–1700* (Mexico City: Centre D'Etudes Mexicaines et Centramericaines, 1988); Ricardo García Cárcel, *Herejía y sociedad en el siglo XVI: la Inquisición en Valencia, 1530–1609* (Barcelona: Ediciones Peninsula, 1980); Ricardo García Cárcel, *Orígines de la Inquisición española: El tribunal de Valencia 1478–1530*, 2nd ed. (Barcelona: Ediciones Peninsula, 1985).
37 Maximiliano Barrio Gozalo, "Burocracia inquisitorial y movilidad social. El Santo Oficio plantel de obispos (1556–1820)," in *Inquisición y sociedad*, ed. Ángel de Prado Moura (Valladolid: Universidad de Valladolid, 1999); Sánchez Rivilla, "Biografía de la cúpula del Santo Oficio: inquisidores generales y consejeros de la suprema: documentación biográfica."
38 See, for example, Gonzalo Cerillo Cruz, "Aproximación al estatuto jurídico de los familiares de la inquisición española," *Manuscrits: Revista d'història moderna*, no. 17 (1999); Gonzalo Cerrillo Cruz, "El capitán de familiares," *Revista de la Inquisición: (intolerancia y derechos humanos)*, no. 2 (1992); Gonzalo Cerrillo Cruz, "Los familiares de la Inquisición en la epoca borbonica," *Revista de la Inquisición* 4 (1995); Cerrillo Cruz, *Los familiares de la Inquisición española* (Valladolid: Junta de Castilla y León, 2000); María del Pilar Domínguez Salgado, "Los familiares del Tribunal de Corte (1665–1820). Primera parte: Origen, trayectoria histórica y estudio sociológico," *Anales del Instituto de Estudios Madrileños* 47 (2007); García Cárcel, "Número y sociología."; Ortega Gómez, "la Inquisición en el mundo rural: los familiares del Santo Oficio del Tribunal de Toledo durante el siglo XVII."; Ricardo García Cárcel, "Número y sociología de los familiares de la inquisición valenciana," in *la Inquisición española. Nueva visión, nuevos horizontes*, ed. Joaquin Pérez Villanueva (Madrid: Siglo XXI, 1980); Lorena Ortega Gómez, "la Inquisición en el mundo rural: los familiares del Santo Oficio del Tribunal de Toledo durante el siglo XVII," in *Campo y campesinos en la España Moderna; culturas políticas en el mundo hispano* (Madrid: Fundación Española de Historia Moderna, 2012); Contreras, *El Santo Oficio.*
39 Bartolomé Bennassar, "Le pouvoir inquisitorial," in *L'Inquisition espagnole XVe–XIXe siècle*, ed. Bartolomé bennassar (Paris: Hachette, 1979), 83.

40 The fiscal's duties are described in some detail in Isabel Martínez Navas, "Un manual para Fiscales del Santo Oficio," *Revista de la Inquisición: (intolerancia y derechos humanos)*, no. 24 (2020).
41 BN, MS. 2440.
42 Knutsen, *Servants of Satan,* 121, 130.
43 Haliczer, *Inquisition and Society*, 145.
44 Lu Ann Homza, *Village Infernos and Witches' Advocates: Witch-Hunting in Navarre, 1608–1614* (University Park: Penn State University Press, 2022).
45 Starr-LeBeau, *In the Shadow of the Virgin*, 151.
46 John Edwards, *Inquisition* (Tempus, 2003), 97.
47 Haim Beinart, *Conversos on Trial. The Inquisition in Ciudad Real* (Jerusalem: The Magnus Press, 1981), 153.
48 Starr-LeBeau, *In the Shadow of the Virgin.*
49 In one notable episode, the bishop of Cuba claimed the right to hold Inquisition himself in his diocese as late as the seventeenth century. Gunnar W. Knutsen, "Witchcraft and Slavery in Cartagena de Indias," *Magic, Ritual, and Witchcraft* 15, no. 2 (2020).
50 The best introduction in English is Manlio Bellomo, *The Common Legal Past of Europe: 1000–1800*, trans. Lydia G. Cochrane (Washington, DC: The Catholic University of America Press, 1995).
51 Alessi Palazzolo, *Prova legale e pena la crisi del sistema tra evo medio e moderno.*
52 John H. Langbein, *Torture and the Law of Proof* (Chicago, IL: University of Chicago Press, 1977).
53 Pedro Ortego Gil, "El arbitrio de los jueces inferiores: su alcance y limitaciones," in *El arbitrio judicial en el Antiguo Régimen: España e Indias, siglos XVI–XVIII*, ed. José Sánchez-Arcilla Bernal (Madrid: Dykinson, 2013).
54 See, for example, José Sánchez-Arcilla Bernal, ed., *El arbitro judicial en el Antiguo Régimen: (España e Indias, siglos XVI–XVIII)* (Madrid: Dykinson, 2013). Massimo Meccarelli, *Arbitrium: un aspetto sistematico degli ordinamenti giuridici in età di diritto comune*, Pubblicazioni della Facoltà di giurisprudenza, (Milano: A. Giuffrè, 1998); Bernard Durand, *Arbitraire du juge et consuetudo delinquendi la doctrine pénale en Europe du XVIe au XVIIIe siècle* Publications de la Société d'histoire du droit et des institutions des anciens pays de droit écrit, (Montpellier: Société d' histoire du droit et des institutions des anciens pays de droit écrit, 1993); Bernard Schnapper, "Peines arbitraires du XIIIe au XVIIIe siecle (Doctrines savantes et usages francais)," *Tijdschrift voor Rechtsgeschiedenis* 42, no. 3–4 (1974).María Paz Alonso Romero, *El proceso penal en Castilla (siglos XIII-XVIII)* (Ediciones Universidad de Salamanca, 1982).
55 Bellomo, *The Common Legal.*
56 Alessi Palazzolo, *Prova legale e pena la crisi del sistema tra evo medio e moderno.*
57 María del Pilar Rábade Obradó, "la toma de decisiones en relación con las denuncias de criptojudíos ante los tribunales de Ciudad Real y Toledo (1483–1504)," *Revista de la Inquisición: (intolerancia y derechos humanos)*, no. 22 (2018): 164.
58 Bellomo, *The Common Legal*, 90–91.
59 Farinacci, *Tractatus de haeresi,* XCIII §96.
60 See, for example, Doris Moreno Martínez, "la discrecionalidad de un inquisidor. Francisco Vaca, ¿el primer abogado de las brujas?," *Revista Internacional de los Estudios Vascos, RIEV*, no. 9 (2012).
61 José Luiz González Novalin, "Las instrucciones de la Inquisición española. de Torquemada a Valdés (1484–1561)," in *Perfiles juridicos de la Inquisición española*, ed. José Antonio Escudero (Madrid: Instituto de Historia de la Inquisición. Universidad Complutense de Madrid, 1989), 98.

62 Gaspar Isidrio de Argüello, *Instrucciones del Santo Oficio de la Inquisición, sumariamente, antiguas y nuevas* (Madrid: Imprenta Real, 1630), fol. 27v.
63 See Eduardo Galván Rodríguez, *El secreto en la Inquisición española* (Gran Canaria: Universidad de Las Palmas de Gran Canaria, 2001).
64 Valdes' Instructions from 1561, §6. de Argüello, *Instrucciones* fol. 28r.
65 Torquemada's instructions from 1488, §5. de Argüello, *Instrucciones* fol. 10r.
66 Valdes' Instructions from 1561, §10. de Argüello, *Instrucciones* fol. 28v.
67 See, for example, Dedieu, *L'Administration de la foi*; Starr-LeBeau, *In the Shadow of the Virgin*; Lynn, *Between Court and Confessional: The Politics of Spanish Inquisitors*, 70. The problems of employees treating documents as their private property wasn't limited to the Spanish Inquisition in this period. Matthieu Pène, "Le temps des archives et la périodisation historique: une histoire découpée en boîtes ?," *Questes* (2016): 39, https://doi.org/10.4000/questes.4315.
68 Susana Cabezas Fontanilla, "Nuevas aportaciones al estudio del archivo del Consejo de la Suprema Inquisición," *Documenta & Instrumenta* 5 (2007).
69 Relación in AHN, Inq, Lib. 865, fols. 50r–100v.
70 John Arnold, *Inquisition and Power: Catharism and the Confessing Subject in Medieval Languedoc*, The Middle Ages Series (Philadelphia: University of Pennsylvania Press, 2001), 2.
71 Jean-Pierre Dedieu, *L'Inquisition* (Paris: Éditions du Cerf, 1987).
72 Dedieu, *L'Inquisition*, 107.
73 For some time the desire to find extra-judicial resolutions to social conflicts that ended up in the courts was held to be a characteristic of so-called 'primitive societies' before the insights of legal anthropology revealed its relevance also to contemporary justice. Simon Roberts, *Order and Dispute: An Introduction to Legal Anthropology*, 2nd ed., Classics of Law & Society Series (Quid Pro, LLC, 2013); Norbert Rouland, *Legal Anthropology* (London: Athlone Press, 1994). In early modern Europe this search for extra-judicial solutions was pervasive.

   For a recent study, see Stéphanie Blot-Maccagnan, *Procédure criminelle et défense de l'accusé à la fin de l'Ancien Régime: étude de la pratique angevine* (Rennes: Presses universitaires de Rennes, 2010). See also the classic, Natalie Zemon Davies, *Fiction in the Archives: Pardon Tales and Their Tellers in Sixteenth-Century France* (Stanford, CA: Stanford University Press, 1987).
74 AHN, Inq, Lib 976, fol. 229r. The *relación* of the eventual *auto* held on 21 February 1639 is in AHN, Inq, Lib 992, fols. 411r–429r.
75 Monter, *Frontiers of Heresy*, 265–67; Knutsen, *Servants of Satan*, 88–89, 119–20.
76 Torquemada's instructions from 1488, §3. Printed in de Argüello, *Instrucciones* fol. 9r.
77 *Relaciones* from Llerena in AHN, Inq, leg. 1988, exp. 3, 2r–6v, and exp. 5, fols. 1r–6v.
78 The Roman Inquisition saw this use of external experts only in the 'wealthier and busier tribunals'. Black, *The Italian Inquisition*, 59.
79 AHN, Inq, Libs 238, 239 and 240.
80 Martínez Navas, "Un Manual," 24.
81 AHN, Inq, Lib 933, fols. 23v–32r.
82 Knutsen, "Where Did the Witches Go?' An updated translated Spanish version is published as Gunnar W. Knutsen, "Después de la condena: supuestas hechiceras y brujas en Valencia después de sus procesos inquisitoriales," in *Mulieres Inquisitionis: la mujer frente a la Inquisición en España*, ed. María Jesús Zamora Calvo (Vigo: Academia del Hispanismo, 2017).
83 Pauline Croft, "Englishmen and the Spanish Inquisition 1558–1625," *The English Historical Review* 87, no. 343 (1972); Gunnar W. Knutsen and Daniel Muñoz Navarro, "Prosecuting the French: Patterns of Trials Against French Defendants

in Valencia, 1566–1686," *Continuity and Change* 25, no. 3 (2010), https://doi.org/doi:10.1017/S0268416010000275; Gunnar W. Knutsen, "Religious Life in Seventeenth Century Norway Seen Through the Eyes of the Spanish Inquisition," *Arv: Scandinavian Yearbook of Folklore* 61 (2005); Werner Thomas, *Los protestantes y la Inquisición en España en tiempos de Reforma y Contrareforma* (Leuven: Leuven University Press, 2001); Werner Thomas, *la represión del protestantismo en España, 1517–1648* (Leuven: Leuven University Press, 2001).

84 See, for example, Knutsen, "Religious Life"; Gunnar W. Knutsen, "El Santo Oficio de la Inquisición en Barcelona y soldados protestantes en el ejercito de Cataluña," *Estudis* 34 (2008); Croft, "Englishmen and the Spanish Inquisition 1558–1625"; Pauline Croft, "English Mariners Trading to Spain and Portugal, 1558–1625," *Mariner's Mirror* 69, no. 3 (1983).

85 Gustav Henningsen, *The Witches' Advocate: Basque Witchcraft and the Spanish Inquisition* (Reno: University of Nevada Press, 1980); Gustav Henningsen, ed., *The Salazar Documents* (Leiden: Brill, 2004); Homza, *Village Infernos*; Knutsen, *Servants of Satan*; Gunnar W. Knutsen, "Topics of Persecution: Witchcraft Historiography in the Iberian World," in *Writing Witch-Hunt Histories: Challenging the Paradigm*, ed. Marko Nenonen and Raisa Maria Toivo (Leiden: Brill, 2014); Gunnar W. Knutsen, "Witchcraft and Slavery."

86 AHN, Inq, Leg 1988, exp. 8, fol. 3.

87 Homza, *Village Infernos*, 39.

88 Gretchen D. Starr-LeBeau, *In the Shadow of the Virgin*; Haim Beinart, *Conversos on Trial. The Inquisition in Ciudad Real* (Jerusalem: The Magnus Press, 1981).

89 See, for example, Jaime Contreras, *Sotos contra Riquelmes: regidores, inquisidores y criptojudíos* (Madrid: Anaya & Mario Muchnik, 1992); Juan Ignacio Pulido Serrano, *Injurias a Cristo: religión, política y antijudaísmo en el siglo XVII: (análisis de las corrientes antijudías durante la Edad Media)* (Alcalá de Henares: Instituto Internacional de Estudios Sefardíes y Andalusíes, 2002); Stanley M. Hordes, "The Inquisition as Economic and Political Agent: The Campaign of the Mexican Holy Office against the Crypto-Jews in the Mid-Seventeenth Century," *Americas: A Quarterly Review of Inter-American Cultural History* 39, no. 1 (1982); R. A. Stradling, *Philip IV and the Government of Spain, 1621–1665* (Cambridge: Cambridge University Press, 1988).

90 See, for example, Ramón Lázaro Dou y de Bassols, *Instituciones del derecho público general de España con noticia del particular de Cataluña y de las principales reglas de gobierno en qualquier [sic] Estado*, 9 vols., vol. 6, Instituciones del derecho público general de España con noticia del particular de Cataluña y de las principales reglas de gobierno en qualquier [sic] Estado (Madrid: en la Oficina de Benito García y Compañía, 1803), III, I, I, 5.

91 For the two tracks of judicial punishment and religious penance and reintegration in the inquisitorial trial, see Dedieu and Knutsen, "la cause de foi."

92 See the Toledo instructions from 1561. de Argüello, *Instrucciones*, fol. 30r.

93 de Argüello, *Instrucciones* fol. 30v.

94 *Relación* in AHN, Inq, Lib 861, fols. 106v–107r.

95 Dedieu and Knutsen, "la cause de foi."

96 Alonso Romero, *El proceso penal.*

97 Beinart, *Conversos on Trial. The Inquisition in Ciudad Real*, 145.

98 The trials become longer over time, and the stipulated trial times from the earliest instructions were routinely flouted as early as the first half of the sixteenth century – even though the instructions containing them remained in vigor and were printed in the legislative compilations of the seventeenth century.

99 Given, *Inquisition and Medieval Society: Power, Discipline, and Resistance in Languedoc*, 26–27.

100 Daniel Lord Smail, *The Consumption of Justice: Emotions, Publicity, and Legal Culture in Marseille, 1264–1423* (Ithaca, NY: Cornell University Press, 2003), 83.
101 Given, *Inquisition and Medieval Society: Power, Discipline, and Resistance in Languedoc*, 26.
102 Black, *The Italian Inquisition*, 116.
103 Black, *The Italian Inquisition*, 53.
104 Friedlander, *The Hammer of the Inquisitors: Brother Bernard Délicieux and the Struggle Against the Inquisition in Fourteenth-Century France*, 16–17.
105 Silvana Seidel Menchi, "The Inquisitor as Mediator," in *Heresy, Culture, and Religion in Early Modern Italy: Context and Contestations*, ed. Ronald K. Delph, Michelle M. Fontaine, and John Jeffries Martin (Kirksville, MO: Truman State University Press, 2006), 174.
106 BN, MS 7341, fol. 182.
107 Pérez García, "Perspectivas," 45–46.
108 AHN, Inq, lib. 936, fol. 73r.
109 AHN, Inq, Lib 27, p. 183.
110 Josef Febrero, *Libreria de escribanos, e instruccion juridica teorico practica de principiantes*, 6 vols (Madrid: en la imprenta de Antonio Perez de Soto, 1769–81), parte 2, tomo 3, p. 187.
111 Beinart, *Conversos on Trial. The Inquisition in Ciudad Real*, 112.
112 One of the obstacles to studying an Inquisition tribunal is making sense of this document flow as many of the archive pieces that have been preserved are fragments that we cannot always be certain were part of a formal trial or simply loose sheets from activities that never resulted in a trial.
113 AHN, Inq, Lib 27, pp. 173–181. Martínez Navas, "Un manual."
114 Given, *Inquisition and Medieval Society*, 40.
115 Henningsen, "The Archives and Historiography."
116 Edwards, *The Inquisitors: The Story of the Grand Inquisitors of the Spanish Inquisition*, 115.
117 AHN, Lib 942, *relación* on fols. 238–50.
118 Dedieu, *L'Administration de la foi*, 344; Homza, *Village infernos*, 166.
119 Lea, *A History* 2, 2, 91.
120 Robert Gellately, "Denunciation as a Subject of Historical Research," *Historical Social Research* 26, no. 2/3 (2001): 28, https://doi.org/10.12759/hsr.26.2001.2/3.16-29.
121 For a rare case study of how ordinary people could be activated as 'sleeper' informants for the Inquisition, see Juan Ignacio Pulido Serrano, "Las voces de la calle: testificaciones inquisitoriales contra portugueses en Madrid durante el siglo XVII," in *la Inquisición vista desde abajo: testificaciones de gente corriente ante el Santo Oficio*, ed. Juan Ignacio Pulido Serrano and William Childers (Madrid: Iberoamericana, 2020).
122 Tiberio Deciani, *Tractatus criminalis D. Tiberii Deciani . . . duobusque tomis distinctus . . . Cum summarijs, & duplici indice: altero quidem rerum, ac verborum omnium, locorumque insignium; altero vero titulorum, qui in utroque tomo continentur* (Turin: Apud haeredem Nicolai Beuilaquae, 1593), Lib. V, cap XX, 1.
123 Deciani, *Tractatus criminalis*, Lib. V, cap XX, 16–17.
124 J. Meseguer Fernández, "Los hechos," in *Historia de la Inquisición en España y America*, ed. Joaquin Pérez Villanueva and Bartolomé Escandell Bonet (Madrid: Editorial Cátolica, 1984), p. 322.
125 Dedieu, *L'Administration de la foi*, 144.

126 Jean-Pierre Dedieu, "Denunciar-denunciarse. la delación inquisitorial en Castilla la Nueva, siglos XVI-XVII," *Revista de la Inquisición*, no. 2 (1992): 96.
127 Black, *The Italian Inquisition*, 57.
128 Dedieu, "Denunciar-denunciarse. la delación inquisitorial en Castilla la Nueva, siglos XVI-XVII," 136–40.
129 Smail, *The Consumption of Justice.*
130 Gellately, "Denunciation as a Subject," 17.
131 Homza, *Village Infernos*, 66–68.
132 Adriano Prosperi, "Notas sobre Inquisición," *Manuscrits: Revista d'història moderna*, no. 17 (1999).
133 Adriano Prosperi, *Tribunali della coscienza inquisitori, confessori, missionari*, Biblioteca di cultura storica (Torino: G. Einaudi, 1996); Stefania Pastore, *Il Vangelo e la spada: l'Inquisizione di Castiglia e i suoi critici (1460–1598)* (Roma: Edizioni di storia e letteratura, 2003, 2003).
134 Berco, *Sexual Hierarchies*, 129.
135 Robert Gellately, *The Gestapo and German Society: Enforcing Racial Policy 1933–1945* (Oxford: Clarendon Press, 1990); Robert Gellately, "Denunciations in Twentieth-Century Germany: Aspects of Self-Policing in the Third Reich and the German Democratic Republic," *Journal of Modern History* 68, no. 4 (2001).
136 Lea, *A History*, vol. 2, 91–101.
137 Dedieu, *L'Administration de la foi*, 278.
138 Dedieu, *L'Administration de la foi*, 144.
139 Lea, *A History*, vol. 2, 457–63.
140 Henningsen, *The Witches' Advocate;* Homza, *Village Infernos.*
141 AHN, Inq, lib 730, fol. 186v.
142 In 1533 this led the *Cortes* of Aragon to protest: Kamen, *The Spanish Inquisition*, 183.
143 Lea, *A History*, vol. 1, 360–65. Some inquisitors were even formally charged for such fraud: Lynn, *Between Court and Confessional*, 288.
144 While the confiscation of property was an important trait of the Spanish Inquisition, it did not originate with the Holy Office. Earlier secular legislation also called for the confiscation of convicted heretics' property, and indeed also in the case of other religious crimes, such as blasphemy. Miguel Pino Abad, *la pena de confiscación de bienes en el derecho histórico español* (Editorial Dykinson, S.L., 2014), 325–49.
145 The instructions of 1561 allowed the support of dependents out of sequestrations and made it less likely that the defendant's family would be reduced to begging in the streets or dying of hunger.
146 AHN, Inq, Leg 2155.
147 The sources contain many references to prisoners who died while imprisoned in all tribunals of the Spanish Inquisition, but those in Logroño were particularly unhealthy. See Iñaki Reguera, "Las cárceles de la Inquisición de Logroño," in *Perfiles juridicos de la Inquisición española*, ed. José Antonio Escudero (Madrid: Instituto de Historia de la Inquisición. Universidad Complutense de Madrid, 1989).
148 §11. Quoted from Pablo Garcia, *Orden de processar en el Santo Oficio, recopilado de las instrucciones antiquas y modernas* (Madrid: la imprenta Real, 1628), fol. 29r.
149 AHN, Inq, Lib 1020, fols. 459v–460r.
150 AHN, Inq, Lib 1027, fols. 400v–403r.
151 AHN, Inq, Lib 930, fol. 359r.

152 The definite edition is Amiel and Lima, *L'Inquisition de Goa.*
153 Conversely, precisely the inability to end the trial by making a satisfactory confession is claimed by Dellon to have driven him to attempted suicide and eternal perdition when he was tried by the Portuguese Inquisition. Dellon, Chapter XXV (p. 178?)
154 Solange Alberro, *Inquisición y sociedad en México, 1571–1700,* Seccion de obras de historia (México: Fondo de Cultura Económica, 1988), 48.
155 Lea, *A History 3*, 3, 37–39.
156 Amiel and Lima, *L'Inquisition de Goa.*
157 The same holds true for the Roman Inquisition. Black, *The Italian Inquisition*, 81.
158 Lea, *A History*, vol. 3, 35.
159 AHN, Inq, Leg 1988, Exp 8, fol. 6r, and Exp. 12, fols 14v–15r, respectively.
160 Farinacci, *Tractatus de haeresi,* CLXXIX §47.
161 Farinacci, *Tractatus de haeresi,* XCIII §96.
162 Three *relaciones* cover her cases as they developed. These are in: AHN, INQ, lib. 989, fols. 264r–305r; lib. 991, fols. 1r–91 and 92r–156r.
163 *Relaciones* in AHN, INQ, leg. 1988, exp 5, fols. 1r–6v and exp. 10, fols. 10r–17v; leg. 1987, exp 8, fols. 1r–5v.
164 Arnold, *Inquisition and Power*, 44.
165 *Relaciones* in AHN, Inq, leg. 1988, exp3, fols. 2r–6v; exp. 5, fols. 1r–6v; and exp. 10, 10r–17v.
166 AHN, Inq, Leg. 134 exp. 5 and 14; Leg. 139, exp. 18; Leg. 150, exp. 15; Leg. 153, exp. 8 and 20; Leg. 154, exp. 8 and 26; Leg. 155, exp. 10; Leg. 177, exp. 6; and Leg. 3223, Document entitled *Memoria de los sambenitos que en 8 de mayo de 1649 años se hallaron en la capilla de Santiago, sita en la iglesia mayor de Burgos, la cual es parroquia de dicha iglesia mayor, de los cuales algunos se leían mal y otros bien.*
167 AHN, Inq, 2776. Document entitled *Relación del auto particular de fe que el domingo siete de julio de este año de 1754 celebró el Santo Oficio de la Inquisición de esta ciudad de Llerena en el convento de religiosas de Santa Clara de ella.*
168 Except in cases of witchcraft.
169 Juan Gil found just a dozen auctions as the result of some 500 confiscations. Juan Gil Fernández, *Los conversos y la inquisición sevillana*, 8 vols (Sevilla: Fundación El Monte, 2000). See also, Jean Pierre Dedieu, "Les morisques de Daimiel et l'Inquisition (1502–1612)," in *Les morisques et leur temps*, ed. Louis Cardaillac (Paris: CNRS, 1983).
170 AHN, Inq, Leg 2075, exp. 14, fols 2r–27v.
171 Relación in AHN, INQ, leg. 2853, document entitled *Memoria de los reos que salieron en el auto particular de fe que el Santo Oficio de la Inquisición de la ciudad y reino de Murcia celebró el día treinta de noviembre de 1724 en la iglesia del convento de San Francisco de dicha ciudad.*
172 His trial is referred in two *relaciones:* AHN, INQ, leg. 3681, exp. 19; and leg. 2480, a document entitled *Relación de causas pendientes de fe en el tribunal del Santo Oficio de la Inquisición de Murcia desde 10 de febrero hasta 4 de mayo de 1688.*
173 Monter, *Frontiers of Heresy*, 32–35.
174 Louis Cardaillac, *Morisques et chrétiens. Un affrontement polémique, 1492–1640* (Paris: Klincksieck, 1977).
175 For confiscations in Spanish law in general, see Pino Abad, *la pena de confiscación.*
176 For the influence of war and of peace treaties on inquisitorial activity, see Knutsen and Muñoz Navarro, "Prosecuting the French: Patterns of Trials Against

French Defendants in Valencia, 1566–1686"; Croft, "Englishmen and the Spanish Inquisition 1558–1625"; Knutsen, "Religious Life"; Knutsen, "El Santo Oficio de la Inquisición en Barcelona y soldados protestantes en el ejercito de Cataluña"; Thomas, *la represión del protestantismo en España, 1517–1648.*

177 Pedro de los Angeles, *Compendio del orden iudicial y practica del Tribunal de religiosos: en que se declara lo que pueden y deuen hazer assi prelados como subditos* (Madrid: Diego Diaz de la Carrera, 1643), 272–79.

178 *Instrucciones de Toledo*, §46–48. Reprinted in de Argüello, *Instrucciones,* 33v.

179 Alonso Romero, *El proceso penal.*

180 An exception appears to be the very early trials in Guadalupe in 1485: Starr-LeBeau, *In the Shadow of the Virgin*, 166–67.

181 The idea that resistance to torture 'purged' the evidence does not appear to have taken hold in the Roman Inquisition. Black, *The Italian Inquisition*, 58.

182 *Instrucciones de Toledo*, §54. Printed in de Argüello, *Instrucciones* 34v. For secular courts, see Alonso Romero, *El proceso penal*, 255–56.

183 There are at least four bundles and 24 books of *cartas acordadas* at the Archivo Historico Nacional in Madrid, in addition to the many who are misplaced in other archival units there. In addition, there are *cartas acordadas* preserved in archives and libraries around the world, such as the British Library in London, the University of Notre Dame, the Archivo Nacional de Chile in Santiago, and others.

184 This was also the case in Italy: 'In January 1559 the Holy Office under Paul IV followed the Spanish Inquisitor-General in instructing confessors that they should not absolve penitents who adhered to heresy, or possessed prohibited books, unless they had first gone to an inquisitor or their bishop and declared themselves penitent, revealed their offence officially, and named any accomplices'. Black, *The Italian Inquisition*, 73. See also Adriano Prosperi, *Tribunali della coscienza inquisitori, confessori, missionari*, Biblioteca di cultura storica, (Torino: G. Einaudi, 1996), Texte imprimé; Prosperi, "Notas sobre Inquisición."

185 See José Goñi Gaztambide, *Historia de la Bula de la Cruzada en España*, Victoriensia Publicaciones del Seminario de Vitoria (Vitoria: Seminario de Vitoria, 1958); Joseph F. O'Callaghan, *Reconquest and Crusade in Medieval Spain*, The Middle Ages Series (Philadelphia: University of Pennsylvania Press, 2003); Patrick J. O'Banion, "For the Defense of the Faith? The Crusading Indulgence in Early Modern Spain," *Archiv fur Reformationsgeschichte* 101 (2010).

186 O'Banion, "For the Defense," 17. See also, Pastore, *Il Vangelo e la spada.*

187 AHN, Inq, Lib 500, fol. 170r. The same *carta acordada* from 1628 and another one from 14 May 1629 are mentioned in a compilation of instructions from the tribunal in Valencia: AHN, Inq, Lib 231, fols. 70r–70v.

188 Conflicts with confessors over this matter were noted by Dedieu in his study of Toledo. Dedieu, *L'Administration de la foi*, 180.

189 All given in summary in AHN, Inq, Lib. 1231, fol. 126r.

3

THE FORMS OF NON-CONVICTION

Sentencing and trial outcomes

Most trials in the Spanish Inquisition ended in convictions. Thousands did not. They all followed the same trial procedures, leading up to the definite vote. This took place after all the evidence had been assembled during the investigation and presented during the trial, and was known as the *consulta de fé*. This description of it as the definite vote is slightly misleading since there could be more than one: as we have seen, at this point, the decision could be made to subject the defendant to torture if there was insufficient evidence to convict. In other words, insufficient evidence wasn't necessarily interpreted as a sign of innocence, and the evidence that had caused the trial and the assumption of guilt in the first place was normally, though not always, still there.

One way forward was then to try to produce further evidence in the form of a confession by torturing the defendant. According to the doctrines of the *ius commune*, this was a potentially dangerous undertaking for the prosecution, since a defendant who refused to confess was considered to have 'purged' the testimony against him. As pointed out earlier, the regulations of the Spanish Inquisition reflected this. Yet, there were ways around this, such as the practice in some secular courts of ordering torture 'with reservation of proof', in which case the evidence assembled against the defendant would be considered intact even if torture did not lead to a confession. The defendant would in these cases be sentenced to 'extraordinary' punishment instead of the ordinary punishment which was unavailable to the judge because of the lack of full proof. This was the doctrine and practice developed by late medieval and early modern judicial theorists; we see echoes of this practice in

DOI: 10.4324/9781003455691-3

how the Holy Office would sometimes sentence a defendant to be penanced after resisting torture, when a confession would have brought reconciliation.

If the defendant was in fact tortured, there would be a second definite vote cast after the results of the torture had been incorporated with the other evidence, unless of course, the defendant had confessed something that he or she had not been accused of, in which case the fiscal would demand to present a new accusation and the whole trial would loop back to an earlier stage. Only after it was clear that no further evidence was forthcoming did the trial move to the final definite vote.

The inquisitors did not vote alone at the definitive vote, and their vote did not always carry the day if they disagreed with the *consultores* and the ordinary. The case would then go to the *Suprema*, which was frequently more lenient than the inquisitors in the local tribunals. If the decision was made to not submit the defendant to torture (or if that had already been done), the sentencing panel had to choose between an array of options of sentences and punishments as outlined earlier. Even when they decided that the defendant was not proven guilty, an outright acquittal was not the only option. A frequent choice was to formally suspend the trial, another was to simply and quietly drop the trial, leaving no formal record of suspension. This could also be done at earlier stages, of the trial, when it became apparent that it would be difficult to legally prove the defendant's guilt. In other cases, the accused was reprehended, sometimes as part of a sentence, in others as part of a suspension, and frequently as the only recorded outcome of a formal trial. We shall deal with all of these, in turn, but start with the somewhat mysterious cautious absolutions, the *absoluciones ad cautelam*.

Absolución ad cautelam

The *absolución ad cautelam* is in many ways the most difficult form of sentence to get to grips with. This is in part because it was less well-defined in early modern legal doctrine than for example suspension or the *absolución de la instancia*. It derives from canon law and is not mentioned in contemporary legal dictionaries or in the Spanish Inquisition's sets of instructions as issued by the inquisitor generals. It appears, rather, primarily in the *cartas acordadas* issued by the *Suprema* to the local tribunals, and then, as far as the present author has been able to ascertain, only in connection with how to deal with two specific groups of defendants: Christian converts to Islam, and Protestants who had never been Catholics and as such had never received any Catholic instruction. The criteria that decided if these persons were reconciled or absolved *ad cautelam* are easy to point out. The important difference in the cases of baptized Christians who had apostatized to Islam was whether their conversion had been completely external or if they had ever thought that they might reach salvation as Muslims. The Inquisition reconciled those who had admitted to at some point having thought that Catholicism might not be the only way to salvation. Those absolved had insisted that their conversion was purely external and that they always maintained their sole belief in salvation in the Catholic Church. In a very similar fashion the Holy Office absolved, from the end of the sixteenth century onwards, all those foreign Protestants who had been raised as Protestants with no Catholic teaching at all. If, on the other hand, they at some point had received religious instruction as Catholics but remained Protestant, they were reconciled, even if they had been raised as Protestants in Protestant countries. Exactly when the *absolución ad cautelam* was introduced is unclear, but as well shall see below, the sources give us some hints.

The second problem with this form of sentence is that its usage changed over time. Just as it is nearly impossible to locate the precise time and the rationale behind its introduction, it appears to be equally unlikely that we will find the specific time and reason for the change in its use. Yet it is clear that it changed because by the eighteenth century, increasing numbers of those convicted by the Inquisition were also absolved *ad cautelam* in addition to the penalties inflicted. This practice appears to have been well known, although certainly not universal, after 1700. Yet it represents a significant change from the tens of thousands of earlier trials for which we have sentencing data. Of those 27,043 sentenced to be penanced and to abjure *de levi* or *de vehementi* before 1700, only 1,272 – slightly less than five per cent – were also recorded to have been absolved *ad cautelam*. On the other hand, from 1700 onwards, the percentage increases significantly, so that a total of 253 sentences – 12 per cent – out of 2,105 include the absolution *ad cautelam* when the defendant was penanced and made to abjure *de levi* or *de vehementi*.[1] Indeed the actual number may have been higher, since these numbers are overwhelmingly based on *relaciones de causes*, and Marisa Pedrós, using *procesos*, found that every person convicted of superstitions in Valencia after 1700 was both absolved *ad cautelam* and made to abjure *de levi*.[2] Earlier *procesos* do not show this pattern, whether from Valencia or from Toledo.

It is hard to escape the conclusion that the *absolución ad cautelam* changed meaning as it went from being used mainly as a sentence in its own right without accompanying punishments, to become a standard part of the sentence in many convictions. Yet, there is also some logic to this latter usage, as those sentenced to abjure were in fact not convicted as heretics, but rather as slightly or vehemently suspect of heresy. It was these suspicions that they swore off with their abjurations, and by the eighteenth century, this was frequently accompanied by the *absolución au cautelam* of whatever censures they might have incurred.

This is the crux of the matter: the *absolución ad cautelam* was a conditional judicial absolution of ecclesiastical censures incurred. Protestants and renegades had most certainly brought upon themselves ecclesiastical censures, even if they had not been legally guilty of heresy in the formal sense of having knowingly and willingly chosen to break with the teachings of the Catholic church. The censures they had incurred could be removed by a confessor for the *forum internum*, but for the *forum externum* they could only be lifted by those with the necessary judicial power. This was so because lifting these censures was considered to be a judicial act, since the imposition of these censures had also been a judicial act. It is possible to argue from this that the *absolución ad cautelam* was in fact not simply an absolution, but also a judicial acquittal specific to the Holy Office. This would be taking it too far. What is not in question is that it is an absolution, but it is also a conditional absolution. In canon law, it means the lifting of ecclesiastical censure, in particular that of excommunication.[3] In the practice of the Spanish Inquisition, we usually find it simply recorded as an absolution *ad cautelam* without any specifics as to what was absolved in the *relaciones de causas*. However, we find it explicitly referring to the lifting of censures in some cases, such as that of the apostate French sailor Antonio Chabana, who had converted to Islam during his captivity in North Africa. He was absolved *ad cautelam* of all the censures he might have incurred.[4]

This form of absolution was not mentioned in the Inquisition's printed instructions since it is not an inquisitorial penance, but an element of canon law more broadly, and it may have possibly been seen as an encroachment on ecclesiastical jurisdiction. In fact, neither in the *Orden de processar* nor in the *Instrucciones del Santo Oficio* does this appear, even though it had been in use in the Spanish Inquisition for decades before these books were printed. It is difficult to give an exact time for when it came into use. A number of letters instructing the inquisitors to use it in cases involving Christian converts to Islam and foreigners raised as Protestants who wished to convert to Catholicism have survived from 1561 and onwards.[5] A letter from the *Suprema* dated 20 June 1570 states that the *absolución ad cautelam* had not been used in the Inquisition before and was therefore an innovation, something usually frowned upon and ordinarily not acknowledged.[6] The letter gives us a tentative dating of its introduction, and the fact that it was used extensively henceforth indicates its utility to the inquisitors. By 1626, instructions were repeated that Englishmen who 'spontaneously' denounced themselves as heretics and declared their desire to convert to Catholicism were to be absolved *ad cautelam*.[7] These instructions were reissued two years later in a *carta acordada* on occasion of the renewed peace with England. This time the orders were that 'spontaneous' heretics who had never been raised or instructed as Catholics could be absolved *ad cautelam* by the *comisarios* without even coming to the tribunal themselves. If, on the other hand, they at some point in life had been instructed as Catholics, they should be brought to the tribunal to be reconciled without *sambenito* or confiscation of property, but with spiritual penance.[8]

There is no doubt that such a sentence was the result of a judicial evaluation of evidence, an evaluation that in the case of renegades and foreigners raised as Protestants could end only with a conviction in the form of reconciliation or a finding of no proven judicial guilt of heresy and subsequent absolution *ad cautelam* from ecclesiastical censures. In this form, as the expression of the finding of no legal guilt, it may even seem logical to characterize the *absolución ad cautelam* as an acquittal, and to group it with the acquittals based on a lack of judicial evidence. In fact, the very word *absolución* in Spanish contains the meanings of both the words 'acquittal' and 'absolution' in English, but this was not an acquittal. It was an absolution, in the same way that a conviction for heresy and subsequent reintegration with the Catholic church upon confession was an absolution.

As alluded to above, one of the two most significant contexts for the question of guilt and absolution was that of Christian converts to Islam, the so-called renegades.[9] The constant war on the Mediterranean was also a competition for souls, where both Christians and Muslims procured conversion by persuasion and force, just as on the Balkans in the same period. How to deal with the tens of thousands of Christians who converted to Islam became a vexing problem as their numbers increased with the success of Barbary corsairs who enslaved more than a million Europeans over the span of two centuries.[10] A harsh line towards these converts would not be conducive to their reintroduction to European society and conversion back to Christianity after their flight or ransom from captivity. A similar problem developed with the permanent establishment of Protestant states. From these states came generations of Europeans who had never been Catholics and hence could not be called heretics in the legal definition as somebody who knowingly chose to follow false doctrine instead of the true teachings of the Catholic church.[11] This change, coupled with the weakening of Spain versus the Protestant powers, led to a situation where a limited toleration for foreign Protestants was accompanied by attempts at facilitating their conversion to Catholicism.[12] Thus, self-confessed 'Lutherans' – the Inquisition's catch-all phrase for all sorts of Protestants – were to be judged by the Holy Office before they could be allowed to convert and be absolved by a confessor.

Consequently, in the sixteenth and seventeenth centuries, the *absolución ad cautelam* was not used by the Holy Office when no offence had been proved: rather, it was most frequently used by the Inquisition when there was evidence of heresy but no legal guilt, such as in the case of supposedly forced conversions to Islam, or men and women who had been raised as Protestants.[13] In neither case could the defendant be said to be a heretic in the formal legal sense of knowing Catholic doctrine but choosing deliberately to follow a different teaching.

This reflected the political and military realities surrounding post-Tridentine Spain, most importantly the permanence of Protestant states and the North

African slavery, both of which the Habsburgs proved incapable of eradicating, despite their best efforts. By the seventeenth century, it was obvious that neither of these were going away, and the Inquisition's policies were adjusted and adapted by absolving those Christians who, while formal heretics, had incurred no personal guilt by choosing to abandon Catholicism and embrace heresy. This goes to the very heart of what heresy was: the deliberate choice of following the wrong theology and rejecting Catholic doctrine. The inquisitors followed Farinacci, Diana and the other jurists in deciding that those baptized defendants who had never been instructed in the Catholic faith could not be considered to have chosen to abandon the true teachings of the Catholic church since they never had access to them.

The question of those 'forced' to convert to Islam was more difficult. There the Inquisition took the pragmatic route and absolved all those who maintained that their conversion had been purely external and hypocritical, never doubting that Christianity was the only way to salvation, and remaining Christians at heart. Those who admitted to ever entertaining some doubts or considering the possibility of obtaining salvation in Islam were reconciled. In these cases, the Inquisition discarded appearances and actions as evidence of faith or of guilt, and only considered the expressed inner state of the defendant's conscience. There is a notable difference here compared to the Inquisition's normal prosecution of baptized Judaizers, Moriscos, and Protestants. There it was precisely the external signs of deviance in the form of fasts, cleanliness, and dietary habits that were used as evidence, and that therefore formed the basis of prosecution.

Both of these groups grew very large and were felt to be problematic during the course of the sixteenth century. This forced the Holy Office to adopt new measures to deal with large groups who did not conform to any of the traditional categories of heretics. This also corresponds well with the appearance of the *absolución ad cautelam* in inquisitorial legislation which we have earlier dated to early in the second half of the sixteenth century. Many, but far from all, of these cases were the result of self-denunciations. However, self-denunciations did not automatically end in absolutions, as some defendants were reconciled instead. An *abecedario* from Valencia states that this was the correct procedure. Those Protestants who made 'spontaneous' self-denunciations ('*espontaneos*' in the parlance of the Holy Office) and who had at some point in their lives been taught or had lived as Catholics should be reconciled, while those who had not should be absolved *ad cautelam*.

Moreover, many converts to Islam and foreign Protestants were absolved *ad cautelam* after having been denounced by others. In short, self-denunciation was not the only reason for this form of absolution, nor did it in itself ensure an absolution. This was in line with instructions: For example, in April 1596, the Inquisition in Valencia was ordered not to allow renegades to be reconciled without prior communication with the *suprema*. They were told to follow previous *cartas acordadas*, and no mention was made of absolutions. We can therefore say that the absolution *ad cautelam* resulted from an evaluation of the evidence, not necessarily tied to a particular form of denunciation or trial, though many – or even most – have been the result of what William Monter calls 'pro-forma appearances before the Holy Office' since the outcome was predictable, and sentences hardly ever carried any real punishment.[14]

As we have seen, the *espontaneos* always figured prominently in the Spanish Inquisition's activities,[15] and it was frequent also in Italy where it was encouraged by 'bishops, parish priests and inquisitors'.[16] The punishment was generally known to be lower the earlier a confession was made during a trial, and the Holy Office solicited such denunciations at times by issuing edicts of faith and edicts of grace. Self-denunciations leading to absolution among the cases studied for this book came generally from the two groups just mentioned, the hundreds of foreign Protestants who had to be formally absolved by the Inquisition in order to be allowed to worship as Catholics in Spain,[17] and the hundreds of Europeans who had been enslaved in North Africa and who had converted to Islam during their captivity.[18] The latter were subjected to judicial proceedings by the Holy Office when they reached Spain after regaining their freedom, frequently after having denounced themselves. However, because they had received valid Christian baptisms, they risked reconciliation rather than absolution ad cauthelam, and their trials were more than mere formalities, since they resulted in sentences and written judicial records that might be used against them in the future, even in the case of an absolution. Furthermore, whether or not the case started with a denunciation or self-denunciation appears to have made little difference to the inquisitors in these cases.

There were several reasons why these men and women chose to denounce themselves. The most important one was to be admitted or re-admitted into the Catholic Church, whether this was motivated by fears of eternal damnation or a desire for social accommodation. An interesting case is that of 13-year-old Angela Marina from 1613. She was one of the children left behind in Spain as the Moriscos were expulsed, and left to be raised by Old Christians, in Angela's case a priest.[19] No wonder then, that she eventually made her way to the Inquisition's tribunal in Valencia to confess that she had lived as a Muslim with her family before the expulsion. Claiming to have forgotten the prayers she had prayed, the duration of the fast she had observed during Ramadan and the other details of Muslim observance, she was given a lawyer and questioned a second time before being absolved *ad cautelam* with the Inquisition as a mere actor of a non-inquisitorial ritual – but also made to swear *de levi*, a purely inquisitorial ritual. One may well think that such a confession was sparked by a genuine desire to become fully Catholic as parents and Islam disappeared into the realm of faint childhood memories. There was certainly little danger of prosecution unless she herself or the priest who had taken her in took the initiative. Even so, the inquisitors followed through with a second interrogation and a curator to serve as her legal guardian and defence lawyer before absolving her three weeks after her initial self-denunciation.[20] There was a similar case brought before them in 1611, when ten-year-old Angela Malech confessed that she had been raised as a Muslim before the expulsion. She did not claim to have forgotten the rites and prayers, but to have understood that they were not good for her salvation. Eight months later, she was absolved *ad cautelam* – without abjuration.[21]

Those who were absolved *ad cautelam* were normally instructed to find a confessor and receive absolution after their trial by the Holy Office, demonstrating the difference between the Inquisition's absolution and that of a regular priest and confession. The use of a conditional absolution thus allowed the inquisitors to absolve the defendant and remove their possible excommunication, without giving up the option to prosecute them in the future if evidence later appeared that suggested or demonstrated different circumstances surrounding their cases.

An *absolución ad cautelam* was certainly no guarantee against harsh penalties. For example, in Murcia, in 1567, four Morisco slaves were tried for attempting to 'go to a Muslim country in order to live as Muslims'. Three of them were reconciled, while one named Luís was absolved *ad cautelam* and sentenced to be whipped a hundred times.[22] Such an absolution was also no hindrance to punishment from secular authorities. In 1621, the tribunal in Cartagena de Indias received a number of English and Dutch sailors as prisoners from the governor with orders that they should receive their confessions 'since he had to hang them' (presumably as pirates).[23] They all duly confessed their heresy, begged for clemency (probably in an effort to save their lives) and were absolved *ad cautelam* and accepted into the Catholic Church before being handed back to the governor to be hanged.

The absolution *ad cautelam* thus differs from the acquittal *de la instancia* in several ways, some of them quite important, the most important being that it in fact belonged to another universe of ritual. It lifted ecclesiastical censures but did not signify innocence. It was used when formal heresy was proven in the sense that a baptized Christian had deviated from Catholic teachings, while there was no proof of guilt in the judicial sense of a conscious and willing decision to deviate from Catholic doctrine after being taught it. It necessitated a confession of wrong-doing – if not personal guilt – since only a confession could permit the lifting of ecclesiastical censures, and it therefore opened the defendant up to the charge of making a false or incomplete confession later. The Sicilian Juan Russo denounced himself as a renegade to the Mallorcan Inquisition in 1611. He stated that his conversion to Islam was 'only by the mouth and not by the heart' and that he never thought he could save his immortal soul as a Muslim. He was then absolved *ad cautelam* and given spiritual penance.[24] Three years later, he was denounced as having said that there was no point confessing to priests, that if a woman went to a priest to confess, the priest would 'ride her', and that he wanted to go to Algiers. To this, the fiscal added the charge that his confession three years earlier had been 'feigned and incomplete'. He was finally reconciled after confessing, his original trial and absolution weighing heavily against him.[25]

Suspensions and dropped cases

In addition to the thousands of defendants who were absolved or acquitted, the Inquisition suspended thousands of other trials. Many other cases were dropped with no recorded formal decision to suspend them in the extant sources. We may assume that a great number of them were formal suspensions, but we have no way of knowing precisely how many. In the following, we shall treat them as two expressions of the same phenomenon, starting with those where we have a formal notice of suspension, moving on to those that were dropped without any such notice coming down to us, and finally looking at those cases ending with a simple reprehension. Most of these are known only from the *relaciones de causas*. Before we do so, however, we should note that a small number of trials stopped because it became clear that the defendant 'was not the person who had committed the crime', as the inquisitors put it when they ruefully reported their release of the Portuguese barber Manuel Rodriguez accused of bigamy from jail in Llerena in 1681.[26] The tribunal in Cuenca gave the same reason for releasing another man also named Manuel Rodriguez,[27] and these are just two examples among several of mistaken identity. It wasn't just the inquisitors who sometimes struggled to identify the accused. In a bigamy case in Barcelona in 1588, it proved impossible to prove if the defendant was the man who under the name of Joan Canaleta had married Joana Canaleta. His allegedly abandoned wife turned out to not be certain that the man who she had denounced was in fact her husband, 'sometimes she says this is the same man that she married at other times she says she can't say for certain'.[28] Another example. The agricultural worker Francisco de San Juan was tried for bigamy in Granada in 1692, and his alleged first wife was brought to the court to examine the defendant. She declared that 'the Francisco de San Juan who is prisoner is not the Francisco de San Juan she married'.[29] This case is interesting, because she made an examination or at least observation of the defendant 'in the usual place', meaning that – despite the secrecy of the proceedings, visual identification was a customary way of producing evidence – and also delays. In the end, although the Holy Office released him, it did not acquit him. This sort of mix-up, arresting the wrong person, was inevitable at a time when methods of identification were weakly developed. To counter this, the Holy Office eventually started recording *señas*, the physical description of the defendant or the suspect who was to be arrested. Sometimes such errors of identification were discovered early, at other times the trial advanced for some time before the defendant was set free, sometimes acquitted, at other times after the suspension of the trial, and yet other times with no other statement in extant records than that of his release. All of this, of course, presupposes that the defendant did not start to confess something despite not being the target of the initial denunciation, as we have seen earlier.

When we examine the cases of suspensions and acquittals from the defendant's point of view, those who saw their cases suspended were left in a somewhat more precarious situation than those acquitted since their trials could be restarted at any point in the future if new evidence appeared.[30] However, in practice, there was not much difference, since they in both cases were released from jail after being sworn to secrecy with their personal economy and reputation damaged, if not destroyed, and remained vulnerable to future denunciation and prosecution. An acquittal, as we shall see later, was no guarantee against future legal proceedings by the Holy Office, even on the basis of some of the same evidence.

Overall, the number of suspended cases mentioned in relaciones de causas was relatively high: slightly over 10 per cent (6,601) of the trials examined for this book ended with a decision to suspend the trial. At 10.2 per cent, the average suspension rate is two and a half times as great as the acquittal rate. Taken together, the acquittal and suspension rates give us the conviction rate, on average 85.9 per cent of all trials with known outcomes.

As we have seen earlier, the instructions of the Holy Office told the inquisitors to suspend the trial or acquit the accused when there was insufficient evidence against them, without giving any indication of how they should distinguish the two outcomes, or if they were completely interchangeable. It is no surprise then, to find the two sentencing modes almost indistinguishable in the court records. There is rarely a clear indication why a suspension was chosen instead of an acquittal, nor does it appear to be possible to systematically say that a certain state or type of evidence consistently led to one or the other outcome, even after reading thousands of case summaries and full trial files. What is more, the two outcomes are frequently grouped together under the same heading in the *relaciones de causas*, and in some of the very short early *relaciones* these cases appear as a single list without even distinguishing who had been acquitted and who simply had seen their case be suspended, clearly signalling a belief that the distinction at that time mattered very little to the readers of the report in the *Suprema*.

From the prosecution's point of view, the suspension of the trial had the great advantage that it enabled a simple resumption of the trial on the appearance of new evidence, allowing the use of previous judicial proceedings as well as evidence. This made it easier and quicker to build the case against the defendant.

Another difference between the two was also quite significant because it afforded the inquisitors more flexibility versus other actors: while an acquittal *de la instancia* could only be issued as a final sentence after a *consulta de fé* with the inquisitors, ordinary and *consultores* collectively deciding a final outcome (or the *Suprema* if it intervened), a trial could also be suspended at any time before that, including unilaterally by the inquisitors alone. Perhaps more than any other trial outcome (apart from a quietly dropped case) a suspension was the ultimate expression of the inquisitors' *arbitrium*, since they could decide it alone. Doing so before it reached the *consulta de fé* could have the added benefit for the inquisitors of sparing them the humiliation of having their work disapproved of by the ordinary and *consultores* if there was insufficient evidence to convict the defendant. A suspension before the *consulta de fé* could consequently be a way for the inquisitors to avoid a formal acquittal. There were other advantages: since a suspension could be decided in the early stages of a trial, it could save vital resources. In addition to freeing up jail cells and relieving the Holy Office of the financial burden of defraying the cost of the imprisonment if the defendant was poor – ever a concern and complaint in inquisitorial correspondence – an early end to a trial released manpower, especially that of scribes and notaries. The speed of writing was one of the bottlenecks that limited the number of trials a tribunal could conduct in a year.

One would very much like to know more of such strategies of sentencing and framing of trials, but the state of the evidence makes this very hard: this is the sort of reasoning before reaching a decision that the inquisitors would be loath to put in writing, and one would find it in letters rather than in trial documents, if, indeed, it ever was recorded.

In addition to the formal suspensions, some cases were simply dropped without any recorded decision to suspend the trial. This practice was in no way unique for the Spanish Inquisition. Jonathan Seitz found that among the many trials for *maleficium* in the Venetian Inquisition, 'almost 60 percent, ended without comment at some point during the trial, perhaps after a handful of witnesses testified and failed to support the accusations offered in the denunciation'.[31] Nor was this limited to the secret trials of early modern Inquisitions: following the ground-breaking work of Bernard Schnapper, William Monter noted that while the French criminal justice system acquitted only 3 per cent of the defendants in the sixteenth century, the courts 'released one prisoner in four or five (about as many as they sentenced to death) in the 1540s, generally because of insufficient evidence'.[32] In other words, insufficient evidence to convict did not necessarily lead to an acquittal in French secular courts, either. In fact, compared to other judicial systems at the time, one of the hallmarks of the Spanish Inquisition was that it generally pursued the formal trials it had started to a formal conclusion, whether that was a conviction, an acquittal or a suspension.

Even so, among the trials before the Holy Office in Spain we also find a number of cases which were simply dropped when the evidence did not support a conviction. The trial of Diego de Montinegro in Sardinia in 1589 can serve as an example. A single witness had claimed that he was circumcised, while another stated that Diego was afraid to go to sea because he feared that 'the Moors would capture him because they would execute him'. He was arrested and interrogated twice under suspicion of being a Muslim before an examination by surgeons revealed that he in their opinion had not been circumcised. After this, he was simply released from jail and went to Spain.[33] Other trials ended when the defendant died or fled.[34] The suspected bigamist Toribio de la Vega Barquera, alias Toribio de Ribera, was more than 60 years old when he was arrested in Cordoba in 1624. His case dragged on for over a year while the inquisitors struggled to prove that he was in fact the man who had married in Villaviciosa 30 years earlier. In the meantime, the old man fell sick and was transferred to the hospital of San Sebastian where he died on 3 May 1625. With his death the case closed, even though, as we have seen, the Holy Office could prosecute the dead.

The Morisco Miguel Matarraz was on trial in a secular court for murder in 1595 when he confessed living as a Muslim and expressed a desire to become a genuine Christian. Brought to the Holy Office in Zaragoza, he changed his mind and his story so many times that the inquisitors simply handed him back to the secular court which promptly hanged him, 'and then the boys stoned him and burned him'. His trial in the Inquisition thus ended without a formal sentence.[35]

Other cases ended when the defendant was remitted to hospital for a lengthy stay, or they were merely brought to an end by 'reprehending' the defendant. Reprehension could be part of a sentence of conviction, but it was also used in the form of 'reprehension without trial' or 'reprehension without sentence'. The concept of reprehending instead of convicting the defendant was part of the characteristics of the Holy Office as an ecclesiastical court. As Dedieu writes, 'At any moment [of a trial] . . . any ecclesiastical judge could abandon the juridical forms and treat the case as one of "paternal reprimand"'.[36]

In total, 130 cases are recorded to have ended with 'reprehension without trial', all of them from the period 1594 to 1628, a short period in the Inquisition's existence.[37] Even more noticeable is that 113 of these cases stem from the tribunal of Cuenca. Only 17 cases in our sources have been recorded to end in this way in the other 20 tribunals: Granada used it once, Zaragoza five times, and Llerena on 11 occasions. As an example of this sort of case, Don Antonio de Villodre, priest in San Clemente, was together with his brother Gómez de Villodre reprehended without trial in Cuenca after he had put chairs next to the chair of the Inquisition's *comisario* at the reading of edicts against banned books. He was told to remove the chairs (and the attempt to gain the same prestige as the *comisario*) and refused, earning him a brief encounter with the Holy Office with the charge of interfering with the operations of the Inquisition.[38] All of these cases were against Spanish Old Christians, many of whom had denounced themselves to the Holy Office.

Much more common was the 'reprehension without sentence', which was recorded in 564 cases – but only 31 of them from Cuenca. This way of ending proceedings was recorded in cases spanning the period from 1577 to 1692. Again, the majority of the defendants dispatched in this way were Spanish Old Christians, but not all of them. There were also *conversos* and Moriscos, as well as Berbers and mulattos and a few Frenchmen. Luís Bernardo was reprehended without sentence in Granada in 1614 for removing the crucifixes and blowing out the candles carried by boys in an evening procession,[39] while Juan de Leon received similar treatment in Llerena in 1600 after breaking several religious images in anger at losing money while gambling.[40] Some of these cases recorded the trial as being suspended as well as the reprehension of the defendant, while the majority did not. Indeed, the tribunal of Murcia frequently put these cases under the heading of 'reprehended', as separate from those reported under the heading 'suspended'. Finally, formal acquittals *de la instancia* frequently included a reprehension, often accompanied by a warning that the defendant's actions and words gave others reasons to suspect him or her of offences against the faith, and an admonishment to live a more Christian life henceforth.

As should be clear by now, the various tribunals of the Spanish Inquisition acted in different ways, and had different styles of recording and reporting the outcome of trials, very much as we would expect when so many of the style manuals and written guides were the private property of individual scribes and notaries and passed down within the families retaining these posts. Furthermore, they were never consistent: styles and ways of acting and reporting changed over time. Further complicating the issue is the fact that the cases recorded as 'reprehended without trial' were reported to Madrid in *relaciones de causas* – trial summaries – where they really should not be included if they ended without trial. This may be the explanation why we have so few such recorded outcomes and only from a few tribunals: The other tribunals may have chosen not to report to the *suprema* such cases that did not go to trial and have reported only those that resulted in a reprehension after a trial, with or without sentence.

In addition to these 594 cases, some 2,162 other trials ended with a reprehension as the only or most substantial part of the sentence. A total of 143 of these had started with a self-denunciation, which clearly was not the main reason for the lenient sentence. As an example of such trials ending with reprehension and nothing more, we have the case of 13-year-old Sebastian

Albert who was found to have been sodomized by Ángelo Mateo. He was tried in Barcelona in 1599, and then reprehended and warned before being turned over to his mother's care, a very mild sentence in a sodomy case.[41] More interesting is the case of Juan Pascual, who received the same sentence at Zaragoza in 1666 for having removed all the *sambenitos* from the church in Falces one night. This was a serious offence against the Holy Office, which placed great emphasis on the permanent exposition of the *sambenitos*.[42] It was an attack on the institution's memory and explicitly aimed at the Inquisition's attempt to perpetuate the infamy of those who had been convicted in the past and hence keeping the population alert to possible misdeeds by their descendants. Juan Pascual told the inquisitors that he had fallen asleep in the church, and when he woke up he found the church to be locked and he was unable to get out. At that point, without having planned this or been induced to do so by others, he spontaneously decided to take the *sambenitos* down and throw them in the well so that they would become unreadable and it would be impossible to replace them. He then declared to the inquisitors that 'some eight years ago he lost his mind, and they brought him to the hospital in Zaragoza to be cured, where he remained with the crazy people for some days and then he ran away, and it appears to him that he had not recuperated well from his loss of mind'. The Inquisition's *commisario* in the village later vouched for his mental infirmity. At this point, it was clear that he could not be convicted, as he had proven that he lacked the mental faculties necessary to be convicted according to canon law. The logical choice then would have been to acquit him. Yet he had committed an offence that was impossible to hide, and indeed, the inquisitors did not try to hide it: they ordered that the *sambenitos* should be replaced with new ones since they were in a poor state. Juan was then 'warned, reprehended and admonished'.[43] He might just as well have been acquitted, and the sources give us no indication why he was not.

Pedro Escanilla Menor had smuggled horses to France with his father, another crime with dubious connection to heresy but which nevertheless fell under the remit of the Holy office since the supply of horses might conceivably aid the military efforts of the Huguenot heretics there.[44] His advocate mounted a successful defence, pointing out that his charge was a minor and claiming that he 'was not responsible for the offence as he was acting on the orders of his father' (which he was obliged to carry out as a Christian son). The witnesses he named dutifully testified that the boy went with his father against his will. This was sufficiently important for the *Suprema* to order that he should be given a sharp warning and his case suspended without sentence. His father, Pedro Escanilla Mayor, was banished and fined, and the horses confiscated.[45]

For the defendant an acquittal was of course a very welcome news, but what of a suspension, or if the case was simply dropped? We see that they went home, perhaps chastised, perhaps even broken by their experience, but it is very difficult to know what then became of them. Unless, of course, their trials were reopened later, which they sometimes were. The trial against Fray Raphael Serra who was charged with soliciting sexual favours from women in the confessional was suspended by the Mallorca tribunal in 1688.[46] Two years later new testimony appeared, and he was arrested again. The first trial, even if it ended in a suspension with the real risk of renewed proceedings, had not been sufficient to change Fray Raphael Serra's behaviour, and he had continued to make unwanted sexual advances to numerous women in the confessional. The renewed trial resulted in a conviction in 1691.[47] What is intriguing is the way he continued to act as if the first trial did not have any impact whatsoever on his way of thinking, going straight back into the same behaviour that caused his arrest and trial in the first place. He behaved as if there was no danger at all and received a quite heavy sentence: being penanced in front of the community of his convent (apart from the novices) as well as on another occasion in front of the ministers of the secret in the Holy Office and 12 confessors, including his prelate. Then he had to abjure *de levi*, was banished for ten years, and confined to a monastery cell for four years, as well as suffering other punishments and penances. Finally, of course, he was deprived of the right to hear confession for both men and women for the rest of his life. After reading his trial summary, one does get the feeling that the members of the tribunal were very cross with him for not taking the hint from his first trial.

We have, then, a number of varied forms of non-convictions in the records of the Holy Office in Spain, even before we come to the actual acquittals. Coming on top of all of these cases of non-convictions, a significant number of convictions resulted in no punishment at all, or a very light punishment, such as fasting every Friday morning for a month. However, these are not the cases that interest us here. We shall now focus on those trials resulting in an acquittal, that is, those were the Inquisition formally acknowledged that the defendant was not proven guilty of the charges levelled against him.

Acquittals

We shall deal with the acquittals in depth in the following chapter, but a brief overview in the context of all non-convictions can be useful. As we have seen earlier, the various instructions and inquisitors' manuals used by the Holy Office contain relatively little information about acquittals, while going into great detail about convictions and sentencing.[48] This reflected not just that the majority of cases ended with a conviction but also (apart from the important distinction between *absueltos* and *suspensos*) that acquittals lacked the many nuances and degrees that characterized convictions and punishments.[49] The Holy Office almost exclusively used conditional acquittals. The reason for using these conditional forms of acquittal was that the Inquisition as a matter of principle endeavoured to avoid ever giving a full and clear acquittal of the imputed crime, as the inquisitors' manuals make clear. For example, Francisco Peña follows the influential medieval inquisitor Eymerich in stating that the inquisitor should take care not to write that the defendant was innocent when writing sentences of acquittals.[50] Nevertheless, in early modern Spanish inquisitorial practice, a conditional acquittal was preferred to a suspension in numerous cases where the inquisitors might otherwise have chosen to suspend the trial, making even a conditional acquittal clearly a decision in favour of the defendant. In any case, an acquittal did not in any way preclude later prosecution if more evidence later surfaced. A document called *Elucidationes Sancti Officii per SS distribuitæ* states of he who has been acquitted *de la instancia*, that 'if more full proof against him appears, he may be apprehended and convicted according to law',[51] in line with Torquemada's earlier instruction.

Almost all acquittals issued by the Spanish Inquisition conform to the recommended use of an acquittal *de la instancia.*[52] Nevertheless, in addition to these, we find a small number of differently phrased acquittals, such as eight cases ending with '*absolución in totum*', all of them from the years 1559–1580, from the tribunals in Zaragoza, Logroño, and the Canary Islands.[53] Two cases from Valencia in 1575 were recorded as ending with a sentence of '*Absuelto diffinitivamente et ab observatione juridici*'.[54] Another 273 cases from various tribunals were simply recorded to have been 'acquitted' with no qualifier, or to have been 'set free', 'let out of jail', 'allowed to go home', or some other such phrase not corresponding to any of the Inquisition's legal categories. Unless otherwise stated, henceforth all those referred to as acquitted had been so *de la instancia.*

The fact that the defendant was acquitted of some charges did not preclude a conviction for other offences at the same time. Such cases are rare, but do exist. They are frequently the result of the defendant doing something in desperation during his imprisonment during the trial, reflecting, perhaps, a belief that it was impossible to escape conviction once one was tried by the Holy Office. For example, Diego Alfonso was acquitted of Judaism by the tribunal in Toledo in 1518, but he was convicted of having broken out of and escaped from the Inquisition's jail. Thus, he was banished for year, even though the court had fund him not guilty of the original charge.[55]

All these conditional acquittals should therefore be considered as genuine acquittals, and not simply as suspended trials. This is clearly brought out by the fact that the inquisitors used suspensions and conditional acquittals in parallel, although it is difficult or even impossible for us to determine why one sentence was chosen over the other. Almost every *relación de causas* that contains acquittals also contains suspended trials, judged by the same tribunal in the same time period. For example, a single *relación de causas* from

Valencia covering trials judged in that tribunal in 1651 reported one acquittal *de la instancia*, two absolutions *ad cautelam*, and four suspended trials.[56] It was therefore not arbitrary if a trial was suspended or ended in a conditional acquittal, even though the motives behind the distinctions can be difficult or even impossible to disentangle after so many of the sources have been lost, frequently leaving us with only short summaries that do not go into the reasons in detail. For the defendant, of course, the acquittal was the most basic fact of the sentence, even if it was conditional. We now turn to that in full in the following chapter.

Notes

1 Of the 15,197 sentenced to be reconciled, 50 were also absolved *ad cautelam*: 30 of 13,673 before 1700, and 20 of 1,503 after 1700.
2 María Luisa Pedrós Ciurana, "Inquisición, magia y sociedad en la Valencia del siglo XVIII," (Unpublished doctoral diss., University of Valencia, 2015).
3 See, for example, Fray Martín de Torrecilla's discussion of absolution: Martin de Torrecilla, *Suma de todas las materias morales arreglada a las condenaciones pontificas de Alexandro VII y Inocencio XI*, vol. 2 (Madrid: Imprenta Real, 1691).
4 AHN, Inq, Leg 2022, Exp 25, fols. 20v–21v.
5 Examples of *cartas acordadas* and ordinary letters containing such instructions can be found in AHN, Inq, Leg 505, exp 2, fol 104; AHN, Inq, Leg 2366, exp. 1; AHN, Inq, Lib 497, fols, 113v–114v, and 244r–246v; AHN, AHN, Inq, Lib 926, fol. 824r; AHN, Inq, Lib 1231, fols. 122r–122v; and AHN, Inq, Lib 1234, fols. 50v–51r; See also Lea, *A History 3*, 3, 463–68.
6 AHN, Inq, Lib 1231, fol. 126v.
7 AHN, Inq, Lib 498, fol. 244r.
8 AHN, Inq, Lib 498, fol. 245v. AHN, Inq, Lib 231, fol. 79v.
9 The classic work is Bartolomé Bennassar and Lucile Bennassar, *Les chrétiens d'Allah: l'histoire extraordinaire des renégats, XVIe et XVIIe siècles* (Paris: Perrin, 1989). See also I.M.R.M.D. Braga, *Entre a cristandade e o islão, séculos XV-XVII: cativos e renegados nas franjas de duas sociedades em confronto* (Instituto de Estudios Ceutíes, 1998); Miguel Angel de Bunes Ibarra, "Reflexiones sobre la conversión al Islam de los renegados en los siglos XVI y XVII," *Hispania Sacra* 42, no. 85 (1990); José Antonio Martínez Torres, "El alimento para ir más alla: Fernand Braudel, el mundo Turco-Berberisco y los estudios sobre cautivos renegados (siglos XVI y XVII)," *Hispania Sacra* 53, no. 108 (2001); Giovanna Fiume, *Schiavitú, religione e libertà nel Mediterraneo tra Medioevo ed età moderna* (Cosenza: L. Pellegrini, 2008); Giovanna Fiume, *Schiavitù mediterranee corsari, rinnegati e santi di età moderna, Sintesi* (Milano: B. Mondadori, 2009); Georgis Plakotos, "The Venetian Inquisition and Aspects of 'otherness'. Judaizers, Muslim and Christian Converts (16th–17th Century)" (D Phil, University of Glasgow, 2004). For the Balkans, see Anton Minkov, *Conversion to Islam in the Balkans: Kisve Bahasi Petitions and Ottoman Social Life, 1670–1730* (Leiden: Brill, 2004); Tijana Krstić, *Contested Conversions to Islam: Narratives of Religious Change in the Early Modern Ottoman Empire* (Stanford, CA: Stanford University Press, 2011).
10 An excellent to introduction to the subject of Europeans enslaved in North Africa is Robert C. Davis, *Christian Slaves, Muslim Masters: White Slavery in*

the Mediterranean, the Barbary Coast, and Italy, 1500–1800, Early Modern History (Houndmills, Basingstoke, Hampshire, and New York: Palgrave Macmillan, 2003).

11 Kelly, "Inquisition and the Prosecution."

12 Knutsen, "El Santo Oficio de la Inquisición en Barcelona y soldados protestantes en el ejercito de Cataluña."

13 The Islamic position was, of course, that there was no such thing as a forced conversion, since Christians were legally tolerated as dhimmi. Furthermore, the slave owners had numerous reasons to keep their Christian slaves from converting. On the other hand, there was a competition for souls in the Mediterranean, and every conversion was a spiritual victory. For discussions of the involuntary nature of these conversions, see Bennassar and Bennassar, *Les chrétiens d'Allah*; de Bunes Ibarra, "Reflexiones."; Maximiliano Barrio Gozalo, "Trasvase de religiones y culturas en el mundo mediterráneo del siglo XVIII: Renegados y conversos," *Cuadernos Dieciochistas*, no. 5 (2004); Braga, *Entre a cristandade e o islão, séculos XV–XVII: cativos e renegados nas franjas de duas sociedades em confronto.*

14 Monter, Frontiers of Heresy, 250.

15 Dedieu, "Denunciar-denunciarse." Lea, *A History*, vol. 3–573 Dedieu, *L'Administration de la foi*, 135–53.

16 Black, *The Italian Inquisition*, 57.

17 Some studies have appeared: Knutsen, "Religious Life"; Knutsen, "El Santo Oficio de la Inquisición en Barcelona y soldados protestantes en el ejercito de Cataluña"; Gustav Henningsen, "I inkvisitionens Net," *Skalk*, no. 5 (1980); Elisabeth Balancy, "Les immigrés français devant le tribunal de l'Inquisition de Barcelone (1592–1692)," in *Les Français en Espagne à l'époque moderne* (Paris: CNRS, 1990); Croft, "Englishmen and the Spanish Inquisition 1558–1625." See also Thomas, *Los protestantes y la Inquisición en España en tiempos de Reforma y Contrareforma*; Thomas, *la represión del protestantismo en España, 1517–1648.*

18 See, for example, Davis, *Christian Slaves, Muslim Masters: White Slavery in the Mediterranean, the Barbary Coast, and Italy, 1500–1800*; Ellen G. Friedman, *Spanish Captives in North Africa in the Early Modern Age* (Madison: University of Wisconsin Press, 1983); W. H. Rudt de Collenberg, *Esclavage et rançons des chrétiens en Méditerranée: 1570–1600: d'aprés les Litterae Hortatoriae de l'Archivio Segreto Vaticano* (Paris: Léopard d'or, 1987); Bennassar and Bennassar, *Les chrétiens d'Allah: l'histoire extraordinaire des renégats, XVIe et XVIIe siècles; Maximiliano Barrio Gozalo, Esclavos y cautivos conflictos entre la Cristiandad y el Islam en el siglo XIII* (Valladolid: Junta de Castilla y León, 2006); Anita Gonzalez-Raymond, *la croix et le croissant: les inquisiteurs des îles face à l'islam, 1550–1700, Collection Sud* (Paris: Editions du Centre national de la recherche scientifique, 1992); Lucia Rostagno, *Mi faccio Turco: esperienze ed immagini dell'islam nell'Italia moderna, Supplemento n 1 a 'Oriente moderno'*, (Roma: Istituto per l'Oriente C.A. Nallino, 1983); Braga, Entre a cristandade e o islão, séculos XV-XVII: cativos e renegados nas franjas de duas sociedades em confronto; L. Scaraffia, *Rinnegati: per una storia dell'identità occidentale* (Laterza, 1993); Mercedes García-Arenal, *Conversions islamiques: identités religieuses en islam méditerranéen* (Maisonneuve et Larose, 2001). For the Balkans, see Minkov, *Conversion to Islam in the Balkans: Kisve bahasi Petitions and Ottoman Social Life, 1670–1730*; Krstić, Contested Conversions to Islam: Narratives of Religious Change in the Early Modern Ottoman Empire.

19 For Morisco children left behind in 1609–14, see José Luis Betrán Moya, "Los niños moriscos antes y después de la expulsión," in *Historia y perspectivas de investigación: estudios en memoria del profesor Angel Rodríguez Sánchez* (Mérida

(Badajoz): Editora Regional de Extremadura, 2002); Ignasi Gironés Guillem, "Relación de los morisquillos y morisquillas presentados en los diferentes pueblos desde la ciudad de Valencia hasta Orihuela, según el bando de 1611," in *30 años de mudejarismo: memoria y futuro (1975–2005): actas [del] X Simposio Internacional de Mudejarismo, Teruel, 14–15–16, septiembre, 2005* (Teruel: Centro de Estudios Mudéjares, 2007); Mario Martínez Gomis, "El control de los niños moriscos en Alicante tras el decreto de expulsión de 1609," *Revista de historia moderna: Anales de la Universidad de Alicante*, no. 1 (1981); François Martinez, "la permanence morisque en Espagne après 1609 (discours et réalités)' (Doctorat d'Etudes Romanes Université Paul-Valéry – Montpellier III, 1997), 242–89.

20 *Proceso* in AHN, Inq, Leg 522, exp. 2. *Relación* in AHN, Inq, Lib 939, fol. 190r.
21 *Proceso* in AHN, Inq, Leg 522, exp 22.
22 *Relación* in AHN, Inq, Leg. 2022, exp. 2, fol. 1v.
23 *Relación* for 1620–1621 in AHN, INQ, lib. 1020, fols. 185r–197v, quote on fols. 196v–197r.
24 *Relación* in AHN, Inquisition, Lib 861, fol. 71.
25 AHN, Inq, Lib 861, fols. 106v–107r.
26 *Relación* in AHN, Inq, Leg. 3681, exp. 9, fol. 10v.
27 ADC, Inq, Leg. 0393, exp. 5591.
28 AHN, INQ, lib. 731, fols. 29v–30r.
29 *Relaciones* in AHN, Inq, Leg 2662 and Leg 1952, exp 4V. The question of correctly identifying a returning husband is a fascinating one, and as Natalie Zemon Davies has argued, a false returning husband might be better liked than the real one. Natalie Zemon Davis, *The Return of Martin Guerre* (Cambridge, MA: Harvard University Press, 1983).
30 Lea, *A History*, vol. 3, 108–11.
31 Seitz, Witchcraft and Inquisition in Early Modern Venice, 54.
32 Monter, *Judging the French Reformation: Heresy Trials by Sixteenth-Century Parlements*, 26. The numbers are from articles by Bernard Schnapper, collected and reprinted in Bernard Schnapper, *Voies nouvelles en histoire du droit la justice, la famille, la répression pénale, XVIe–XXe siècles, Publications de la Faculté de droit et des sciences sociales de Poitiers* (Paris: Presses universitaires de France, 1991), Texte imprimé.
33 AHN, Inq, Lib 782, fol. 159r.
34 The Holy Office both could and did prosecute and convict the dead as well as the absent. However, by the middle of the sixteenth century, only trials for formal heresy were carried forward against the dead. Suspicion of heresy was held to be extinguished by death, and so the many crimes that involved only suspicion of heresy were no longer prosecuted against the reputation, bones and property of the dead. Lea, *A History*, vol. 3, 84–85; Bruno Aguilera Barchet, "El procedimiento de la Inquisición española," in *Las estructuras del Santo Oficio*, ed. Bartolomé Escandell Bonet and Joaquín Pérez Villanueva, Historia de la Inquisición en España y América (Madrid: BAC, 1993), 526–58.
35 AHN, Inq. Lib 990, fols 19v–20r.
36 Dedieu, L'Administration de la foi, 75–76.
37 For the purpose of this study these been counted as cases, although one can argue that they should be deducted from the total number of cases as they were reported as not going to trial.
38 *Relación* in AHN, Inq Leg 1931, exp 14.
39 *Relación* in AHN, Inq, Leg 1953, exp. 60.
40 *Relación* in AHN, Inq, Leg 1988, exp 54B, fols. 60v–61r.

41 Relación in AHN, inq, Lib 731, fols. 378r–378v. For sentencing in sodomy cases, see Berco, Sexual Hierarchies; Carrasco, Inquisición y represión sexual en Valencia. Historia de los sodomitas, 1565–1785.
42 *Instrucciones de Toledo*, §81. Printed in de Argüello, *Instrucciones*, 38.
43 'habría como ocho años se hallo falta de juizio y le llebaron a curar al hospital del la ciudad de Caragoça, donde estuvo con los locos algunos días y se huyo, y q le parecía no hacia convalecido bien de la día falta de juizio'. 'advertido reprehendido y conminado'. *Relación* in AHN, Inq, Lib 839, fols. 90r–91r.
44 Monter, Frontiers of Heresy.
45 Their cases are referred in two *relaciones* from 1628 and 1629 since the cases went to the *Suprema* for sentencing. AHN, Inq, Lib. 991, fols 913r- 944v; and Lib. 992, fols, 1r–33v.
46 *Relación* in AHN, Inq, lib 863, fols. 42r–46v.
47 *Relación* in AHN, Inq, lib 863, fols. 311r–313v.
48 A modern study of the Inquisition's sentences devotes some pages to acquittals, but shows limited interest in the subject. María del Camino Fernández Giménez, *la sentencia inquisitorial* (Madrid: Editorial Complutense, 2000).
49 For these subtleties, see Dedieu and Knutsen, "la cause de foi."
50 Nicolás Eymerich, *El manual de los inquisidores* (Barcelona: Muchnik Editores, 1996), 179–81.
51 AHN, Inq, Lib 26, fol. 82.
52 For the use of *absoluciones de la instancia* in Castillian secular courts, see Ortego Gil, "Innocentia praesumpta." There are no similar studies for the Inquisition, or for the Valencian, Mallorcan or Catalan judicial systems.
53 *Relaciónes* in AHN, Inq, lib. 988, fols. 70r–71v and 106r–109r; AHN, Inq, leg. 1829/N. 1C, fols. 1r–8v; AHN, Inq, lib. 833, fols. 155r–162r. and 442r–473v.
54 *Relación* in AHN, INQ, lib. 936, fols. 143v–145r.
55 *Proceso* in AHN, Inq, Leg 133, exp. 1.
56 AHN, Inq, Lib 941, fols. 346r–399r.

4

ACQUITTAL

Absolución de la instancia

The *absolución de la instancia* was the favoured form of acquittal in the Spanish Inquisition, and it can be hard to get to grips with because it in many of its formal characteristics resembles a suspension of the trial. Before we get to the details that in some ways cloud the central facts, it will be useful to set our why this was a finding fundamentally in favour of the defendant. First because it states that it was not possible to legally prove that the defendant was guilty of the charges produced by the promotor fiscal of the Holy Office. Second, because it gave the defendants the possibility of procuring written instruments declaring that they had been found not guilty of this instance of the crime(s) they had been accused of, and of having this proclaimed to the crowd at an auto da fe. These were often in their thousands, and that meant that there were potentially thousands of witnesses to the fact that he had been acquitted.

The problem, of course, was that this acquittal referred to what had been seen and heard, while there was no way of knowing if the defendant believed something contrary to the teachings of the Catholic Church even if he or she had not said or done anything heretical in this instance. It is at this point that this decision starts to look less like an acquittal since it could at any point be set aside and the case reopened in line with Torquemada's instructions from 1484. As we have stated before, this was a formal aspect of all inquisitorial practice, and no sentence or condemnation was final, and therefore this should not be allowed to overshadow what the *absolución de la instancia* actually meant. Furthermore, given the near impossibility of disproving heresy completely, it is hard to imagine any more absolute acquittal being acceptable.

DOI: 10.4324/9781003455691-4

Nevertheless, the *absolución de la instancia* was not the only formulation of acquittal used by the Holy Office in Spain. It was, however, the original form of acquittal used by the Spanish Inquisition, it was the only one to see extensive use, and the one exclusively referred to in its rules and regulations. In the same way as the use of torture that frequently preceded it, the *absolución de la instancia* was not exclusive to the Inquisition; it was also used in Castilian secular courts in lieu of a formal full acquittal regulated by law. According to the early modern Spanish judicial manuals studied by future inquisitors at the Castilian universities, the acquittal *de la instancia* was used when the accusation had not been proven, but there had been genuine reasons to suspect the defendant.[1] This form of acquittal came from the world of theoretical jurisprudence, and was not set down in secular law in Spain, even though it was in fact used by secular courts.[2] It was an acquittal of the accusation in that specific instance, but it left the way open for a new trial for the same crime if new evidence would appear in the future. Although the trial could not be resumed and the acts produced during these judicial proceedings were not valid for a new trial, the evidence presented could be used in a new trial. A nineteenth-century Spanish legal dictionary states that the *absolución de la instancia* is a legal device which 'suspends rather than finalises the trial'.[3] These interpretations of the conditional acquittal should not be directly transferred from secular courts to the Holy Office, since the Inquisition had another legal device for this which secular courts lacked, and that was the formal suspension of the trial which we dealt with in the previous chapter. Furthermore, Torquemada's instructions from Valladolid in 1488 made it clear that a case could be tried again if new evidence appeared, no matter what the original sentence had been. Thus, not even an unconditional acquittal would have prevented a new trial in the Inquisition.

Another attraction of the *absolución de la instancia* for judges in Spanish secular courts was that it allowed the court to force the defendant to pay part or all of the costs of the trial.[4] Again, this did not apply to the Inquisition, where the defendants were obliged to bear the cost of their own imprisonment even when acquitted, but under no circumstances were they supposed to pay the cost of the trial,[5] one of the reasons why the Holy Office was virtually always in financial dire straits. In sum, the acquittal *de la instancia* was to secular courts what a suspension was to the Holy Office. Thus, neither reason normally given why a Spanish judge might choose to acquit *de la instancia* instead of issuing a full acquittal applies to the Holy Office. Nevertheless, it was frequently used by the inquisitors, even when the acquittal was publicly and dramatically announced at an auto da fe. We find a total of 2,421 such acquittals recorded among our cases, from 1485 to 1758, virtually the whole period under study.

In keeping with the flexible way that the inquisitors approached sentencing, we sometimes find contradictory sentences here also. For example, in

1562, the tribunal in Murcia reported that five persons had been '*absueltos de la ynstancia libremente*' (freely acquitted *de la instancia*), while another three had been '*absueltos de la ynstancia con abjuración de vehementi*', in addition to pecuniary punishment and loss of office.[6] The latter sentences thus combined an acquittal with swearing off the suspected heresy at an *auto da fe* as if they had been penanced!

The acquittals

With 2,529 proper acquittals among 65,102 trials with known outcomes, we have sufficiently large numbers to produce some interesting statistics on the phenomenon. Perhaps the most noteworthy thing about these cases is that there is a great variation in the acquittal rates of the various tribunals of the Spanish Inquisition. The variation between the different offences is much smaller than one might expect.

Unsurprisingly, perhaps, of the 2,451 acquittals in this study where we know the accusation, no more than 281 were accused of Judaizing. In total, some 2.5 per cent of all those 11,445 who were primarily accused of being Judaizers and where we know the outcome of the trial were acquitted.[7] The corresponding numbers are slightly higher for the other two major heresies: more than 6.2 per cent of those accused of being Protestants were acquitted, while 3.1 per cent of those charged with following Muslim religious precepts were acquitted.

However, this picture has to be adjusted somewhat, since significant numbers of those tried for the two latter offences were in fact self-denunciating converts from Protestantism to Catholicism or Christian Europeans who had converted to Islam while enslaved in North Africa – or both. We have discussed these cases earlier, and also the difficulty of delineating them clearly from all other sorts of cases. If we cautiously try to deduct these cases to only look at those who were subject to a hostile denunciation and prosecution, the acquittal rate for all those charged as Protestants jumps to 8.1 per cent, while that for alleged Muslims increases to more than 3.5 per cent. Yet, these figures must be treated with care since it is so difficult to disentangle the self-denunciations and discover which ones were made without the threat of a hostile denunciation and which were made simply to pre-empt being informed upon by an unfriendly third party.

Another way of looking at this might be the consistency. Even though the acquittal rate for those accused of Protestantism was two and a half to three times that of those accused of Judaizing, in the end. all offences show a global acquittal rate of somewhere between 2.5 and 6.2 (or 8.1 if you will) per cent, entirely in line with the general acquittal rate of 3.9 per cent. The only offence that really can be said to differ slightly from the others is Protestantism, which has a somewhat higher acquittal rate. This apart, there is no really significant difference by offence when viewed across all tribunals.

TABLE 4.1 Acquittal rates by offence in trials with known offences and outcomes

Offence	*Trials*	*Acquittals*	*Per cent*
J (Judaism)	11,445	281	2.5
M (Islam)	12,884	400	3.1
L (Protestantism)	5,191	320	6.2
A (Illuminism)	289	8	2.8
P (Propositions)	15,602	756	4.8
S (Superstitions)	4,701	128	2.7
O (Opposing the Inquisition)	4,906	196	4.0
C (Soliciting in confession)	1,580	45	2.8
B (Bigamy)	3,794	138	3.6
V (Various offences)	3,125	179	5.7
Total	63,517	2,451	3.9

The four offences that show markedly lower than average acquittal rates are thus Judaizing, Illuminism (very small numbers), superstitions, and confessors soliciting in the confessional. None of these are particularly surprising. The acquittal rate for Judaizers would probably be even lower if we had better data for the first decades of the Inquisition's operations.[8] Superstition was a difficult material which brought the Holy Office much trouble and hand-wringing, especially after a witchcraft scandal brought new and stricter rules on how to deal with diabolical witchcraft in 1614, including a prohibition on confiscating convicted witches' property.[9] That priests were soliciting sexual favours in the confessional was a massive problem for the Catholic church, and, significantly, the Inquisition appears to have been loath to acquit those accused of this offence once proceedings had been initiated. Instead, this offence shows the highest percentage of suspended cases 19.9 per cent, which gives a conviction rate of 77.2 per cent. We can only speculate why these cases ended in this way. Two hypotheses might be put forward. First, the confessors' behaviour was so morally reprehensible that the inquisitors didn't want to acquit them even if there was no provable criminal guilt. Second, we can speculate that the inquisitors spared them the ignominy of having their cases put before the ordinary and *consultores* if the evidence against them was too weak to support a conviction. Both are possible, and not mutually exclusive, but ultimately we can never know.

Indeed, when we look at acquittals and suspensions together, they do not always follow each other closely. At 10.2 per cent, the average suspension rate is two and a half times as great as the acquittal rate. Taken together, the acquittal and suspension rates give us the conviction rate, on average 85.9 per cent. It bears repeating that this is the conviction rate after the inquisitors had discarded an estimated 95 per cent of the alleged offences that had to come to their attention by way of denunciations.

TABLE 4.2 Conviction, acquittal, and suspension rates by offence

Offence	*Convictions*	*Acquittals*	*Suspensions*
J (Judaism)	87.3%	2.5%	10.2%
M (Islam)	88.8%	3.1%	8.1%
L (Protestantism)	90.8%	6.2%	3.0%
A (Illuminism)	87.9%	2.8%	9.3%
P (Propositions)	84.7%	4.8%	10.5%
S (Superstitions)	77.6%	2.7%	19.7%
O (Opposing)	88.1%	4.0%	7.9%
C (Soliciting)	77.3%	2.8%	19.9%
B (Bigamy)	89.3%	3.6%	7.1%
V (Various offences)	75.5%	5.7%	18.8%
All offences	85.9%	3.9%	10.2%

The three offence categories of superstitions, solicitation, and various have significantly lower conviction rates than all offences taken together, yet, of those, only one – the hodgepodge of offences classified as various – has a higher acquittal rate than average. As said before, the general suspension rate is two and a half times that of the acquittal rate, and for superstitions, the suspension rate is almost eight times as high. However, for those charged with Protestantism, the numbers are reversed, with more than twice as many formally acquitted as suspended. There is thus no correlation between the use of suspensions and acquittals in the sentencing of these trials when we look at them by offence.

When we look at the acquittal rate by the tribunal, the first thing that becomes apparent is the existence of important differences between the various tribunals of the Spanish Inquisition. The differences are striking, with several tribunals showing acquittal rates far above the average, while others show few or even no recorded acquittals at all. Nor is it easy account for these differences in geographic terms. If we look at islands, for example, Canarias, Sardinia, and Sicily are above the average acquittal rate, but Mallorca is below. In the Americas, Lima and Mexico are slightly below the average, while Cartagena de Indias is far above it. If we look at the peninsular coast, Barcelona is far above the average, while neighbouring Valencia is far below it. Nor do we get any clearer view if we look at tribunals in the interior or along the French border: in both cases, there is significant variation.

We cannot thus explain these differences in purely geographic terms, by distance from the centre or proximity to hostile borders or foreign shipping. If we try to look at population patterns, neither French immigration nor Morisco settlement is useful in distinguishing between tribunals with high and low acquittal rates. It is also impossible to explain this difference simply by the disparity of the types of offences tried by the various tribunals in their districts (again tied to population patterns as was our previous point), since the tribunals with the highest acquittal rates have higher general acquittal rates than those found for any single offence across all tribunals. The fact of the matter is that some tribunals of the Spanish Inquisition acquitted a higher percentage of their defendants than other tribunals across the spectrum of offences.

Furthermore, as Table 4.3 shows, there is no clear connection between the numbers of acquittals and suspensions. A high rate of acquittal does not necessarily entail a large number of suspensions, and vice versa. A (relatively) low conviction rate does not by necessity indicate a high acquittal rate. The lack of any discernible systematic quality to the differences between tribunals and between offences appears to point to the internal judicial workings of the courts as the reason for the observed differences, rather than any external influences.

Finally, to avoid boring the reader by giving a statistical overload – quite easy given the amount of data available in EMID – we shall simply look at the distributions in time of acquittals in four tribunals. There are temporal differences in acquittal rate for the Spanish Inquisition as a whole, in particular, the historic high acquittal rates are in the 1560s, 1570s, and 1580s. Yet this aggregate view turns out to be an aggregate that is not representative of

TABLE 4.3 Conviction, suspension, and acquittal rates by tribunal (trials with known outcome)

Tribunal	*Convictions*	*Acquittals*	*Suspensions*
Barcelona	77.0%	9.1%	13.9%
Canarias	90.2%	5.5%	4.3%
Cartagena	82.8%	7.8%	9.4%
Cordoba	88.8%	1.7%	9.5%
Corte	84.0%	0.0%	16.0%
Cuenca	83.7%	3.7%	12.6%
Granada	85.2%	3.7%	11.1%
Lima	84.9%	3.6%	11.5%
Llerena	85.5%	5.7%	8.8%
Logroño	83.8%	2.3%	13.9%
Mallorca	78.9%	3.1%	18.0%
Mexico	92.5%	3.7%	3.8%
Murcia	87.0%	3.1%	9.9%
Santiago	90.1%	4.8%	5.1%
Sardinia	79.5%	10.3%	10.1%
Sevilla	90.6%	3.2%	6.2%
Sicilia	88.2%	6.6%	5.2%
Toledo	88.0%	3.6%	8.4%
Valencia	84.5%	1.4%	14.0%
Valladolid	87.0%	2.8%	10.2%
Zaragoza	85.0%	2.9%	12.1%
All tribunals	85.9%	3.9%	10.2%

all tribunals. When we zoom in to view the development in the individual tribunals we soon run into a lack of sources, which means that we have to deal with numbers that are too small to produce reliable statistics.

The four tribunals studied here (Barcelona, Granada, Santiago and Zaragoza) have been chosen because they are from different parts of Spain, with different populations, geography, and borders, and are thus subject to different types of cases and political influences. The period chosen is 1560 to 1700, a period when we know more than a hundred trials per decade for each of these four tribunals. The perceptive reader will notice that this is almost exactly the period for which we have *relaciones de causes*, which indeed are the mainstay of this as almost every other statistical approximation to the Spanish Inquisition.

What we thus see is a variation from no acquittals at all (Granada for several decades of the seventeenth century) to the acquittal of one defendant in five (Barcelona 1570s and 1580s). In fact, the variation over time within Barcelona (from 20 to 1 per cent) is greater than that observed earlier between any two tribunals and between offences. Nor is Barcelona the only tribunal with great variation in trial outcomes over time: Santiago varies between 0 and 14 per cent, and Granada goes from a high of 12 per cent to

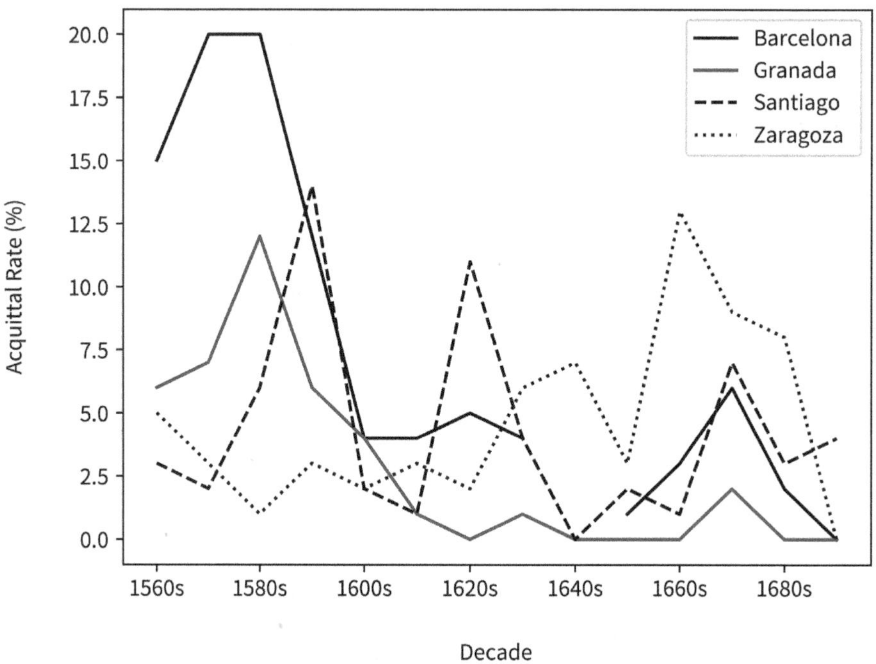

FIGURE 4.1 Percentage of acquittals 1560–1700, by decade, from Barcelona, Granada, Santiago de Compostela and Zaragoza.

a low of 1 per cent. The historically highest acquittal rates of the Holy Office as a whole for the period 1560–1690 is reflected in the data from three of the fourth tribunals, but not from the fourth. Let us at this point repeat that this statistic is based on robust numbers of hundreds of cases. Unfortunately, we do not have sufficiently robust data for all these tribunals for the periods before 1560 and after 1700, nor for every other tribunal in this period. It is thus impossible at this point to say if the relatively high numbers of acquittals observable in the final decades of the sixteenth century are connected with the new regulations issued by Inquisitor General Valdes in 1561, but the trajectory of Zaragoza suggests caution in searching for common reasons for changes in acquittal rates across all tribunals. The rather dissimilar trajectories sketched by the various tribunals indicate that outside influences have not had the same or at least simultaneous effect on trial outcomes across all tribunals of the Spanish Inquisition.

If we want to dig deeper into the numbers, we can as an example take a look at Barcelona in the 1560s, 70s and 80s. There we find that it was not a single type of offence that resulted in a high number of acquittals, the acquittal rate is extremely high across the board. Only clerics tried for soliciting in the confessional and Muslims are excepted from this trend and saw high conviction rates these two decades. Most of the latter were slaves and Christians who had converted to Islam in North Africa (renegades). In other words, we are looking at a wholesale crisis for the Holy Office on Barcelona, which failed to prove its accusations, or select winning cases across a wide range of offences for three decades. William Monter memorably dubbed the Barcelona Holy Office 'inquisitors with short arms'. He made reference to the tribunal's 'inability to convict Catalans of any serious offences, and for a long time after 1578, its inability to execute any resident of Catalonia for any reason whatsoever'.[10] Yet, Monter referred to the Inquisition's lack of ability to inflict severe penalties which the Holy Office needed local secular authorities to carry out, and not the breakdown of the prosecution's case in one-fifth of all trials. Indeed, the crisis of the Holy Office in Catalonia these decades also manifests itself in the numerous prosecutions for opposing the Holy Office, trials which came to make up some 25 per cent of all the business of the Inquisition in Catalonia these three decades. A number of these cases were prosecutions of alleged false witnesses who had previously testified against others who were acquitted of other offences. Several of these purported false witnesses were thereafter acquitted of the charge of false testimony! For example, the brothers Diego and Antonio Baura accused their stepfather before the Holy Office in Barcelona in 1574 or early 1575 of having a French language Bible, having given a horse to a Lutheran minister and other things that would indicate that he was a Protestant. Their stepfather, however, proved that he was a good Christian by *abonos* (effectively character witnesses), and other witnesses convinced the tribunal that his two stepsons were his mortal enemies who had wanted to kill him. After the acquittal of their stepfather, the two Baura brothers were in their turn prosecuted as false witnesses. They were able to prove that one of their stepfather's witnesses was their mortal enemy and they claimed to have only told the tribunal what they had seen and heard. They were both acquitted since it was impossible to prove that they had lied.[11] This family squabble – if that is the right word for this enmity – thus left the Barcelona tribunal with three unsuccessful prosecutions resulting in as many acquittals in a single year, tying up a not inconsiderable part of the court's resources.

It should be clear at this point that the acquittals resulted from cases involving all types of offences, in every tribunal and throughout the history of the institution. What then of the accused?

The acquitted

The Spanish Inquisition prosecuted men, women, and children. Foreigners and Spaniards, for trifles and for deadly offences. These were not all equal before the law. Yet the results were sometimes not what we would expect. For example, the acquittal rate for women is slightly lower than the one for men, as shown in Table 4.4. Women were not tried for the same offences as men: some 75 per cent of all women who were tried by the Spanish Inquisition were accused of one of just three offences. These were superstitions, Islamic practices, and Judaizing. Given the nature of these offences, it is also no surprise that many of them were tried not as single defendants but as part of chain trials where the evidence against each defendant increased whenever one of her co-defendants confessed. This may have contributed to lowering the acquittal rate, and was, of course, one of the factors that the inquisitors probably looked at when deciding whether to prosecute or not. Chain trials greatly facilitated convictions and made the collection of evidence much more economical since only the first case had to be built from the ground up.

A little more than 3 per cent of all prosecuted women were acquitted, while exactly 4 per cent of the men were found not guilty. The conviction rate for women is also slightly higher than that for men. Though the differences are small, they are to some degree unexpected, since women were at a formal advantage when it came to claiming a lack of legal responsibility for their actions, as we have discussed earlier. Since they were thought to be, and

TABLE 4.4 Acquittal rates by gender (trials with known gender and outcome)

Gender	*Convictions*	*Acquittals*	*Suspensions*
M	85.9%	4.0%	10.1%
F	86.4%	3.2%	10.4%

were legally classified as, less rational than men, they could fall back on this as a defence and claim that their lack of understanding had made them err. This was also enshrined in canon law, yet, as our numbers show, this did not lead to a higher acquittal rate.

Figure 4.2 shows the impact of age on sentencing. As it shows clearly, the percentages of acquittals and suspensions varies with age. Both the number of acquittals and suspensions nearly double, and the rate of convictions falls from over 90 per cent for the very young to 82 per cent for the very old.

Surprisingly, minors have the lowest acquittal rates, 2.1 per cent for those under 18, and 2.9 per cent for those between 18 and 24. One might expect that the legal age of majority at 25 years of age would have an impact on the finding of guilt. It appears to do so by decreasing the conviction rate to 86, 8 per cent. This is more than a little surprising since minors were held to be less accountable for their actions, and even more so in heresy trials where intent was the main factor in determining guilt and the lack of reason carried with it a lack of capacity for guilt. One reason for this may be the same as for women: that they were more likely than men to be tried as part of a

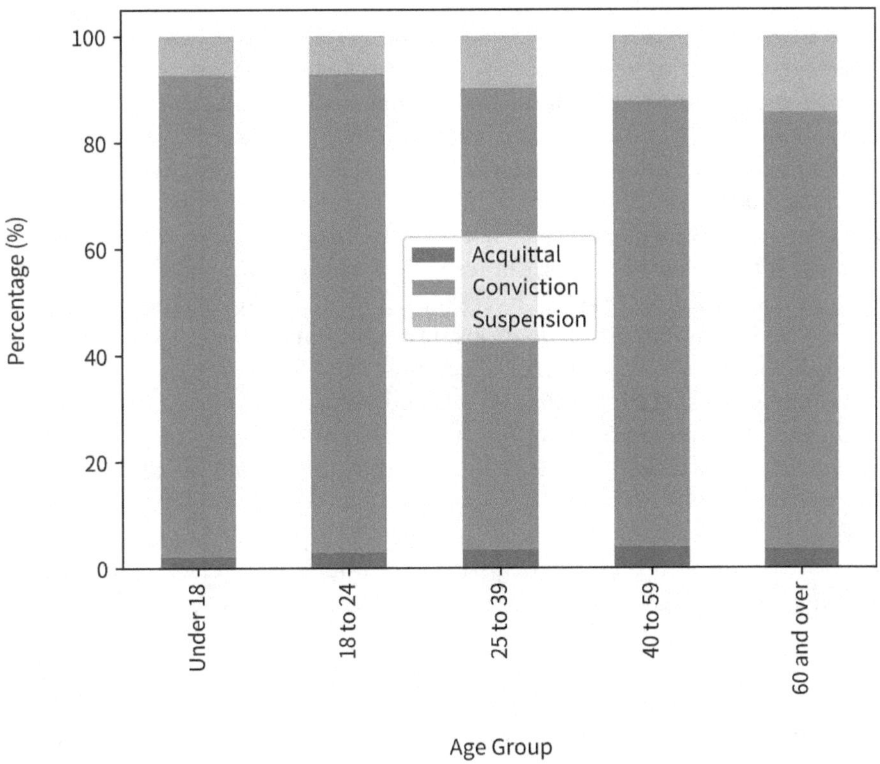

FIGURE 4.2 Trials with known age and outcome, separated by age groups.

chain of trials involving purported complicities in offences such as Judaizing, Muslim practices, or even sodomy, rather than as single individuals. In such cases, every admission of guilt from an alleged accomplice constituted evidence against them, lessening the need for external witnesses or even their own confession.

This statistic has not been broken down by gender because there is little differentiation between the genders, and the development over time is the same. The only real difference is that the acquittal rate for women is somewhat lower than that for men across all age groups.

The development sketched above also holds good across all offences, with two exceptions. The first is that of superstitions which is the only offence category where the very young had the same likelihood of being convicted as the very old: both had a 79 per cent likelihood of being convicted, with those between 25 and 59 having an increased probability of being found guilty. Here the under-18s had a 4.3 per cent chance of being acquitted while the over-60s had just a 1.8 per cent chance. They had, however, a correspondingly greater likelihood of seeing their cases suspended so that the likelihood of a conviction was no greater.

The other exception to the tendency towards lower conviction rates with higher age is that of those prosecuted for impeding the Holy Office in its operations in various ways. Here we find a conviction rate of 85 per cent among the youngest and oldest defendants, with a slightly higher rate for those between 18 and 24 years of age. Precisely, the latter group saw a rise in their acquittal rate and a decrease in the suspension rate, with acquittals reaching as high as 5.4 per cent, while hovering between 3 and 4 per cent for the other age groups for this offence. We shall come back to the significance of these differences a bit later, suffice it here to point out that being a minor did not make a conviction less likely once a formal trial was under way.

One of the notable preoccupations, not to say obsessions, of early modern Spanish society was that of *raza*, race, most notably the presence or absence of Jewish or Muslim blood, that is, if an individual had any Muslim or Jewish ancestors. This biological conception of religion did not originate with the Holy Office, but it did eventually deeply influence the actions of the Spanish Inquisition.

For many defendants this information has been recorded in the sources we have at our disposal; for the majority, it is not. It is patently clear that the vast majority of those for whom no such information was entered belong to the majority population of Spanish Old Christians. For foreigners, gipsies, Moriscos, non-Spanish converts from Islam, *conversos* and others, their provenance from a (suspect) minority group was systematically entered, while for the Spanish Old Christians, this was much less systematic.[12] Nevertheless, we have a total of 28,313 cases where we know both the trial outcome and the racial classification the inquisitors made of the defendant.

When studied, these contain some small surprises, such as the much higher acquittal rate among the deported Granadian Moriscos (8.7 per cent) compared to other Moriscos (3.2 per cent), and the similarly high acquittal rate among recent converts from Islam of North African origin (7.0 per cent) compared to other recent converts from Islam (1.8 per cent). Yet, when we look at the bigger picture, these are the only two minority groups where we have both robust numbers and significant variance in acquittal rates. Somewhat similarly, we find that non-Spanish Old Christians had a higher acquittal rate (7.3 per cent) than Spanish Old Christians (4.3 per cent). For most other groups, the acquittal rate tends to hover close to the average or be based on too small numbers to be of significance.

What is interesting here is that the connection between the defendant's origins and the final sentence appears to be the opposite of what one would expect for a tribunal infamous for its xenophobia and use of outsiders for exemplary punishment. One obvious reason for this is simply that these trials were the result of a previous evaluation of evidence where flight risk was part of the calculation when deciding whether or not to initiate formal trial proceedings and arrest the suspect. Foreigners and the internally exiled had of course fewer local roots and might in any case be transient. Any hesitation from the Holy Office might make a formal trial impossible as the suspect left or fled, as many documents extant in the archives make amply clear. Locals also ran away, of course, but they had much stronger bonds to the local area, frequently owned property, or had sentimental reasons to return.[13] In these cases, the Holy Office could take its time in building a case before striking, thus lowering the likelihood that the prosecution would end in a failure.

When we look at the European defendants, we also see some interesting contrasts. What, for example, to make of the fact that 8.2 per cent of all Sicilians tried on Sicily were acquitted, but only 2.9 per cent of the Sicilians tried elsewhere were found not guilty? (On the other hand, 11.8 per cent of the latter group saw their trials suspended, versus 6.5 per cent of the first group. In both cases, exactly 85.3 per cent were convicted.) Given the general percentages, it is not surprising that just a single one of the 43 Hungarians tried was acquitted and another one saw his trial suspended. It is, perhaps, a little bit more so that not a single one of the 80 Swedes was acquitted or saw his trial suspended. In general, the two nationalities to fare best are the French, and the Swiss. Somewhat surprisingly, the Irish come off as badly as the English, and these have the highest conviction rates by far. However, they were convicted of very different offences: the English were overwhelmingly protestants and convicted as one might expect of the heretical enemy. Yet the Catholic Irish, who were overwhelmingly welcomed to Spain and given privileges that no other nation could aspire to,[14] fared almost as badly once tried by the Holy Office.

TABLE 4.5 Selected nationalities with rates of acquittal, suspension, and conviction[15]

Nationality	*Acquittals*	*Suspensions*	*Convictions*
Low Countries	4.1%	5.9%	90.0%
French	7.0%	8.6%	84.4%
German	4.3%	4.1%	91.6%
English	2.7%	1.7%	95.6%
Irish	1.7%	3.0%	95.3%
Italian[16]	4.7%	11.6%	83.7%
Portuguese	2.0%	12.8%	85.2%
Swiss	9.6%	0.8%	89.6%

Summing up our findings so far, we find that minors and women, the two groups who according to the legal rules should have a better chance at demonstrating a lack of guilt in any offence they might have committed, were in fact less likely to be acquitted than adults and males, respectively. This would seem to imply that appealing to a lack of mental capacity was not a particularly effective means of legal defence in the Spanish Inquisition, even though it was one of the most clearly defined ones. We might flip this argument around and think that the legal protections for minors and women made the inquisitors select for prosecution only cases with somewhat stronger evidentiary basis than what they considered sufficient for groups that had weaker legal protections. We also find that foreigners and the internally displaced Granadian Moriscos had high acquittal rates. This might reflect any number of things, perhaps most convincingly that they were arrested on flimsier evidence since they represented obvious flight risks. On the other hand, they were less likely to be able to pay for their own stay in the Inquisition's jail and thus a burden on the already strained economy of most of the Holy Office's tribunals in Spain. This was a serious, but not necessarily sufficient, disincentive to prosecute them. As outsiders, they would obviously have been excellent material for exemplary punishment without offending local sensibilities, but without local roots, they may also have been deemed to represent less of a threat if the offences they were accused of were not particularly serious.[17] The inquisitors were also aware that outsiders were particularly vulnerable to malicious and false denunciations and in less of a position to defend themselves since they lacked the local network to produce witnesses to the regularity of their churchgoing, confession and participation in Catholic rites.

In the end, it appears likely that during the selection of cases to go to trial, the inquisitors took cognizance of the means of defence of the defendant to a higher degree than many of us have previously thought, and that this had a profound effect on which cases they chose for prosecution. Otherwise, it becomes difficult to explain why those with the best means of a defence were less frequently able to effectively defend themselves during the trial. Similarly, the high acquittal rates of outsiders seem inexplicable unless we go back to the first evaluation of evidence and the decision to prosecute or not, because just as those groups with the strongest legal protections have fewest acquittals, those groups most disadvantaged in their capacity to defend themselves do in fact have the highest acquittal rates of all. When the weakest do well and the protected do poorly it is evident that they did not start from a level playing field. All evidence point back to the care taken before undertaking the prosecution of a formal inquisitorial trial.

What did an acquittal mean?

The way the inquisitors avoided issuing unconditional acquittals means that even an acquittal did not formally signify anything beyond an absolute lack of evidence of guilt in the particular instance brought before the court. The word absolute may seem somewhat rash, but the fact is that the Holy Office convicted people not just for offences but also for the suspicion of heresy which they then had to swear off. The bar for acquittal was thus quite high once a formal trial had been initiated. In any modern judicial system, such a finding would of course have resulted in a sentence of not guilty. This was also in marked contrast to Spanish secular courts, which did issue unconditional acquittals in addition to the conditional acquittal *de la instancia*, and also subscribed to the doctrine of the *cosa juzgada*, which meant that a final verdict settled the matter and did not allow for a retrial of the facts, quite unlike the Holy Office, which, as we saw, could always retry a case no matter what the original sentence.[18]

That the Holy Office issued such conditional acquittals instead of a full acquittal even when there was every reason to believe that the defendant was innocent, or that no crime had even been committed, was a point of principle and tradition stretching back to medieval inquisitorial practice, rather than a decision tied to whatever case being tried. Yet, as we have noted before, the inquisitors did not need to issue even such a limited acquittal. They could simply drop or suspend cases, always keeping pressure on the defendant who was released with the great uncertainty whether or not the case would be reopened. Even a conditional acquittal must therefore be seen as a decision clearly favouring the defendant, indicating belief in his or her absolute innocence combined with a principled refusal to officially acknowledge that innocence.

In fact, even the reading of a sentence of acquittal after it had been passed would usually be preceded by an attempt to get the defendant to incriminate himself one final time, as we have seen earlier. As the reader will remember from the beginning of this book, both Juan Beltrano and Simón Maestrich from Maastricht were questioned once more as if they had been called in for another round of interrogations before their acquittals were read to them.

From their trembling limbs and streaming tears, we understand that an acquittal – even conditional – could mean a great deal to the defendants. If they were informed of it. In at least one case, the inquisitors decided explicitly not to inform the defendant that he had been acquitted. On 16 September 1652, the Toledo tribunal decided that Juan Capua should be acquitted *de la instancia* 'although it shall not be stated to him that he is acquitted'.[19] Consequently, he was set free without knowing what state his case was in, and – contrary to the Inquisition's own rules – he was not afforded the option to have his acquittal read publicly to the crowd at an auto da fe. Again, one may wonder why the Holy Office did not simply suspend the case. There is a calculated callousness in both how the inquisitors tried one last time to force those they had acquitted to confess, and in deliberately withholding the information about his acquittal from a man. Yet, acquit they did, and not just suspend.

Means of defence

These acquittals came in trials where the defendants had limited means of defending themselves. In heresy trials, there was no confrontation with witnesses and no way the accused or his advocate could question the prosecution witnesses.[20] It is common to state that the defendant was not invited to submit his own evidence pertaining to the alleged offences, yet both Beinart and Starr-Lebeau show that the defendants and their advocates did in fact do exactly that, and we shall see some examples next.[21] In theory, the only evidence the defendant was allowed to produce was names of witnesses to his own good life and conduct (*abonos*). Sometimes the inquisitors were willing to hear a significant number of such witnesses, even though they had no obligation to hear them all. In the case of Joan Libra in 1574 or 1575, the tribunal heard more than 30 witnesses in his favour, though this was undoubtedly influenced by his status as familiar of that Holy Office. He was duly acquitted.[22] The most effective form of defence was *tachas*, which demonstrated enmity and rendered witness testimony formally inadmissible, effectively destroying the prosecution's evidentiary basis for its allegations of law-breaking by the defendant.[23] 'The result, ordinarily, was the elimination of this testimony', writes María del Pilar Rábade Obradó, one of the very few to have studied this defence.[24] However, this was only so when the defendant correctly identified the witness and proved the *tachas* beyond any doubt.

Tachas were not only the most effective defence, but they were also the only formal way to openly challenge the evidence gathered against them. This defence was complicated by the fact that the witnesses were anonymous. In the trials, their testimony was rendered in the form of 'witness no. 1, a 60-year-old male', 'witness no. 2, 13-year-old unmarried female', and so on. Even so, some defendants successfully defended themselves by correctly identifying the witnesses and proving pre-existing enmity towards them. Damian

Martin, for instance managed to free himself from a charge of heretical propositions in Barcelona in 1619 by presenting favourable witnesses to his own character and partly discrediting the nine witnesses against him.[25] Similarly, Pedro da Belenda freed himself of the same charge in Santiago five years later by proving enmity with the witnesses who testified against him.[26] Alonso del Cañi was tried in Cordoba in 1580 for having had intercourse with a woman and her daughter, and having said that if a woman urinated after sleeping with a man, his brother could then go to bed with her without sinning. He 'proved enmity with the witnesses . . . and he also proved that he had been charged with and set free by a competent judge for the incest'.[27] In other words, the witnesses were not just his enemies, but they had denounced him, among other things, for a crime outside the Inquisition's jurisdiction, for which he had already been acquitted by the proper court. These acquittals show us that the Holy Office was used to settle scores, to transact enmities, just as we would expect a free system of justice to be. In this context, it did not really matter if the denunciation led to a conviction since the trial and imprisonment could be ruinous even to those acquitted.

The French immigrant Juan Carrera was less fortunate than Alonso del Cañi when he was tried by the same tribunal the same year. Denounced for heretical propositions which made him suspected of Protestantism, he 'did not confess, and defended himself by proving some enmity with the witnesses and good testimony about his own person'. Even so, he was tortured, probably because he was French and hence believed to be more susceptible to Protestant sympathies.[28] Only after maintaining his innocence under torture was he formally acquitted.[29] We find the same inequality a few years earlier in the same tribunal. The Morisco Juan de Varea and the Old Christian Pedro de Chichilla were both tried for heretical propositions in 1579, and both proved enmity with the witnesses. Only Juan de Varea needed a round in the torture chamber to convince the inquisitors that he was in fact innocent.[30] The bar for acquitting foreigners, Moriscos, and conversos appears to have been significantly higher than that for the acquittal of Spanish Old Christians, despite their higher acquittal rate.[31]

The guanche Bastian Rodriguez had previously been convicted of the proposition of simple fornication (i.e. saying that sex between unmarried partners was not a mortal sin) by the Holy Office on the Canaries when he was denounced by two witnesses in 1586 for having said that it was not a mortal sin to have sexual intercourse with a midwife. He was acquitted after proving enmity with the two who denounced him and that they were disreputable persons, and that the 'only words he had said were that it was a greater sin to have intercourse with one's mother or relative than with one's midwife'.[32] One can only wonder what brought him to such rumination in public.

On occasion, the defendants' statements convinced the inquisitors to gather further evidence. For example, the Frenchman Guillen Grimant was acquitted of bigamy in Barcelona in 1574 or 1575 when the inquisitors were confronted by a notarized document from France that his first wife was dead. The inquisitors then proceeded to prosecute his denouncer.[33] Twenty years later in Granada, Juan Rodríguez Osorio was less fortunate in his trial for bigamy. The inquisitors acknowledged that when the case came to *prueba* and the examination of evidence by the prosecution and the defence, he had proven that his first wife was dead before he married again and thus had not committed bigamy. Yet they did not acquit him, deciding instead to release him from jail and suspend the case. A probable explanation is that it was obvious that he could not be convicted and that taking the trial to the state where he could be acquitted would bind up resources that could more profitably be employed elsewhere. The difference between these two cases may simply have been at what point the exculpatory information was introduced to the court.

As we have seen, the few formal defences open to the defendants apart from gender and age, were claims of drunkenness, passion, madness, simplicity, or faulty education. A heretic was, after all, someone who after being baptized and instructed as a Christian, willingly and knowingly followed erroneous doctrine. Some managed to convince the court that they were too simple-minded to be punished, just as the doctrine would lead us to expect.

Drunkenness figures occasionally as a defence, and not always successfully.[34] An example of a successful defence comes from Logroño in 1621. Francisco Ruiz denied having said that the devil had more power than God. He had, he claimed, said that 'God had more power than the devil, and he could not have said the opposite unless he had been drunk, or his companions had been so drunk that they misunderstood him'. The inquisitors decided to reprehend him without a sentence.[35] A Frenchman named Jorge Luis was acquitted for stating heretical propositions in Murcia in 1570. The inquisitors noted that he 'appeared to have been drunk' when he stated that there was no need for priests and that the Virgin Mary 'did not have more substance than other women'.[36]

Madness was also a reason for acquittals in the Inquisition, notably studied by Sara T. Nalle in a uniquely documented case.[37] However, while it normally meant that the defendant escaped conviction, it did not always lead to an acquittal. Frequently the defendant was remitted to a madhouse or hospital where conditions might be significantly worse than in the Inquisition's jail. Of one Pedro Ortiz we are informed from Barcelona in 1578 that he 'was regarded as insane and was handed over to the hospital where he completely lost his mind'.[38] As one might expect, the majority of those dismissed as mentally ill had ended up in the Inquisition because of careless talk rather than adherence to any formally heterodox doctrine. In 1623, the inquisitors in Cordoba were alerted to the presence of a man named Pedro who among many other things allegedly had told boys that fornication and masturbation was not a sin, that being a saint meant only proclaiming God's greatness, and that the human body was the image of God and perfect in every movement, even when illicitly touching animals. On 4 September 1623, the inquisitors dismissed him as insane and ordered that he be locked up in the city's madhouse.[39] As a madman, he could not be convicted of the heretical propositions he was accused of making, and he was acquitted. However, madness did not automatically result in an acquittal. In the case of Thomas de Salamanca tried for blasphemy in the same tribunal nine years later, the appearance of madness made the inquisitors suspend the case and release the defendant, rather than acquit him.[40] Pedro Lopez was locked up in the madhouse in Seville instead of being acquitted by the Inquisition after presenting proof that he was both 'insane and drunk' when he flogged a crucifix in 1635.[41] Ten years earlier, the wandering Pedro Lopez de la Parra was deemed to be too ignorant to be punished when he had fenced in some biscuits and a cross on the ground and worshipped them as Holy Hosts. Instead of conviction and punishment, the inquisitors decided that he should receive religious instruction and the Eucharist[42]

Doctor Juan Baptista Bernabeu had been convicted in 1567 of Judaizing. His sentence included four years as soldier on the galleys, and perpetual banishment from the inquisitorial district of Murcia.[43] Three years later, he was charged with violating his galley sentence and entering Murcia several times. He proved to the inquisitors that he had received licenses from his generals to do so. With this, he was acquitted of having violated his galley sentence. However, he was ordered to refrain from leaving the galleys and availing himself of such licenses in the future.[44] While this case illustrates how a convict of the Holy Office could use his influence to ease the consequences of a conviction, it also shows how a defendant might be able to produce evidence that proved no criminal guilt even when the facts of the case indicated a crime, such as a violation of banishment and galley sentence. As a converso and convicted Judaizer Doctor Bernabeu was not somebody likely to receive lenient treatment at the hands of the Holy Office, yet here he was able to achieve an acquittal instead of the perpetual sentence as a galley rower that the inquisitors had threatened if he violated his original sentence.

If the defendant was deceased, either in the case of a trial against the 'memory and reputation' of somebody, or if the defendant died during the course of the trial, the obligation of mounting a defence rested on the relatives of the accused. We can see that they frequently did. For example, after Francisca Rodríguez Hidalga died in the Inquisition's jail in Llerena at the age of 25 in 1581, her memory and reputation were defended by her sister who did so sufficiently well to have Francisca acquitted *de la instancia*. Her acquittal was read aloud at the *auto da fe* in Llerena on 1 July 1582, and whatever remained of possessions were secured for the family.[45]

Reasons given

Many of the acquittals were the result of the defence mechanisms we have just seen. However, discovering which ones were successful in any single case is not always straightforward. As with other Inquisitions, we have few traces of the internal discussions and reasonings behind sentencing – or indeed other decisions made during a trial.[46] These votes on sentences were recorded in voting protocols called *libros de votos* before they were later copied to the trial manuscript. The only such books of votes over sentencing preserved are from the Canaries, *corte* and the *suprema*, and these generally indicate what these decisions were, without recording any information about why those particular decisions were reached.

We also have several thousand trial manuscripts preserved, yet most of these do not contain more than the outcome of the vote. Sometimes we find the votes, or the summary of the voting, sometimes we also find the sentence and information of how it was read to the defendant. At other times, this information is missing, having been ripped out from the preserved trial manuscript, or simply never put there by a negligent scribe.

What we have then, when these sources are preserved, is the outcome, not the reasoning behind the vote. This is not peculiar for the Spanish Inquisition. In fact, it was the same in Castilian secular courts, where the reason for the sentence was never given, nor did the sentences specify the legislation on which the decision was based.[47] This was also the case in Valencian secular courts, which likewise passed sentence without recording any valuation of the evidence, or stating the doctrine or jurisprudence used to reach the court's decision,[48] and it was so in all other Spanish courts. Yet the important fact here is the practice of secular courts in Castile since the inquisitors were Castilian, educated in Castile, and frequently had served in Castilian courts before becoming inquisitors.

In fact, most inquisitorial *procesos* conform closely to the models set forth by Spanish jurists for general use in the Spanish judicial system. Gabriel de Monterroso writes that the sentence *absolución de la instancia* should have the following form: 'I pass the following judgement, after considering the acts and the merits of this trial, that so-and-so did not prove his claim and petition'.[49] Similarly, Álvarez Posadilla later gave the correct form of writing a sentence as, 'I pass the following judgement, after considering the acts and the merits of this trial, to which I refer as far as necessary, that I have to declare and I do declare that the *promotor fiscal* proved his claim sufficiently'.[50] Inquisitorial sentences closely follow these models, frequently using the exact same phrase 'We pass the following judgement, after considering the acts and the merits of this trial'.

It is thus little surprise that the sentences as recorded in the *procesos* are frequently of little use in understanding the outcome of the trial, which instead must be sought in the proceedings. For example, the vote in favour of acquittal of Francisco Torremani in Valencia in 1575 was simply given as 'they voted and were of the opinion that the above-mentioned should be acquitted'.[51] Benita Lopez was acquitted by the *suprema* the same year after the local tribunal in Toledo had delivered a split sentence: the inquisitors wanted to convict her of bigamy while the ordinary and *consultores* voted to seek more information about her first marriage. The *suprema* voted to acquit her *de la instancia*. In none of the recorded votations was any explanation for the vote entered.[52] Thus we have to make our own judgement of how they arrived at this decision from the evidence as presented in the trial document.

Some *procesos* are more informative. For example, the trial against Francisco de Mesegar ended with an acquittal because 'the fiscal did not prove his accusation and lawsuit [querella] and we have to declare it as not proven and that Francisco de Mesegar did prove his exceptions and defences. In consequence we must acquit him and we do acquit him of that which the fiscal has requested'.[53] The case against Diego López Perea contains a voting record which shows that the reason for his acquittal was that his resistance during torture cleared the suspicions raised against him, even though his flight cast doubts on his innocence.[54] Juan Redondo was acquitted because of 'the variations in the testimony of his wife and daughter, and other just causes', which led the Inquisition to choose 'mercy' over 'rigour'.[55] The majority of the preserved *procesos* that ended with acquittal are, however, silent on the reasons for the decision, just as in secular courts.

What is peculiar to the Holy Office in Spain, however, is the existence of the reports that the inquisitors sent to their superiors in the *Suprema* in Madrid, the *relaciones de causas*. These evolved over time and were initially simply lists of completed trials. The information contained in them quickly expanded, and it eventually became quite voluminous as the number of trials went down. While these documents were unique in the sense that they were reports of trials that had been sentenced, they followed the form a very common way of summing up trials before sentencing, known in both Spain and other countries using the *ius commune*. The practice of summing up the judicially relevant content of a trial conducted by a single or several judges before it was voted on by the full court of judges was a common practice in early modern Europe, for example in France where the judge who handled the actual trial functioned as the *rapporteur* for the assembled judges who later passed sentence.[56] The job of preparing the *relación* that the court would use as its basis for the final vote on the sentence was in Spanish courts normally done by jurists who held the post of *relator*, a somewhat lower and hence cheaper office to buy than that of a judge.[57] The specific form of the *relación de causas* was consequently well known to the jurists who staffed the Holy Office, and not particular to the Inquisition. It signified a document that contained all the juridically relevant information that had been produced during the trial proceedings and which had relevance at the time of sentencing. In it would be all the evidence (or lack of it) and the various mitigating and aggravating circumstances which had direct legal significance. The main difference between the *relaciones* prepared in the Spanish Inquisition and those produced in other Spanish courts was that until the second half of the sixteenth century, those from the Holy Office contained only completed trials that had already been sentenced. By 1655, it was noted that it was 'newly agreed' that the fiscal should submit to the *Suprema* monthly summaries of all pending trials and the state that they were in.[58] Because of this the *relaciones* at first also contained very little information about each case before gradually becoming more informative since the Suprema was not initially expected to make judicial decisions based on the information contained in them.

From the second half of the sixteenth century onwards, the *relaciones de causas* therefore contained what the tribunals of the Holy Office considered to be the legally significant information about the trials held. Henceforth, they were more than just brief summaries of the cases tried; they were also justifications for the activities undertaken by the inquisitors and the costs incurred by the tribunal. Thus, in the *relaciones de causas* the tribunal frequently spelled out to the *Suprema* the reasons behind the decision to acquit the defendant, pointing out the weaknesses in evidence or the mitigating circumstances in the case as they saw them. This is a consequence of the function of the *relación de causas*, which was to allow the *Suprema* to monitor the performance and activity of local tribunals, and to send them comments on what should be improved. Marginal comments such as 'should have been given more punishment' or 'this appears excessive' dot the margins of many *relaciones de causas* which have passed the *suprema's* review. To avoid such reprimands, it was important for the local tribunals to make their decisions intelligible, or simply to put them in the best possible light. Thus, they needed to justify why they had acquitted the defendants after first having decided that there was sufficient evidence to presume their guilt and subject them to the rigours of a full inquisitorial trial.

It is precisely this need on the tribunal's part to explain the eventual outcome of the trial to the *Suprema* which makes this source the most valuable of those that we have access to in order to understand the reasoning behind the acquittals. There is very little information in the *relación* which is not also in the trial manuscript, but what is often implicit in the *proceso* is sometimes spelled out in the case summary because it needed to be explained and justified concisely and convincingly to demonstrate that the tribunal had performed well. This is an important point, since the *relaciones de causas* are sometimes written off as less valuable sources than the *procesos*, and more suited for quantitative than qualitative analysis since they generally contain much less information. In this case, however, the opposite is true, and the *relaciones de causas* are indispensable for qualitative analysis and not just valuable for the quantitative studies for which they have become so famous.

The most obvious reason for acquittals was simply that the inquisitors judged the cases brought before them according to law. For all their apparent corruption, fanaticism, callousness, and venality, the inquisitors were at the end of the day trained jurists who oversaw a large number of varied cases against diverse defendants within a judicial system which did afford the defendant at least some, if limited, opportunities to refute the charges in meaningful ways.

The most effective means of defence was the use of *tachas* to prove enmity with the witnesses, but this was only possible if the defendant could guess their identity. It remains speculative just how many those cleared of the charges against them were acquitted because they managed to mount a successful defence since most acquittals have left no justification. Many were undoubtably acquitted simply because the inquisitors found the evidence they themselves had assembled insufficient to convict the defendant even of the suspicion of heresy. In the end, there is no doubt that the Holy Office generally did follow its own evidentiary rules and that successful defences were mounted which undermined the prosecution's case by removing sufficient amounts of the assembled evidence from consideration to make a conviction impossible.

We have already seen examples of acquittals due to the difficulty of identifying the correct person in bigamy cases. Getting correct information on absent spouses could also be a challenge. In 1589, in Barcelona, Juan Torre Coll was accused of bigamy by his first wife and was acquitted because he was able to produce written evidence from the prior of the hospital in Manresa that stated – incorrectly, as it were – that his first wife had passed away after an illness in that hospital. Having been misinformed about the death of his first wife he did not commit a punishable crime by remarrying. This case is also (as are many bigamy cases) noteworthy for the extensive use of written evidence: wedding registers from two different cities and a death certificate from a third were submitted and decided the case, rather than simply the witnesses which usually was the most significant form of evidence in the Holy Office.[59]

At times, it was simply stated in the written opinions that the evidence that had been gathered during the proceedings was not credible, even when faced with a defendant who would almost universally be considered suspect in the faith. Take, for instance, the case of Balthasar de Narvaez, one of the Granadian Moriscos forcibly resettled in other parts of Spain after the Alpujarras rebellion, was put down. In 1585, he was denounced to the Holy Office in Llerena by another Morisco who claimed that Balthasar de Narvaez had prayed Muslim prayers, eaten halal food, and so on. After this, he was arrested and interrogated, and formally charged with following Islamic religious precepts. He denied all the allegations throughout his trial. The inquisitors had decided to arrest him, interrogate him, and charge him based on the testimony of a single witness. The tribunal, including those same inquisitors, decided to acquit him, stating that they 'believed that the witness had no credibility whatsoever'.[60]

Similarly, the Frenchman Antonio Giuan was acquitted of sodomy in Barcelona in 1574 or 1575 because he proved 'bastantissimamente' that his accuser Joan de Sant Benet was 'simpleminded and without any understanding'. In fact, the inquisitors state, during questioning the accuser, was 'unable to count to the number four, even when using his fingers', in addition to failing other 'tests which were conducted with relation to his stupidity'. For this reason, his accuser was also acquitted of his confessed sodomy with Antonio.[61] A man who could not count to four or decide if he was 3, 50, or 23 years old could not be used as a witness, and his own confession was equally useless as evidence. The same year saw a further acquittal in the same tribunal for sodomy, this time of Juan Antonio de la Piedra who had been accused by his wife of sodomising her. According to the *relación*, he proved that she was 'an adulteress' and that she hated or at least disliked him. There were also 'other circumstances', as well as 'variations and contradictions' in his wife's testimony. All of this combined with his steadfast refusal to confess led to his acquittal.[62] What is particularly interesting about this group of three cases is that they contrast the flimsy evidence needed to prosecute with the much higher standard required to convict. These are not cases where the failure to produce more evidence during the trial led to an acquittal. They are examples of the 'destruction' of the initial evidence, to use the phrase María Paz Alonso Romero employs when describing the defendant's ability to defend him or herself.[63] The cases of Antonio Giuan and Joan de Sant Benet are particularly interesting in this regard, since Frenchmen were among the Barcelona tribunal's favourite victims, and for long periods, the only defendants they could persuade local authorities to execute after a capital conviction.[64]

The Morisco Francisco Torromani was acquitted in Valencia in 1575 after having been prosecuted and tortured on the basis of the testimony of a single witness. With no confession during torture, he was acquitted, in line with the rules laid out by the instructions.[65] In the case of Thomas Jana on Sardinia the inquisitors based their acquittal on the opinion that 'there did not remain sufficient evidence against the defendant' after the defence had discredited the majority of the witnesses.[66] Inquisitor Muñoz of Barcelona was harsh when he considered the evidence for witchcraft that the secular courts had assembled against Margarita Olivera:

> The four witnesses are women, two testified under torture before an incompetent[67] judge. All four have been hanged, and there is no reason to look at the trial records of other witches to see if there is any evidence of her guilt, for in her own trial records there is none[68]

The Morisco Joan Marchani was acquitted in Valencia in 1572 after his father who had denounced him refused to ratify his own testimony, saying that he had been mistaken about seeing his son perform Muslim ceremonies.[69] It is far from the only case where the reader suspects a family quarrel, but one is also left to wonder if the father had sufficient knowledge of the Inquisition to know that the danger for his son was real enough to be a significant bargaining chip, but limited enough to be manageable if he did not ratify his own testimony.

Sometimes no defence was necessary, and in the case of Francesch Veynat, the *relación* states that 'he did not want to' make a formal defence. It was not necessary: the seven witnesses named by the denouncer did not support his allegations of blasphemy, and Francesch Veynat was acquitted.[70]

False witnesses were prosecuted, and occasionally given harsh sentences. Maria Reoli was given a hundred lashes of the whip and banished for life from Valencia in 1573 after making false accusations of Lutheran sympathies. Her victim was acquitted.[71] Two years later, Nofre Borroy, Bartholome Carron, and Lorenco Torromani, all three Moriscos from Azaneta, were sentenced to 200 lashes of the whip each, and up to lifetime service as galley slaves after giving false testimony against other Moriscos, accusing them of living as Muslims.[72] Yet, persecuting alleged false witnesses was also difficult, as we saw in the cases of the brothers Antonio and Domingo Baura and their stepfather.

The miller Joan Sancho from Castellon de la Plana was acquitted after the *calificadores* found no evidence of heresy in the evidence against him. He had been denounced for owning papers written in Arabic and using them to discover enchanted treasures, as well as going to a Morisca fortune teller. The documents were discovered by a priest who came to his home because of the noise and screams as he was beating his wife and threatening to kill her. She was later one of the witnesses against him. He explained that his trips to the mountains were to find firewood, not enchanted treasure, and that the paper in Arabic letters had been a gift to him as a young boy just after his brother died, from a Morisco who said it would keep him safe. He named some 70 witnesses in his defence and 5 of them were questioned. Despite the evidence of a history of receiving Morisco guest (they travelled to see him on behalf of their lord who used his mill), possessing papers in Arabic with Muslim prayers and an admitted visit to a Morisca fortune teller he was acquitted of both superstitions and any suspicion of Muslim practices. The *calificadores* stated simply that his actions were those of a person of ill repute (*persona mal mirada*), but no heresy. The tribunal agreed, there was no crime against the faith, and he was acquitted *de la instancia*.[73]

Gaspar Pastor was tried because criminal justice officers found Arabic papers on his person when they were searching him for weapons. As a Morisco, he was naturally suspected of using these writings for religious purposes and was handed over to the Inquisition. There he was able to prove that he had found the papers after they had fallen out of the hat of another Morisco, immediately before his arrest. Indeed, he proved that he had not even had time to find out what they were, and he was acquitted.[74]

Arnau Som was acquitted of the charges of being a Huguenot because the witnesses could not be ratified. The defendant, the denouncer, and other witnesses were French, and the alleged offences were committed in France. When the witnesses could not be found to confirm and ratify their original depositions, these lost all evidentiary value. There was thus no legally admissible evidence at all against Arnau Som, who claimed to be a catholic who had been captured by the Huguenots and escaped to Catholic territory at his first opportunity.[75]

Cases involving enmity frequently led to the destruction of evidence when defence witnesses proved enmity between the witnesses and the defendant, and hence the inadmissibility of their testimony. This again could lead to the prosecution of the witnesses in the first case as suspect of false testimony. An example of how complex this could be are the two cases of Pere Roger and Leonard Frage, reported from Barcelona in 1575. Pere denounced Leonard, claiming to have seen him sing psalms with the Huguenots in France and that 'he took him for a Lutheran'. Leonard proved enmity with Pere and was acquitted. Based on the evidence furnished by the witnesses to their enmity, the inquisitors with the ordinary and *consultores* voted to try Pere for false testimony. He for his part named witnesses that proved sufficient enmity with the witnesses produced by Leonard to destroy their evidentiary value. Faced with his insistence that he was not moved by hatred and had only told the inquisitors what he had heard and seen, they were forced to acquit him as well.[76] Indeed, those acquitted after having been charged with false testimony in order to target their enemies universally held to this explanation. Again, it proved virtually impossible for the Holy Office to prove that they had deliberately lied as long as they simply claimed to have told what they had seen and heard without claiming any other knowledge of their target's guilt or innocence. In this context, it is easy to see why some trials inevitably ended in acquittals.

Notes

1 Ortego Gil, "Innocentia praesumpta."
2 Pérez García, "Perspectivas," 82.
3 *Diccionario razonado de legislación y jurisprudencia*, Quoted in Ortego Gil, "Innocentia praesumpta," 112.
4 Ortego Gil, "Innocentia praesumpta," 79. Bernhard Schnapper finds the same motive for conditional acquittals in Bordeaux: Bernard Schnapper, "la répression pénale au XVIe siècle au Bordeaux," *Recueils de mémoires et travaux publiés para la Société d'Histoire du Droit* VIII (1971): 67–69.

5 This was not always respected by the tribunals and we find more than 4.000 trials were the defendant was ordered to pay the expenses or 'extraodinary expenses' of the Holy Office.
6 *Relación* in AHN, Inq, Leg. 2022, exp. 1, fol. 1r.–1v.
7 For clarity the alleged offence in the following refers to the main accusation in the trial. Many, if not most, defendants were accused of multiple crimes: for example, a charge of heresy was usually also accompanied by some accusations of heretical propositions. To avoid confusion and in order to count every trial only once in the statistics, the main point of the accusation has been chosen here.
8 Monter, *Frontiers of Heresy*; Starr-LeBeau, *In the Shadow of the Virgin: Inquisitors, Friars, and Conversos in Guadalupe, Spain.*
9 See, for example, Henningsen, *The Witches' Advocate*; Homza, *Village* Infernos; Knutsen, *Servants of Satan.*
10 Monter, Frontiers of Heresy, 110.
11 Relación of the Baura brothers cases in AHN, Inq, Lib 730, fols. 283v–284r.
12 This was because the person of the defendant was of paramount importance for interpreting his words and actions and understanding if they might be heretical or not. See Dedieu and Knutsen, "La cause de foi."
13 This has been particularily well studied by Jean Pierre Dedieu in *L'Administration de la foi.*
14 See, for example, Enrique García Hernán, *Irlanda y el rey prudente* (Madrid: Ediciones del Laberinto, 2000); Enrique García Hernán, *Irlanda y la monarquía hispánica: Kinsale, 1601–2001: guerra, política, exilio y religión* (Madrid: Universidad de Alcalá: Consejo Superior de Investigaciones Científicas, 2002); Martín Murphy, "Estudiantes y comerciantes irlandeses en Sevilla, 1598–1798," in *Los extranjeros en la España Moderna: actas del I Coloquio internacional, celebrado en Málaga del 28 al 30 de Noviembre de 2002*, ed. Pilar Pezzi Cristóbal and María Begoña Villar García (Málaga: 2003); R. A. Stradling, *The Spanish Monarchy and the Irish Mercenaries: The Wild Geese in Spain, 1618–68* (Dublin: Irish Academic Press, 1994).
15 Among the German, Dutch, English, and Swiss defendants, there were significant numbers who were *absuelto ad cautelam*, with all the complications that entail for calculating conviction rates. See above, Chapter 3.
16 Excluding the tribunals on Sicily and Sardinia.
17 Thomas, *la represión del protestantismo en España, 1517–1648.*
18 Pérez García, "*Perspectivas*"; Alonso Romero, *El proceso penal.*
19 AHN, Inq, Leg 33, exp. 13.
20 An important exception is that trials for bestiality and sodomy in the Crown of Aragon were conducted according to the rules of secular courts. In these trials, there was direct confrontation between the defendant and the accusers during the trial. See the instructions for how to proceed in such cases in the Inquisition in Barcelona: AHN, Inq, Lib. 499, fols. 788v–792v.
21 Beinart, *Conversos on Trial*; Starr-LeBeau, *In the Shadow of the Virgin.*
22 AHN, Inq, Lib 730, fols. 785v–786v.
23 Rábade Obradó, "la toma de decisiones en relación con las denuncias de criptojudíos ante los tribunales de Ciudad Real y Toledo (1483–1504)." See also, Aguilera Barchet, "El procedimiento."
24 Rábade Obradó, "la toma de decisiones en relación con las denuncias de criptojudíos ante los tribunales de Ciudad Real y Toledo (1483–1504)," 163.
25 *Relación* in AHN, Inq, Lib 732, fols. 332v–333r.
26 AHN, Inq, Leg 2041, Exp 64.
27 AHN, Inq, Leg 4972, Exp 1, 28, fol. 6r.
28 Monter, *Frontiers of Heresy*, 234–50.

29 AHN, Inq, Leg 4972, Exp 1, 28, fol. 6v–7r.
30 A second Morisco, Juan Çenote, was also tried for the same offence that year. He also denied the charge and was absolved after maintaining his innocence under torture. However, in his case, there is no mention of discrediting the witnesses. AHN, Inq, Leg 4972, Exp 1, 29, fols. 2v–3r and 5v.
31 However, when studying sodomy trials Cristian Berco found that foreigners were in fact more likely to be acquitted or have their cases suspended. Berco, *Sexual Hierarchies*, 110–11.
32 *Relación* in AHN, Inq, Leg 1829, 1N and 1K.
33 *Relación* in AHN, Inq, Lib 730, fols. 281v–282v.
34 Legg til eksempel på dette.
35 AHN, Inq, Lib 836, fol. 269r–270r.
36 AHN, Inq, Leg. 2022, exp. 4, fol. 4r. The lenience here is notable since he was a Frenchman hence highly suspicious of being a protestant, especially when we consider that this acquittal came at the height of the scare of Protestant contagion from France. See Knutsen and Muñoz Navarro, "Prosecuting the French: patterns of trials against French defendants in Valencia, 1566–1686."
37 Sara Tilghman Nalle, *Mad for God: Bartolomé Sánchez, the Secret Messiah of Cardenete* (Charlottesville: University Press of Virginia, 2001).
38 AHN, INQ, Lib. 730, fol. 317r.
39 AHN, Inq, Leg 4972, exp 10, fols. 14v–15v.
40 AHN, Inq, Leg 4972, Exp 1, 2, fols. 1v–2r.
41 AHN, Inq, Leg 4972, Exp 1, 3, fols. 29v–30r.
42 AHN, Inq, Leg 4972, Exp 1, 40, fols. 9v–10r.
43 AHN, Inq, Leg. 2022, exp. 2, fol. 1r.
44 AHN, Inq, Leg. 2022, exp. 4, fol. 4r.
45 AHN/INQ, leg. 1988, exp. 13, 1r–15v, and exp. 15, 1r–8v.
46 Seitz writes, for example, 'The Venetian Holy Office's internal debates are almost universally lost to us, if they were ever put to paper'. Seitz, *Witchcraft and Inquisition*, 238.
47 Alonso Romero, *El proceso penal*, 260–62.
48 Pérez García, *Perspectivas*, 77. However, Nuria Verdet has recently shown that Francisco Jerónimo de León used his own sentences to argue points of judicial doctrine, and hence extensively comment on the reasons for his sentences in print, though not in court. nuria Verdet Martínez, "Francisco Jerónimo de León. Cultura, poticia y prática administrativa en la Valencia de los austrias menores' (Universitat de Valencia, 2014), 90–111.
49 'Fallo atento los autos y méritos deste processo, que el dicho fulano no provó su pedimiento y demanda'. Gabriel de Monterroso y Alvarado, *Pratica civil y criminal y instrución de escrivanos, dividida en nueve tratados* (Madrid: Pedro Madrigal, 1591), 12r.
50 'Fallo atento a los autos y méritos del proceso, a que en lo necesario me refiero, que debo declarar, y declaro que el promotor fiscal probó su acción en bastante forma'. J.Á. Posadilla, *Practica criminal por principios, ó Modo y forma de instruir los procesos criminales de las causas de oficio*, vol. 2 (Madrid, 1815), 429.
51 *Proceso* in AHN, Inq, Leg 551, exp. 31. The *relación* gives no reason at all for his acquittal. It is in AHN, Inq, Lib 936, fol. 130v.
52 *Proceso* in AHN, Inq, Leg 26, exp. 10.
53 *Proceso* in AHN, Inq, Leg. 111, exp. 18.
54 *Proceso* in AHN, Inq, Leg 169, exp. 9.
55 *Proceso* in AHN, Inq, Leg 196, exp. 26.
56 Shennan, The parlement of Paris.

57 See, for example, Johannes-Michael Scholz, "Relatores et magistrados. de la naissance du juge moderne au XIXe siècle espagnol," in *Les figures de l'administrateur: institutions, réseaux, pouvoirs en Espagne, en France et au Portugal, 16e–19e siècle*, ed. Robert Descimon, Jean-Frédéric Schaub, and Bernard Vincent (Paris: Éditions de l'École des hautes études en sciences sociales, 1997).
58 Martínez Navas, "Un Manual," 23.
59 AHN, INQ, lib. 731, fols. 42v–43r.
60 AHN, Inq, Leg 1988, exp 21, fol. 10r.
61 AHN, Inq, Lib 730, fol. 280r.
62 AHN, Inq, Lib 730, fol. 280v.
63 Alonso Romero, *El proceso penal.*
64 Monter, *Frontiers of Heresy*, 106–24.
65 *Proceso* in AHN, Inq, Leg 555, exp. 31.
66 AHN, Inq, Lib 782, fols 162v–163v.
67 The word 'incompetent' is used here in the narrow sense of lacking jurisdiction.
68 BN, MS 2440, fol. 82r.
69 AHN, Inquisition, Lib 936, fol. 318r.
70 AHN, Inq, Lib 730, fol. 282v.
71 AHN, Inq. Lib 936, fol. 73r.
72 AHN, Inq, Lib 936, fol. 138r.
73 Proceso in AHN, Inq, Leg 551, exp. 13.
74 AHN, Inq, Lib 936, fol. 361r.
75 AHN, Inq, Lib 730, fol. 284v.
76 AHN, Inq, Lib 730, fols. 282v–283v.

5

CONCLUSION

The acquittals came from all types of offences, in all tribunals and through the entire history of the institution. The variations we have seen are probably more the result of internal differences within tribunals and their immediate surroundings, political pressure, and the interests of individual inquisitors. We frequently think of the Spanish Inquisition as a well-oiled and efficient machine. As Lu Ann Homza reminds us, it wasn't always so:

> Far from being an effective bureaucracy, the Inquisition in this episode was fragmented and diffident, with its employees pursuing different tracks simultaneously. New evidence about the tribunal's notaries just cements the impression of incompetence.[1]

What she uncovered is unusually well documented, but it may not be exceptional. The Inquisition's internal documents are rife with stories of lost papers, employees busy with everything except their jobs, and inquisitors who were entangled in personal conflicts. In other words, the Spanish Inquisition was very much an early modern Spanish institution, and the results of its efforts were as one should expect from such an institution.

Theory and practice

Two things should have become clear from reading the previous chapters. The first is that the eventual acquittal of a defendant was above all linked to an evaluation of the available evidence at the end of the trial. Acquittals were the result of internal operations within the Holy Office. More precisely, they resulted from the observation of the rules of evidence on the part of those

DOI: 10.4324/9781003455691-5

making up the Inquisition's sentencing panels. One cannot always say the converse; that the conviction of the defendant was the result of the correct application of judicial rules and legislation, although that certainly appears to have been the case in many or even the majority of trials. Yet it is clear that the Holy Office at times did bend, twist, or even break the law when it suited it, such as with Lucero's trials in Cordoba and Sarmiento's burning of convicted witches in Barcelona. When an inquisitorial tribunal did so, it was to obtain a conviction, not an acquittal. It may be objected here that the Suprema did not agree with Lucero's and Sarmiento's actions, but it was unable to stop these trials and certainly unwilling to overturn the convictions afterwards.

The second thing which should be apparent at this stage is the importance of the selection of which cases to bring to trial. This explains the relatively low acquittal rate, the otherwise puzzling fact that those with the most significant legal protections against convictions – women and children – were in fact least likely to be acquitted, while those most vulnerable in a judicial system where local roots were so important to secure an acquittal – foreigners and the internally displaced – were in fact those most frequently acquitted.

Yet, as we have seen, an acquittal wasn't a foregone conclusion even when there was insufficient evidence to convict the defendants. The case could legally just as well be suspended. There was a clear distinction between these two outcomes in the legislation of the Holy Office, although, as we have seen, paragraph 54 of the 1566 instructions from Toledo stated that if the inquisitors believed that the defendant had sufficiently purged the evidence against him after resisting torture, he should be acquitted. In essence, even here, after torture, the decision was left to the *arbitrium* of the inquisitors and the sentencing panel. They could acquit him, suspend the trial, or convict him to be penanced as a suspect of heresy. And no matter what decision they reached, Inquisitor General Torquemada's 1484 instructions from Seville ensured that the trial could always be reopened in the future. The difference between an acquittal and a suspension was therefore a question of arbitrary justice. Ultimately, one cannot meaningfully evaluate acquittals without also talking of suspensions, the other main form of non-conviction.

Suspension and acquittal

It is difficult in the extreme to pinpoint exactly why some trials ended with an acquittal instead of a suspension, and vice versa. There were, in fact, no hard-and-fast rules for how the inquisitors should decide. Furthermore, for almost every suspended case, one can find an acquittal with the same lack of evidence. Even the total lack of evidence did not always lead to an acquittal.

However, in some cases, it seems clear that the trial was suspended not just because of a lack of evidence but also because the court became uncertain that they had arrested and tried the right person. Instead of acquitting the person in front of them they frequently chose to release him and suspend the case, perhaps in the hope of being able to arrest the correct person at some time in the future – though no such case has yet to come to light. Occasionally is simply stated that the defendant was released from jail, such as when it became clear that the Portuguese barber Manuel Rodriguez 'was not the person who had committed the crime' as the inquisitors put it when they dolefully reported his release from jail after a trial for bigamy Llerena in 1681.[2] The tribunal in Cuenca gave the same reason for releasing another man also named Manuel Rodriguez,[3] and these are just two examples among several of mistaken identity. And it wasn't just the inquisitors who struggled to identify the accused. In a bigamy case in Barcelona in 1588, Joan Puig was acquitted because it proved impossible to prove that he was the man who under the name of Joan Canaleta had married Joana Canaleta. Not many years passed since the wedding, since he was 23 years old at the time of his trial. Yet even his allegedly abandoned wife turned out to not be certain that the man who she had denounced was in fact her husband, and nor were the witnesses, 'even though he looked like him': 'sometimes she says this is the same man that she married at other times she says she can't say for certain'. Joan languished in jail and denied ever having had another name or married his accuser until the Holy Office decided to acquit him because of the 'perplexity' of knowing if he had in fact contracted both marriages.[4] There are a number of such cases, and we have already talked of Franciso de San Juan, whose alleged first wife was unable to identify him when brought to the court to examine the defendant, and the two shoemakers from Albuquerque named Diego Díaz who were both reconciled for Judaism at the same auto da fe. Three more examples. Antonio Rodriguez and Juan Beltrán were both tried in Granada in 1623. The latter was accused of uttering heretical propositions. In the *relación* to the *Suprema*, the tribunal recorded their doubts that Juan Beltrán was the person that the witnesses had testified against, and reported that the witnesses had not presented themselves for the actual trial. At this point, one might expect an acquittal of the man who might not be the one they sought, and against whom there was no legal evidence. Instead, the trial was just suspended. He was not alone in this, as we have just alluded to. The Portuguese Antonio Rodriguez was simultaneously being prosecuted by the same court as a Judaizer. He declared his innocence, produced defence witnesses, and the Inquisition's surgeon confirmed in his testimony that the defendant had, in fact, not been circumcised. His case was also suspended.[5] The refusal to acquit Juan Beltrán may be the most puzzling, yet that of Antonio Rodriguez also gives reason for pause. Thirty-seven years later, in the same tribunal, Simón Rodríguez Cáceres successfully defended himself against charges of Judaism by claiming that the charges and the evidence presented against him must be against 'another person'. The tribunal agreed, reconciling Simón

Rodríguez Díaz instead. Yet, again the trial against Simón Rodríguez Cáceres was only suspended even though they had found and punished the other Simón Rodríguez – the one that they really sought – and they had absolutely no reason to imagine that they would ever reopen the case against Simón Rodríguez Cáceres against who there was no evidence at all. Read together these three cases indicate an absolute refusal to acquit a defendant. If the difference between an acquittal and a suspension was the state of the evidence at the end of the trial, then one would expect Juan Beltrán to be exonerated since there was no legal evidence against him, and one would be less surprised to see Antonio Rodriguez' case suspended since there remained testimony against him, despite the lack of physical evidence and a confession.

The trial of Simón Rodríguez Cáceres is in another class entirely, and one might be forgiven for thinking that the Granada tribunal acquitted no-one after reading this. Yet, as we have seen earlier, while 11 per cent of the trials were suspended in that tribunal, Granada acquitted 3.7 per cent of all the known defendants, very close to the average for the whole institution. Just not in this period: in the years between 1606 and 1677, only four cases ended in an acquittal, while 438 were suspended. For the Spanish Inquisition as a whole in these years, the corresponding figures are 558 acquittals and 3,632 suspensions.[6] Clearly, we are dealing with a change in judicial practice within this tribunal during the first half of the seventeenth century, as indicated by Figure 4.1, in the previous chapter. In the sixteenth century and again at the final of the seventeenth century, defendants were more likely to be acquitted. Changes in sentencing and acquittal rates in Granada appear to above all reflect local conditions rather than central commands and policy changes, quite in line with what William Monter suggested for Barcelona. This then puts into question how fruitful aggregate statistic for the whole institution are if they to a great degree are reflections of local changes within single tribunals rather than evidence of changes for the Spanish Inquisition as a whole. Fortunately, the reality is not quite so bleak, but there are regional and temporal differences that will have to be explained by local circumstances, whether they are demographic, political, or simply the change of personnel.

Precisely in this period in another tribunal, we see a case that initially was bound for an acquittal yet ended in suspension some months later: Manuel Díaz Fernández was tried as a Judaizer in Cordoba in 1645. On 5 June, the tribunal reported to the *Suprema* that the case had been voted on 28 May, and that the decision had been to acquit the defendant. On 4 June, the day before the cut-off date of the *relación*, the fiscal appealed the acquittal.[7] The next notice we have is from another *relación* written at the start of 1646, summing up all activities of the preceding year. Here it is simply and briefly stated that the trial against Manuel Díaz Fernández had been suspended.[8] The same occurred with his wife, doña Leonor de Faro, and their daughter doña Beatriz Manuel. From a later *relación*, we learn that they had all been convicted and reconciled as Judaizers in subsequent trials in 1647, after Manuel Díaz Fernández had died in jail.[9] During the two years that he was jailed, the sentencing changed from acquittal, via suspension to reconciliation. It is fair to assume that new information was produced in the latter stages of the trial, resulting finally in a conviction, but what made the tribunal decide that a suspension was a better sentence than an acquittal?

Consequences of acquittal

Did an acquittal make a defendant more careful, make him change his ways, and modify his behaviour? Did it have a silencing effect, making him bind his tongue or did it cause him to be more careful in how and when he spoke? Did it have such effects on others who observed the trial from the outside, never quite sure what was going on? Gretchen Starr-Lebeau has argued convincingly that convictions of Judaizers silenced even the Old Christians (who had not been the targets of the Inquisition's trials) in some of their conflicts with authorities in Guadalupe. But what of acquittals? There is no easy or obvious method to measure the impact of acquittals in any meaningful way, but we have some evidence of the possible consequences of acquittals. As so often is the case with the Spanish Inquisition, the available evidence points in contradictory directions. For example, a promising theological career could be crushed by the fact of an inquisitorial trial, even if it ended with an acquittal.[10] Denouncing theological opponents to the Holy Office was an effective way of dealing with rivals and ensuring that Spanish theology remained conservative. On the other hand, the fact that some of those acquitted chose the maximum possible publicity for their acquittals by having them read aloud at *autos de fe* is a clear indication that they believed this would be a useful and effective way of clearing their names and going some way towards restoring their reputations. A public declaration of acquittal by the Holy Office in front of thousands would be unforgettable and give the defendant access to many witnesses who could confirm that he or she had in fact been acquitted. The public exoneration of the 52-year-old widow Ángela de la Vega y Torres for Judaism in 1727 was nothing short of spectacular. The tribunal in Valladolid reported:

> She was at the auto with a palm leaf, where she heard her sentence of acquittal and the conditions of her false accusers. On the next the day she came out on a white horse among the ministers of the Holy Office and with the palm leaf, behind the false witnesses on who the sentence of 200 lashes of the whip was being executed.[11]

This was truly a remarkable demonstration of innocence! Using a trial in the Holy Office to tar the reputation of Ángela de la Vega y Torres again would be very difficult indeed after such a show of judicial victory and demonstrated innocence. Even so, her acquittal was just conditional: she was acquitted *de la instancia*.

Another form of evidence to the effect of an acquittal on the defendant's later life is that some of those acquitted were later convicted by the Inquisition. This again points in various directions, for in some cases, it is a question of the same offences and new evidence, while in others the defendant was convicted of new acts committed after the first trial. In the latter cases, we clearly deal with persons who were not intimidated by their first trial experiences, who did not change their ways of thinking and acting substantially just because they had been tried by the Spanish Inquisition.

However, for those who were first acquitted and then later convicted of the same offence, the time after the first trial must have been very taxing, indeed. In particular, if they knew that they had been initially denounced for something that they had actually done or said, the wait for the inevitable knock on the door must have weighed on them.

Conclusion

We have shown that the post-Torquemada Inquisition acquitted a meaningful portion of those defendants that the inquisitors had decided to prosecute among the much larger group of people denounced to the Inquisition. An even larger number of trials were formally suspended. There are a number of important conclusions to draw from this, not least that the inquisitors did in fact follow judicial procedures to the degree that they produced thousands of acquittals, and they did not conform to the caricature that is so often drawn of them as doing whatever it took to avoid admitting that they had prosecuted an innocent man or woman.

Every acquittal may be taken as an admission of error, which is what these critics have done, and in that case, the Spanish Inquisition admitted its errors thousands of times, occasionally even putting them on public display at the *autos de fe*. However, an acquittal can also be taken as a sign that the inquisitors did not wish to punish the innocent and that while they were too quick and eager to arrest and charge people on flimsy evidence, they were too conscientious to convict them when further evidence was not produced. Whatever interpretation one favours, and one need not necessarily stick to a single one over the whole period for every inquisitor and every defendant, one must remember that the same inquisitors chose to arrest, prosecute, and acquit these defendants. The prosecutions and acquittals are not the result of completely different groups of people with varying priorities or different values.

The acquittals were the result of the Holy Office working and functioning as the inquisitors believed it should.

Was the delator who had started the case satisfied when the person he or she had denounced to the Holy Office was acquitted? Perhaps not, but even in the case of an acquittal, his or her vengeance had been served. An inquisitorial trial entailed the loss of freedom, income, and property while it ran its course; losses which even a public acquittal at an *auto da fe* could not make good, even if it could go some way towards rescuing the defendant's reputation. As a means of transacting enmity, the Holy Office was unparalleled: free and with low risk, though false witnesses were occasionally prosecuted. The best outcome for the malicious delator would, of course, be a conviction that destroyed his or her enemy, which is one of the reasons why the most effective weapon was to tell the Inquisition the truth. Even so, an inquisitorial trial that ended with an acquittal was a sufficiently costly and humbling experience for its victim that it served vengeance quite well. It 'mattered little what was the outcome of the case, the fact of imprisonment was remembered and handed down through generations while the fact of its being causeless was forgotten', writes Henry Charles Lea.[12] Against this the only really effective counter would be the public showing of innocence at an *auto da fe*, but there were other methods.

The Venetian Julio Bautista was acquitted in Toledo in 1566. Upon his acquittal, he petitioned the *suprema* for a written confirmation of his acquittal and a translation of his sentence to show his parents and his friends to demonstrate his innocence and 'for the world to know how much virtue is administered in this holy house'. The *Suprema* ordered that he should be given the documentation he requested.[13] A similar request was made in the same tribunal in 1572 by the Portuguese Francisco Herrero who had converted to Islam in captivity, writing to the inquisitors that 'you know from my life's story how I need an instrument which could juridically show that I have already been purged in this holy tribunal'. The inquisitors acquiesced.[14] These two men show us that to them their acquittals were meaningful – but also that their supposedly secret trials continued to cause them trouble even after they had been judicially decided in their favour.[15] An inquisitorial trial affected the life of a defendant long after the judicial proceedings were over, even when he was cleared of the charges. Those who had been acquitted as opposed to simply released or having a suspended trial had the great advantage of being able to stand before their neighbours in triumph as an acquitted defendant at an *auto da fe*, or to have a written instrument announcing that he had been acquitted in the most severe tribunal of all for all to see whenever he was accused of some malfeasance or his Catholicism was questioned. It certainly did not make up for the suffering of a wrongful prosecution, but it did put the defendant on a path towards full reintegration in Catholic society – with the blessing of the Holy Office.

Notes

1 Homza, Village Infernos, 186.
2 *Relación* in AHN, Inq, Leg. 3681, exp. 9, fol. 10v.
3 ADC, Inq, leg. 0393, exp. 5591.
4 AHN, INQ, lib. 731, fols. 29v–30r.
5 The *relación* from Granada in 1623 exists in two copies: AHN, Inq, Leg. 1952, exp. 4E; and AHN, Inq, Leg. 1953, exp. 69.
6 Numbers from EMID.
7 AHN, Inq, Leg 2415.
8 AHN, Inq, Leg 4972, Exp. 1.44, fol. 10v.
9 AHN, Inq, Leg 4972, Exp. 1.50.
10 Dedieu, L'Administration de la foi, 298.
11 AHN, INQ, leg. 3259. Document entitled Memoria de las personas que fueron despachadas por este Santo Oficio de la Inquisición de Valladolid en el auto particular de fe que se celebró en la iglesia del convento de San Pablo, Orden de Predicadores, de dicha ciudad, el sábado 30 de mayo de 1727, día del glorioso San Fernando, rey de España.
12 Lea, *A History*, vol. 1, 357.
13 *Proceso* in AHN, Inq, Leg 199, exp. 39.
14 *Proceso* in AHN, Inq, Leg 101, exp 19.
15 In a similiar vein, Henry Charles Lea recounts how Catalan local officials 'refused to leave the prison without a formal declaration that they had not been arrested for heresy' after having been arrested bu the Holy Office in one of the interminable conflicts between the Inquisition and secular authorities. Lea, *A History*, vol. 1, 470.

SOURCES CONSULTED

Abbreviations used in source

A.Cat.Gr: Archivo de la Catedral de Granada
ADC: Archivo Diocesano de Cuenca
AHN: Archivo Histórico Nacional
Inq: Sección de Inquisición
Leg: Legajo
Lib: Libro
Exp: Expediente
BK: British Library
BNM: Bibliotheca Nacional de España
BPRM: Biblioteca del Real Palacio de Madrid

Primary sources

A.Cat.Gr, Libro de Actas II
A.Cat.Gr, Libro de Actas IV
A.Cat.Gr, Libro de Actas V
ADC, Inq, Leg. 0393
AHN, Inq, Leg. 1
AHN, Inq, Leg. 100
AHN, Inq, Leg. 101
AHN, Inq, Leg. 102
AHN, Inq, Leg. 103
AHN, Inq, Leg. 104
AHN, Inq, Leg. 105

AHN, Inq, Leg. 106
AHN, Inq, Leg. 107
AHN, Inq, Leg. 108
AHN, Inq, Leg. 109
AHN, Inq, Leg. 110
AHN, Inq, Leg. 111
AHN, Inq, Leg. 112
AHN, Inq, Leg. 113
AHN, Inq, Leg. 114
AHN, Inq, Leg. 115
AHN, Inq, Leg. 116
AHN, Inq, Leg. 117
AHN, Inq, Leg. 118
AHN, Inq, Leg. 119
AHN, Inq, Leg. 120
AHN, Inq, Leg. 121
AHN, Inq, Leg. 122
AHN, Inq, Leg. 123
AHN, Inq, Leg. 124
AHN, Inq, Leg. 125
AHN, Inq, Leg. 126
AHN, Inq, Leg. 127
AHN, Inq, Leg. 128
AHN, Inq, Leg. 129
AHN, Inq, Leg. 130
AHN, Inq, Leg. 131
AHN, Inq, Leg. 132
AHN, Inq, Leg. 133
AHN, Inq, Leg. 1330
AHN, Inq, Leg. 134
AHN, Inq, Leg. 135
AHN, Inq, Leg. 136
AHN, Inq, Leg. 137
AHN, Inq, Leg. 138
AHN, Inq, Leg. 139
AHN, Inq, Leg. 140
AHN, Inq, Leg. 141
AHN, Inq, Leg. 142
AHN, Inq, Leg. 143
AHN, Inq, Leg. 144
AHN, Inq, Leg. 1449
AHN, Inq, Leg. 145
AHN, Inq, Leg. 146

AHN, Inq, Leg. 147
AHN, Inq, Leg. 148
AHN, Inq, Leg. 149
AHN, Inq, Leg. 150
AHN, Inq, Leg. 151
AHN, Inq, Leg. 152
AHN, Inq, Leg. 153
AHN, Inq, Leg. 1535
AHN, Inq, Leg. 154
AHN, Inq, Leg. 155
AHN, Inq, Leg. 156
AHN, Inq, Leg. 157
AHN, Inq, Leg. 158
AHN, Inq, Leg. 159
AHN, Inq, Leg. 1593
AHN, Inq, Leg. 160
AHN, Inq, Leg. 161
AHN, Inq, Leg. 162
AHN, Inq, Leg. 163
AHN, Inq, Leg. 164
AHN, Inq, Leg. 165
AHN, Inq, Leg. 166
AHN, Inq, Leg. 167
AHN, Inq, Leg. 168
AHN, Inq, Leg. 1680
AHN, Inq, Leg. 169
AHN, Inq, Leg. 17
AHN, Inq, Leg. 170
AHN, Inq, Leg. 171
AHN, Inq, Leg. 1716
AHN, Inq, Leg. 172
AHN, Inq, Leg. 173
AHN, Inq, Leg. 174
AHN, Inq, Leg. 1743
AHN, Inq, Leg. 1747
AHN, Inq, Leg. 175
AHN, Inq, Leg. 1755
AHN, Inq, Leg. 176
AHN, Inq, Leg. 177
AHN, Inq, Leg. 178
AHN, Inq, Leg. 179
AHN, Inq, Leg. 180
AHN, Inq, Leg. 181

AHN, Inq, Leg. 182
AHN, Inq, Leg. 1829
AHN, Inq, Leg. 183
AHN, Inq, Leg. 184
AHN, Inq, Leg. 185
AHN, Inq, Leg. 186
AHN, Inq, Leg. 187
AHN, Inq, Leg. 188
AHN, Inq, Leg. 189
AHN, Inq, Leg. 19
AHN, Inq, Leg. 190
AHN, Inq, Leg. 191
AHN, Inq, Leg. 192
AHN, Inq, Leg. 193
AHN, Inq, Leg. 1931
AHN, Inq, Leg. 194
AHN, Inq, Leg. 195
AHN, Inq, Leg. 1952
AHN, Inq, Leg. 1953
AHN, Inq, Leg. 196
AHN, Inq, Leg. 197
AHN, Inq, Leg. 198
AHN, Inq, Leg. 1987
AHN, Inq, Leg. 1988
AHN, Inq, Leg. 199
AHN, Inq, Leg. 200
AHN, Inq, Leg. 201
AHN, Inq, Leg. 202
AHN, Inq, Leg. 2022
AHN, Inq, Leg. 203
AHN, Inq, Leg. 204
AHN, Inq, Leg. 2042
AHN, Inq, Leg. 205
AHN, Inq, Leg. 206
AHN, Inq, Leg. 2063
AHN, Inq, Leg. 207
AHN, Inq, Leg. 2071
AHN, Inq, Leg. 2072
AHN, Inq, Leg. 2074
AHN, Inq, Leg. 2075
AHN, Inq, Leg. 208
AHN, Inq, Leg. 209
AHN, Inq, Leg. 210

AHN, Inq, Leg. 2103
AHN, Inq, Leg. 2105
AHN, Inq, Leg. 2106
AHN, Inq, Leg. 211
AHN, Inq, Leg. 212
AHN, Inq, Leg. 213
AHN, Inq, Leg. 2135
AHN, Inq, Leg. 214
AHN, Inq, Leg. 215
AHN, Inq, Leg. 216
AHN, Inq, Leg. 2164
AHN, Inq, Leg. 217
AHN, Inq, Leg. 218
AHN, Inq, Leg. 219
AHN, Inq, Leg. 220
AHN, Inq, Leg. 221
AHN, Inq, Leg. 222
AHN, Inq, Leg. 2223
AHN, Inq, Leg. 2224
AHN, Inq, Leg. 2225
AHN, Inq, Leg. 2226
AHN, Inq, Leg. 223
AHN, Inq, Leg. 2232
AHN, Inq, Leg. 224
AHN, Inq, Leg. 2243
AHN, Inq, Leg. 2244
AHN, Inq, Leg. 225
AHN, Inq, Leg. 2255
AHN, Inq, Leg. 226
AHN, Inq, Leg. 227
AHN, Inq, Leg. 228
AHN, Inq, Leg. 229
AHN, Inq, Leg. 2297
AHN, Inq, Leg. 23
AHN, Inq, Leg. 230
AHN, Inq, Leg. 231
AHN, Inq, Leg. 232
AHN, Inq, Leg. 233
AHN, Inq, Leg. 234
AHN, Inq, Leg. 2364
AHN, Inq, Leg. 2368
AHN, Inq, Leg. 2372
AHN, Inq, Leg. 2374

AHN, Inq, Leg. 2375
AHN, Inq, Leg. 2377
AHN, Inq, Leg. 2378
AHN, Inq, Leg. 2379
AHN, Inq, Leg. 2392
AHN, Inq, Leg. 2395
AHN, Inq, Leg. 2397
AHN, Inq, Leg. 24
AHN, Inq, Leg. 2404
AHN, Inq, Leg. 2405
AHN, Inq, Leg. 2406
AHN, Inq, Leg. 2407
AHN, Inq, Leg. 2409
AHN, Inq, Leg. 241
AHN, Inq, Leg. 2415
AHN, Inq, Leg. 2416
AHN, Inq, Leg. 2418
AHN, Inq, Leg. 2419
AHN, Inq, Leg. 2421
AHN, Inq, Leg. 2422
AHN, Inq, Leg. 2423
AHN, Inq, Leg. 2424
AHN, Inq, Leg. 2425
AHN, Inq, Leg. 2426
AHN, Inq, Leg. 2427
AHN, Inq, Leg. 2428
AHN, Inq, Leg. 2429
AHN, Inq, Leg. 2430
AHN, Inq, Leg. 2431
AHN, Inq, Leg. 2432
AHN, Inq, Leg. 2432
AHN, Inq, Leg. 2433
AHN, Inq, Leg. 2434
AHN, Inq, Leg. 2435
AHN, Inq, Leg. 2436
AHN, Inq, Leg. 2437
AHN, Inq, Leg. 244
AHN, Inq, Leg. 2440
AHN, Inq, Leg. 2441
AHN, Inq, Leg. 2442
AHN, Inq, Leg. 2444
AHN, Inq, Leg. 2445
AHN, Inq, Leg. 2449

AHN, Inq, Leg. 2452
AHN, Inq, Leg. 2453
AHN, Inq, Leg. 2454
AHN, Inq, Leg. 2455
AHN, Inq, Leg. 2456
AHN, Inq, Leg. 2457
AHN, Inq, Leg. 2458
AHN, Inq, Leg. 2459
AHN, Inq, Leg. 2460
AHN, Inq, Leg. 2461
AHN, Inq, Leg. 2462
AHN, Inq, Leg. 2479
AHN, Inq, Leg. 2485
AHN, Inq, Leg. 2486
AHN, Inq, Leg. 2498
AHN, Inq, Leg. 25
AHN, Inq, Leg. 250
AHN, Inq, Leg. 2500
AHN, Inq, Leg. 2501
AHN, Inq, Leg. 2503
AHN, Inq, Leg. 2506
AHN, Inq, Leg. 2511
AHN, Inq, Leg. 2514
AHN, Inq, Leg. 2515
AHN, Inq, Leg. 2519
AHN, Inq, Leg. 2524
AHN, Inq, Leg. 2544
AHN, Inq, Leg. 2545
AHN, Inq, Leg. 255
AHN, Inq, Leg. 2550
AHN, Inq, Leg. 2551
AHN, Inq, Leg. 2555
AHN, Inq, Leg. 256
AHN, Inq, Leg. 2560
AHN, Inq, Leg. 2561
AHN, Inq, Leg. 2562
AHN, Inq, Leg. 2563
AHN, Inq, Leg. 2564
AHN, Inq, Leg. 2564
AHN, Inq, Leg. 2565
AHN, Inq, Leg. 2566
AHN, Inq, Leg. 2567
AHN, Inq, Leg. 2568

AHN, Inq, Leg. 2569
AHN, Inq, Leg. 2570
AHN, Inq, Leg. 2571
AHN, Inq, Leg. 2572
AHN, Inq, Leg. 2573
AHN, Inq, Leg. 2574
AHN, Inq, Leg. 2575
AHN, Inq, Leg. 2576
AHN, Inq, Leg. 2577
AHN, Inq, Leg. 2578
AHN, Inq, Leg. 2579
AHN, Inq, Leg. 2580
AHN, Inq, Leg. 2581
AHN, Inq, Leg. 2583
AHN, Inq, Leg. 2584
AHN, Inq, Leg. 2585
AHN, Inq, Leg. 2586
AHN, Inq, Leg. 2587
AHN, Inq, Leg. 2588
AHN, Inq, Leg. 26
AHN, Inq, Leg. 2601
AHN, Inq, Leg. 2602
AHN, Inq, Leg. 2603
AHN, Inq, Leg. 2606
AHN, Inq, Leg. 2615
AHN, Inq, Leg. 2616
AHN, Inq, Leg. 2617
AHN, Inq, Leg. 2619
AHN, Inq, Leg. 262
AHN, Inq, Leg. 2620
AHN, Inq, Leg. 2622
AHN, Inq, Leg. 2624
AHN, Inq, Leg. 2632
AHN, Inq, Leg. 2633
AHN, Inq, Leg. 2634
AHN, Inq, Leg. 2634
AHN, Inq, Leg. 2635
AHN, Inq, Leg. 2635
AHN, Inq, Leg. 2636
AHN, Inq, Leg. 2636
AHN, Inq, Leg. 2637
AHN, Inq, Leg. 2637
AHN, Inq, Leg. 2638

AHN, Inq, Leg. 2638
AHN, Inq, Leg. 2639
AHN, Inq, Leg. 2639
AHN, Inq, Leg. 2640
AHN, Inq, Leg. 2640
AHN, Inq, Leg. 2641
AHN, Inq, Leg. 2641
AHN, Inq, Leg. 2642
AHN, Inq, Leg. 2643
AHN, Inq, Leg. 2644
AHN, Inq, Leg. 2645
AHN, Inq, Leg. 2646
AHN, Inq, Leg. 2647
AHN, Inq, Leg. 2648
AHN, Inq, Leg. 2649
AHN, Inq, Leg. 265
AHN, Inq, Leg. 2650
AHN, Inq, Leg. 2651
AHN, Inq, Leg. 2652
AHN, Inq, Leg. 2653
AHN, Inq, Leg. 2654
AHN, Inq, Leg. 2655
AHN, Inq, Leg. 2656
AHN, Inq, Leg. 2657
AHN, Inq, Leg. 2658
AHN, Inq, Leg. 2659
AHN, Inq, Leg. 2660
AHN, Inq, Leg. 2661
AHN, Inq, Leg. 2662
AHN, Inq, Leg. 2663
AHN, Inq, Leg. 2664
AHN, Inq, Leg. 2665
AHN, Inq, Leg. 2666
AHN, Inq, Leg. 2667
AHN, Inq, Leg. 2668
AHN, Inq, Leg. 2669
AHN, Inq, Leg. 2670
AHN, Inq, Leg. 2671
AHN, Inq, Leg. 2672
AHN, Inq, Leg. 2673
AHN, Inq, Leg. 2674
AHN, Inq, Leg. 2675
AHN, Inq, Leg. 2676

AHN, Inq, Leg. 2677
AHN, Inq, Leg. 2680
AHN, Inq, Leg. 2682
AHN, Inq, Leg. 2686
AHN, Inq, Leg. 2691
AHN, Inq, Leg. 2692
AHN, Inq, Leg. 27
AHN, Inq, Leg. 2700
AHN, Inq, Leg. 2714
AHN, Inq, Leg. 2715
AHN, Inq, Leg. 2716
AHN, Inq, Leg. 2720
AHN, Inq, Leg. 2721
AHN, Inq, Leg. 2722
AHN, Inq, Leg. 2723
AHN, Inq, Leg. 2724
AHN, Inq, Leg. 2725
AHN, Inq, Leg. 273
AHN, Inq, Leg. 2730
AHN, Inq, Leg. 2731
AHN, Inq, Leg. 2732
AHN, Inq, Leg. 2733
AHN, Inq, Leg. 2734
AHN, Inq, Leg. 2738
AHN, Inq, Leg. 2739
AHN, Inq, Leg. 2740
AHN, Inq, Leg. 2741
AHN, Inq, Leg. 2742
AHN, Inq, Leg. 2743
AHN, Inq, Leg. 2744
AHN, Inq, Leg. 2746
AHN, Inq, Leg. 2747
AHN, Inq, Leg. 2748
AHN, Inq, Leg. 2749
AHN, Inq, Leg. 2750
AHN, Inq, Leg. 2751
AHN, Inq, Leg. 2752
AHN, Inq, Leg. 2753
AHN, Inq, Leg. 2755
AHN, Inq, Leg. 2757
AHN, Inq, Leg. 2758
AHN, Inq, Leg. 2759
AHN, Inq, Leg. 2760

AHN, Inq, Leg. 2761
AHN, Inq, Leg. 2762
AHN, Inq, Leg. 2763
AHN, Inq, Leg. 2764
AHN, Inq, Leg. 2765
AHN, Inq, Leg. 2766
AHN, Inq, Leg. 2768
AHN, Inq, Leg. 2769
AHN, Inq, Leg. 2770
AHN, Inq, Leg. 2771
AHN, Inq, Leg. 2772
AHN, Inq, Leg. 2773
AHN, Inq, Leg. 2774
AHN, Inq, Leg. 2775
AHN, Inq, Leg. 2776
AHN, Inq, Leg. 2777
AHN, Inq, Leg. 2778
AHN, Inq, Leg. 2779
AHN, Inq, Leg. 2780
AHN, Inq, Leg. 2781
AHN, Inq, Leg. 2782
AHN, Inq, Leg. 2783
AHN, Inq, Leg. 2784
AHN, Inq, Leg. 2785
AHN, Inq, Leg. 2786
AHN, Inq, Leg. 2787
AHN, Inq, Leg. 2788
AHN, Inq, Leg. 2789
AHN, Inq, Leg. 2790
AHN, Inq, Leg. 2791
AHN, Inq, Leg. 2792
AHN, Inq, Leg. 2792
AHN, Inq, Leg. 28
AHN, Inq, Leg. 28
AHN, Inq, Leg. 2888
AHN, Inq, Leg. 2889
AHN, Inq, Leg. 2892
AHN, Inq, Leg. 2895
AHN, Inq, Leg. 2896
AHN, Inq, Leg. 2897
AHN, Inq, Leg. 2899
AHN, Inq, Leg. 2900
AHN, Inq, Leg. 2902

AHN, Inq, Leg. 2903
AHN, Inq, Leg. 2904
AHN, Inq, Leg. 2905
AHN, Inq, Leg. 2906
AHN, Inq, Leg. 2907
AHN, Inq, Leg. 2908
AHN, Inq, Leg. 2909
AHN, Inq, Leg. 2910
AHN, Inq, Leg. 2911
AHN, Inq, Leg. 2912
AHN, Inq, Leg. 2913
AHN, Inq, Leg. 2914
AHN, Inq, Leg. 2915
AHN, Inq, Leg. 2916
AHN, Inq, Leg. 2916
AHN, Inq, Leg. 2917
AHN, Inq, Leg. 2918
AHN, Inq, Leg. 2919
AHN, Inq, Leg. 2920
AHN, Inq, Leg. 2921
AHN, Inq, Leg. 2922
AHN, Inq, Leg. 2923
AHN, Inq, Leg. 2925
AHN, Inq, Leg. 2926
AHN, Inq, Leg. 2927
AHN, Inq, Leg. 2928
AHN, Inq, Leg. 2929
AHN, Inq, Leg. 2931
AHN, Inq, Leg. 2943
AHN, Inq, Leg. 2946
AHN, Inq, Leg. 2955
AHN, Inq, Leg. 2959
AHN, Inq, Leg. 2961
AHN, Inq, Leg. 2962
AHN, Inq, Leg. 2963
AHN, Inq, Leg. 2964
AHN, Inq, Leg. 2966
AHN, Inq, Leg. 2967
AHN, Inq, Leg. 2968
AHN, Inq, Leg. 2969
AHN, Inq, Leg. 2970
AHN, Inq, Leg. 2979
AHN, Inq, Leg. 2980

AHN, Inq, Leg. 2982
AHN, Inq, Leg. 2983
AHN, Inq, Leg. 2984
AHN, Inq, Leg. 2985
AHN, Inq, Leg. 2986
AHN, Inq, Leg. 2987
AHN, Inq, Leg. 2988
AHN, Inq, Leg. 2989
AHN, Inq, Leg. 2990
AHN, Inq, Leg. 2991
AHN, Inq, Leg. 2992
AHN, Inq, Leg. 2993
AHN, Inq, Leg. 2995
AHN, Inq, Leg. 2998
AHN, Inq, Leg. 2999
AHN, Inq, Leg. 3
AHN, Inq, Leg. 30
AHN, Inq, Leg. 3000
AHN, Inq, Leg. 3001
AHN, Inq, Leg. 3002
AHN, Inq, Leg. 3003
AHN, Inq, Leg. 3004
AHN, Inq, Leg. 3005
AHN, Inq, Leg. 3006
AHN, Inq, Leg. 3008
AHN, Inq, Leg. 3010
AHN, Inq, Leg. 3011
AHN, Inq, Leg. 3012
AHN, Inq, Leg. 3013
AHN, Inq, Leg. 3014
AHN, Inq, Leg. 3015
AHN, Inq, Leg. 3016
AHN, Inq, Leg. 3017
AHN, Inq, Leg. 3018
AHN, Inq, Leg. 3019
AHN, Inq, Leg. 3020
AHN, Inq, Leg. 3022
AHN, Inq, Leg. 3023
AHN, Inq, Leg. 3024
AHN, Inq, Leg. 3025
AHN, Inq, Leg. 3026
AHN, Inq, Leg. 3027
AHN, Inq, Leg. 3029

AHN, Inq, Leg. 3030
AHN, Inq, Leg. 3031
AHN, Inq, Leg. 3032
AHN, Inq, Leg. 3033
AHN, Inq, Leg. 3034
AHN, Inq, Leg. 3036
AHN, Inq, Leg. 3041
AHN, Inq, Leg. 3048
AHN, Inq, Leg. 3058
AHN, Inq, Leg. 3059
AHN, Inq, Leg. 3060
AHN, Inq, Leg. 3067
AHN, Inq, Leg. 3068
AHN, Inq, Leg. 3069
AHN, Inq, Leg. 3085
AHN, Inq, Leg. 3086
AHN, Inq, Leg. 3092
AHN, Inq, Leg. 31
AHN, Inq, Leg. 3105
AHN, Inq, Leg. 3109
AHN, Inq, Leg. 3110
AHN, Inq, Leg. 3116
AHN, Inq, Leg. 3117
AHN, Inq, Leg. 3118
AHN, Inq, Leg. 3119
AHN, Inq, Leg. 3120
AHN, Inq, Leg. 3121
AHN, Inq, Leg. 3122
AHN, Inq, Leg. 3123
AHN, Inq, Leg. 3124
AHN, Inq, Leg. 3125
AHN, Inq, Leg. 3127
AHN, Inq, Leg. 3128
AHN, Inq, Leg. 3129
AHN, Inq, Leg. 3130
AHN, Inq, Leg. 3131
AHN, Inq, Leg. 3132
AHN, Inq, Leg. 3133
AHN, Inq, Leg. 3134
AHN, Inq, Leg. 3135
AHN, Inq, Leg. 3137
AHN, Inq, Leg. 3138
AHN, Inq, Leg. 3139

AHN, Inq, Leg. 3144
AHN, Inq, Leg. 3145
AHN, Inq, Leg. 3146
AHN, Inq, Leg. 3148
AHN, Inq, Leg. 3149
AHN, Inq, Leg. 3150
AHN, Inq, Leg. 3152
AHN, Inq, Leg. 3153
AHN, Inq, Leg. 3154
AHN, Inq, Leg. 3155
AHN, Inq, Leg. 3156
AHN, Inq, Leg. 3157
AHN, Inq, Leg. 316
AHN, Inq, Leg. 3161
AHN, Inq, Leg. 3162
AHN, Inq, Leg. 3163
AHN, Inq, Leg. 3163
AHN, Inq, Leg. 3164
AHN, Inq, Leg. 3170
AHN, Inq, Leg. 3172
AHN, Inq, Leg. 3175
AHN, Inq, Leg. 3184
AHN, Inq, Leg. 3189
AHN, Inq, Leg. 3190
AHN, Inq, Leg. 3191
AHN, Inq, Leg. 3193
AHN, Inq, Leg. 3194
AHN, Inq, Leg. 3197
AHN, Inq, Leg. 32
AHN, Inq, Leg. 3208
AHN, Inq, Leg. 3209
AHN, Inq, Leg. 3211
AHN, Inq, Leg. 3212
AHN, Inq, Leg. 3214
AHN, Inq, Leg. 3215
AHN, Inq, Leg. 3216
AHN, Inq, Leg. 3217
AHN, Inq, Leg. 3218
AHN, Inq, Leg. 3219
AHN, Inq, Leg. 3221
AHN, Inq, Leg. 3222
AHN, Inq, Leg. 3223
AHN, Inq, Leg. 3224

AHN, Inq, Leg. 3225
AHN, Inq, Leg. 3226
AHN, Inq, Leg. 3227
AHN, Inq, Leg. 3228
AHN, Inq, Leg. 3229
AHN, Inq, Leg. 3230
AHN, Inq, Leg. 3232
AHN, Inq, Leg. 3233
AHN, Inq, Leg. 3234
AHN, Inq, Leg. 3235
AHN, Inq, Leg. 3237
AHN, Inq, Leg. 3238
AHN, Inq, Leg. 3239
AHN, Inq, Leg. 3240
AHN, Inq, Leg. 3242
AHN, Inq, Leg. 3243
AHN, Inq, Leg. 3244
AHN, Inq, Leg. 3246
AHN, Inq, Leg. 3247
AHN, Inq, Leg. 3248
AHN, Inq, Leg. 3249
AHN, Inq, Leg. 3250
AHN, Inq, Leg. 3251
AHN, Inq, Leg. 3253
AHN, Inq, Leg. 3254
AHN, Inq, Leg. 3255
AHN, Inq, Leg. 3256
AHN, Inq, Leg. 3257
AHN, Inq, Leg. 3258
AHN, Inq, Leg. 3259
AHN, Inq, Leg. 3260
AHN, Inq, Leg. 3261
AHN, Inq, Leg. 3262
AHN, Inq, Leg. 3263
AHN, Inq, Leg. 3264
AHN, Inq, Leg. 3265
AHN, Inq, Leg. 3272
AHN, Inq, Leg. 33
AHN, Inq, Leg. 34
AHN, Inq, Leg. 35
AHN, Inq, Leg. 36
AHN, Inq, Leg. 3681
AHN, Inq, Leg. 37

AHN, Inq, Leg. 3716
AHN, Inq, Leg. 3734
AHN, Inq, Leg. 38
AHN, Inq, Leg. 38
AHN, Inq, Leg. 40
AHN, Inq, Leg. 41
AHN, Inq, Leg. 4104
AHN, Inq, Leg. 42
AHN, Inq, Leg. 43
AHN, Inq, Leg. 4320
AHN, Inq, Leg. 44
AHN, Inq, Leg. 4442
AHN, Inq, Leg. 45
AHN, Inq, Leg. 46
AHN, Inq, Leg. 47
AHN, Inq, Leg. 4760
AHN, Inq, Leg. 48
AHN, Inq, Leg. 486
AHN, Inq, Leg. 49
AHN, Inq, Leg. 495
AHN, Inq, Leg. 496
AHN, Inq, Leg. 497
AHN, Inq, Leg. 4972
AHN, Inq, Leg. 499
AHN, Inq, Leg. 518
AHN, Inq, Leg. 519
AHN, Inq, Leg. 520
AHN, Inq, Leg. 521
AHN, Inq, Leg. 522
AHN, Inq, Leg. 523
AHN, Inq, Leg. 524
AHN, Inq, Leg. 525
AHN, Inq, Leg. 526
AHN, Inq, Leg. 527
AHN, Inq, Leg. 528
AHN, Inq, Leg. 529
AHN, Inq, Leg. 530
AHN, Inq, Leg. 531
AHN, Inq, Leg. 5323
AHN, Inq, Leg. 5324
AHN, Inq, Leg. 5327
AHN, Inq, Leg. 533
AHN, Inq, Leg. 534

AHN, Inq, Leg. 535
AHN, Inq, Leg. 536
AHN, Inq, Leg. 537
AHN, Inq, Leg. 538
AHN, Inq, Leg. 539
AHN, Inq, Leg. 540
AHN, Inq, Leg. 541
AHN, Inq, Leg. 542
AHN, Inq, Leg. 543
AHN, Inq, Leg. 544
AHN, Inq, Leg. 551
AHN, Inq, Leg. 69
AHN, Inq, Leg. 70
AHN, Inq, Leg. 71
AHN, Inq, Leg. 72
AHN, Inq, Leg. 73
AHN, Inq, Leg. 74
AHN, Inq, Leg. 75
AHN, Inq, Leg. 76
AHN, Inq, Leg. 77
AHN, Inq, Leg. 78
AHN, Inq, Leg. 79
AHN, Inq, Leg. 80
AHN, Inq, Leg. 81
AHN, Inq, Leg. 82
AHN, Inq, Leg. 83
AHN, Inq, Leg. 84
AHN, Inq, Leg. 85
AHN, Inq, Leg. 86
AHN, Inq, Leg. 87
AHN, Inq, Leg. 88
AHN, Inq, Leg. 89
AHN, Inq, Leg. 90
AHN, Inq, Leg. 91
AHN, Inq, Leg. 92
AHN, Inq, Leg. 93
AHN, Inq, Leg. 94
AHN, Inq, Leg. 95
AHN, Inq, Leg. 97
AHN, Inq, Leg. 97
AHN, Inq, Leg. 98
AHN, Inq, Leg. 99
AHN, Inq, Lib. 1020

AHN, Inq, Lib. 1021
AHN, Inq, Lib. 1022
AHN, Inq, Lib. 1023
AHN, Inq, Lib. 1027
AHN, Inq, Lib. 1028
AHN, Inq, Lib. 1029
AHN, Inq, Lib. 1030
AHN, Inq, Lib. 1031
AHN, Inq, Lib. 1032
AHN, Inq, Lib. 1064
AHN, Inq, Lib. 1065
AHN, Inq, Lib. 1066
AHN, Inq, Lib. 1067
AHN, Inq, Lib. 1082
AHN, Inq, Lib. 1170
AHN, Inq, Lib. 1171
AHN, Inq, Lib. 1172
AHN, Inq, Lib. 1173
AHN, Inq, Lib. 1174
AHN, Inq, Lib. 1174
AHN, Inq, Lib. 1175
AHN, Inq, Lib. 1176
AHN, Inq, Lib. 1177
AHN, Inq, Lib. 1178
AHN, Inq, Lib. 1178
AHN, Inq, Lib. 1179
AHN, Inq, Lib. 1180
AHN, Inq, Lib. 1181
AHN, Inq, Lib. 1182
AHN, Inq, Lib. 1241
AHN, Inq, Lib. 1263
AHN, Inq, Lib. 1327
AHN, Inq, Lib. 1330
AHN, Inq, Lib. 1449
AHN, Inq, Lib. 236
AHN, Inq, Lib. 238
AHN, Inq, Lib. 239
AHN, Inq, Lib. 240
AHN, Inq, Lib. 573
AHN, Inq, Lib. 574
AHN, Inq, Lib. 575
AHN, Inq, Lib. 577
AHN, Inq, Lib. 586

AHN, Inq, Lib. 730
AHN, Inq, Lib. 731
AHN, Inq, Lib. 732
AHN, Inq, Lib. 733
AHN, Inq, Lib. 734
AHN, Inq, Lib. 735
AHN, Inq, Lib. 736
AHN, Inq, Lib. 740
AHN, Inq, Lib. 741
AHN, Inq, Lib. 768
AHN, Inq, Lib. 769
AHN, Inq, Lib. 782
AHN, Inq, Lib. 783
AHN, Inq, Lib. 785
AHN, Inq, Lib. 787
AHN, Inq, Lib. 788
AHN, Inq, Lib. 789
AHN, Inq, Lib. 790
AHN, Inq, Lib. 791
AHN, Inq, Lib. 791
AHN, Inq, Lib. 792
AHN, Inq, Lib. 792
AHN, Inq, Lib. 794
AHN, Inq, Lib. 796
AHN, Inq, Lib. 802
AHN, Inq, Lib. 805
AHN, Inq, Lib. 809
AHN, Inq, Lib. 810
AHN, Inq, Lib. 811
AHN, Inq, Lib. 812
AHN, Inq, Lib. 815
AHN, Inq, Lib. 816
AHN, Inq, Lib. 817
AHN, Inq, Lib. 819
AHN, Inq, Lib. 820
AHN, Inq, Lib. 821
AHN, Inq, Lib. 831
AHN, Inq, Lib. 833
AHN, Inq, Lib. 834
AHN, Inq, Lib. 835
AHN, Inq, Lib. 836
AHN, Inq, Lib. 837
AHN, Inq, Lib. 838

AHN, Inq, Lib. 839
AHN, Inq, Lib. 860
AHN, Inq, Lib. 861
AHN, Inq, Lib. 862
AHN, Inq, Lib. 863
AHN, Inq, Lib. 864
AHN, Inq, Lib. 865
AHN, Inq, Lib. 866
AHN, Inq, Lib. 873
AHN, Inq, Lib. 874
AHN, Inq, Lib. 875
AHN, Inq, Lib. 876
AHN, Inq, Lib. 880
AHN, Inq, Lib. 882
AHN, Inq, Lib. 890
AHN, Inq, Lib. 891
AHN, Inq, Lib. 893
AHN, Inq, Lib. 894
AHN, Inq, Lib. 895
AHN, Inq, Lib. 896
AHN, Inq, Lib. 898
AHN, Inq, Lib. 899
AHN, Inq, Lib. 900
AHN, Inq, Lib. 901
AHN, Inq, Lib. 902
AHN, Inq, Lib. 911
AHN, Inq, Lib. 912
AHN, Inq, Lib. 917
AHN, Inq, Lib. 918
AHN, Inq, Lib. 936
AHN, Inq, Lib. 937
AHN, Inq, Lib. 938
AHN, Inq, Lib. 939
AHN, Inq, Lib. 940
AHN, Inq, Lib. 941
AHN, Inq, Lib. 942
AHN, Inq, Lib. 943
AHN, Inq, Lib. 944
AHN, Inq, Lib. 974
AHN, Inq, Lib. 988
AHN, Inq, Lib. 989
AHN, Inq, Lib. 990
AHN, Inq, Lib. 991

AHN, Inq, Lib. 992
AHN, Inq, Lib. 993
AHN, Inq, Lib. 994
AHN, Inq, Lib. 995
AHN, Inq, Lib. 996
AHN, Inq, Lib. 997
AHN, Inq, Lib. 998
BL, Add MS 21477
BL, Egerton MS 1508
BL, Egerton MS 1887
BL, Egerton MS 2058
BNM, Mss 6751
BPRM Mss 1846

BIBLIOGRAPHY

Aguilera Barchet, Bruno. "El procedimiento de la Inquisición española." In Las estructuras del Santo Oficio, Historia de la Inquisición en España y América, edited by Bartolomé Escandell Bonet and Joaquín Pérez Villanueva, vol. II, 334–58. Madrid: BAC, 1993.

Alberro, Solange. Inquisición y sociedad en México, 1571–1700. México: Fondo de Cultura Económica, 1988a.

______. *Inquisition et societe au Mexique: 1571–1700*. Mexico City: Centre d'Etudes Mexicaines et Centramericaines, 1988b.

Alcoberro, Agustí. "Cacera de bruixes, justícia local i Inquisició a Catalunya, 1487–1643: alguns criteris metodològics." *Pedralbes* 2, no. 28 (2008): 485–504.

Alejandre, Juan Antonio. *El veneno de Dios. la Inquisición de Sevilla ante el delito de solicitación en confesión*. Madrid: Siglo Veintiuno, 1994.

Alessi Palazzolo, Giorgia. *Prova legale e pena la crisi del sistema tra evo medio e moderno*. Storia e diritto. Napoli: Jovene, 1979.

Alonso Romero, María Paz. *El proceso penal en Castilla (Siglos XIII-XVIII)*. Salamanca: Ediciones Universidad de Salamanca, 1982.

Amiel, Charles, and Anne Lima, eds. *L'inquisition de Goa: la relation de Charles Dellon (1687), Collection Magellane*. Paris: Editions Chandeigne, 1997.

Anaya Hernández, Luis Alberto, and Francisco T. Fajardo Spínola. "Los estudios sobre la Inquisición de las Islas Canarias. Estado de la cuestión y perspectivas." In *Actas de la II reunión científica de la Asociación española de historia moderna Moratalla 1992*, 149–61, Murcia: Universidad de Murcia, 1993.

Arnold, John. *Inquisition and Power: Catharism and the Confessing Subject in Medieval Languedoc*. The Middle Ages Series. Philadelphia: University of Pennsylvania Press, 2001.

Balancy, Elisabeth. "Les immigrés français devant le tribunal de l'Inquisition de Barcelone (1592–1692)." In *Les français en Espagne à l'époque moderne*, 45–69. Paris: CNRS, 1990.

Barrio Gozalo, Maximiliano. "Burocracia inquisitorial y movilidad social. El Santo Oficio plantel de obispos (1556–1820)." In *Inquisición y sociedad*, edited by Ángel de Prado Moura, 107–38. Valladolid: Universidad de Valladolid, 1999.

______. "Trasvase de religiones y culturas en el mundo Mediterráneo del siglo XVIII: Renegados y conversos." *Cuadernos Dieciochistas*, no. 5 (2004): 13–49.

______. *Esclavos y cautivos conflictos entre la cristiandad y el Islam en el siglo XIII.* Valladolid: Junta de Castilla y León, 2006.
Beinart, Haim. *Conversos on Trial. The Inquisition in Ciudad Real.* Jerusalem: The Magnus Press, 1981.
Bellomo, Manlio. *The Common Legal Past of Europe: 1000–1800.* Translated by Lydia G. Cochrane. Washington, DC: The Catholic University of America Press, 1995.
Bennassar, Bartolomé. "Aux origines du caciquisme: Les familiers de l'Inquisition en Andalousie au XVIIe siècle?" *Cahiers du monde hispanique et luso-brésilien*, no. 27 (1976): 63–71.
______. "Le pouvoir inquisitorial." In *L'inquisition espagnole XVe – XIXe siècle*, edited by Bartolomé Bennassar, 75–104. Paris: Hachette, 1979.
______, and Lucile Bennassar. *Les chrétiens d'Allah: L'histoire extraordinaire des renégats, XVIe et XVIIe siècles.* Paris: Perrin, 1989.
Berco, Cristian. *Sexual Hierarchies, Public Status: Men, Sodomy, and Society in Spain's Golden Age.* Toronto: University of Toronto Press, 2007.
Bethencourt, Francisco. "The Auto da Fe: Ritual and Imagery." *Journal of the Warburg and Courtauld Institutes* 55 (1992): 155–68.
______. *The Inquisition: A Global History, 1478–1834.* Translated by Jean Birrell. Cambridge: Cambridge University Press, 2009.
Betrán Moya, José Luis. "Los niños moriscos antes y después de la expulsión." In *Historia y perspectivas de investigación: Estudios en memoria del profesor Angel Rodríguez Sánchez*, 295–300. Mérida (Badajoz): Editora Regional de Extremadura, 2002.
Black, Christopher F. *The Italian Inquisition.* New Haven, CT: Yale University Press, 2009.
Blot-Maccagnan, Stéphanie. *Procédure criminelle et défense de l'accusé à la fin de l'ancien Régime: Étude de la pratique angevine.* Rennes: Presses Universitaires de Rennes, 2010.
Braga, I.M.R.M.D. *Entre a Cristandade E O Islão, Séculos XV-XVII: Cativos e renegados nas franjas de duas sociedades em confronto.* Ceuta: Instituto de Estudios Ceutíes, 1998.
Cabezas Fontanilla, Susana. "Nuevas aportaciones al estudio del archivo del Consejo de la Suprema Inquisición." *Documenta & Instrumenta* 5 (2007): 31–49.
Cameron, Euan. *Waldenses: Rejections of Holy Church in Medieval Europe.* New York: Wiley, 2001.
Cardaillac, Louis. *Morisques et chrétiens. Un affrontement polémique, 1492–1640.* Paris: Klincksieck, 1977.
Caro Baroja, Julio. *El señor inquisidor, y otras vidas por oficio.* Madrid: Alianza Editorial, 1968.
Carrasco, Rafael. *Inquisición y represión sexual en Valencia. Historia de los sodomitas, 1565–1785.* Barcelona: Laertes, 1985.
Castrillo Benito, Nicolas. *El 'Reginaldo Montano': Primer libro polemico contra la Inquisición española.* Madrid: CSIC, 1991.
Cerrillo Cruz, Gonzalo. "El capitán de familiares." *Revista de la Inquisición: (intolerancia y derechos humanos)*, no. 2 (1992): 135–46.
______. "Los Familiares de la Inquisición en la epoca borbonica." *Revista de la Inquisición* 4 (1995): 177–204.
______. "Aproximación al estatuto jurídico de los familiares de la Inquisición española." *Manuscrits: Revista d'història moderna*, no. 17 (1999): 141–58.
______. *Los familiares de la Inquisición Española.* Valladolid: Junta de Castilla y León, 2000.
Contreras, Jaime. *El Santo Oficio de la Inquisición en Galicia, 1560–1700. Poder, sociedad y cultura.* Madrid: Akal Editor, 1982.

______. *Sotos Contra Riquelmes: Regidores, Inquisidores y Criptojudíos*. Madrid: Anaya & Mario Muchnik, 1992.

______, and Jean Pierre Dedieu. "Geografia de la Inquisición Española: la formación de los distritos, 1470–1820." *Hispania* 40, no. 144 (1980): 37–93.

______. "Estructuras geograficas del Santo Oficio En España." In *Las estructuras del Santo Oficio*, *Historia de la Inquisición en España y America*, edited by Joaquin Pérez Villanueva and Bartolomé Escandell Bonet, vol. II, 3–47. Madrid: Biblioteca de autores Cristianos, 1993.

Croft, Pauline. "Englishmen and the Spanish Inquisition 1558–1625." *The English Historical Review* 87, no. 343 (1972): 248–63.

______. "English Mariners Trading to Spain and Portugal, 1558–1625." *Mariner's Mirror* 69, no. 3 (1983): 251–66.

Cruselles Gómez, José María. "La primera contabilidad inquisitorial. El fondo del Archivo del Reino de Valencia (1482–1527)." In *El primer siglo de la Inquisición española: Fuentes documentales, procedimientos de análisis, experiencias de investigación*, 221–50. València: Universitat de València, 2013.

Cuadro García, Ana Christina. "Acción inquisitorial contra los judaizantes en Córdoba y crisis eclesiástica (1482–1508)." *Revista de historia moderna: Anales de la Universidad de Alicante*, no. 23 (2003): 11–28.

Davis, Natalie Zemon. *The Return of Martin Guerre*. Cambridge, MA: Harvard University Press, 1983.

______. *Fiction in the Archives: Pardon Tales and Their Tellers in Sixteenth-Century France*. Stanford, CA: Stanford University Press, 1987.

Davis, Robert C. *Christian Slaves, Muslim Masters: White Slavery in the Mediterranean, the Barbary Coast, and Italy, 1500–1800*. Early Modern History. Houndmills, Basingstoke, Hampshire, and New York: Palgrave Macmillan, 2003.

de Argüello, Gaspar Isidrio. *Instrucciones del Santo Oficio de la Inquisición, Sumariamente, Antiguas y nuevas*. Madrid: Imprenta Real, 1630.

de Bunes Ibarra, Miguel Angel. "Reflexiones sobre la conversión al Islam de los renegados en los siglos XVI y XVII." *Hispania Sacra* 42, no. 85 (1990): 181–98.

Deciani, Tiberio. *Tractatus criminalis D. Tiberii Deciani . . . Duobusque tomis distinctus . . . Cum summarijs, & duplici indice: Altero quidem rerum, ac verborum omnium, locorumque insignium; Altero vero titulorum, Qui in utroque tomo continentur*. Turin: Apud haeredem Nicolai Beuilaquae, 1593.

Dedieu, Jean Pierre. "Les quatre temps de l'Inquisition." In *L'inquisition espagnole, XVe-XIXe siècle*, edited by Bartolome Bennassar, 15–41. Paris: Hachette, 1979.

______. "Les morisques de Daimiel et l'Inquisition (1502–1612)." In *Les morisques et leur temps*, edited by Louis Cardaillac, 496–522. Paris: CNRS, 1983.

______. "L'inquisition et le droit. Analyse formelle de la procedure inquisitoriale en cause de foi." *Melanges de la Casa de Velázquez* 23 (1987a): 227–51.

______. *L'inquisition*. Paris: Éditions du Cerf, 1987b.

______. *L'administration de la foi: L'Inquisition de Toléde (XVIe-XVIIIe siécle)*. Madrid: Casa de Velázquez, 1989.

______. "Denunciar-denunciarse. La delación inquisitorial en Castilla la Nueva, siglos XVI-XVII." *Revista de la Inquisición*, no. 2 (1992): 95–108.

______, and Gunnar W. Knutsen. "La cause de foi dans l'Inquisition espagnole." *Annales*, no. 1 (2023): 1–26.

de los Angeles, Pedro. *Compendio del orden iudicial y practica del tribunal de religiosos: En que se declara lo que pueden y deuen hazer assi prelados como subditos*. Madrid: Diego Diaz de la Carrera, 1643.

de Monterroso y Alvarado, Gabriel. *Pratica civil y criminal y instrución de escrivanos, dividida en nueve tratados*. Madrid: Pedro Madrigal, 1591.

de Torrecilla, Martin. *Suma de todas las materias morales arreglada a las condenaciones pontificas de Alexandro VII y Inocencio XI*, Vol. 2. Madrid: Imprenta Real, 1691.

Domínguez Salgado, María del Pilar. "Los familiares del tribunal de Corte (1665–1820). Primera parte: Origen, trayectoria histórica y estudio sociológico." *Anales del Instituto de Estudios Madrileños* 47 (2007): 667–87.

Dou y de Bassols, Ramón Lázaro. *Instituciones del derecho público general de España con noticia del particular de Cataluña y de las principales reglas de gobierno en qualquier [sic] estado. Instituciones del derecho público general de España con noticia del particular de Cataluña y de las principales reglas de gobierno en qualquier [sic] estado.* 9 vols. Madrid: en la Oficina de Benito García y Compañía, 1803.

Durand, Bernard. *Arbitraire du juge et consuetudo delinquendi la doctrine pénale en Europe du XVIe au XVIIIe siècle.* Montpellier: Société d'histoire du droit et des institutions des anciens pays de droit écrit, 1993.

Edwards, John. "Trial of an Inquisitor: The Dismissal of Diego Rodriguez Lucero, Inquisitor of Cordoba, in 1508." *Journal of Ecclesiastical History* 37, no. 2 (1986): 240–57.

______. *Inquisition.* Stroud: Tempus, 2003.

______. *The Inquisitors: The Story of the Grand Inquisitors of the Spanish Inquisition.* Stroud: Tempus, 2007.

Eymerich, Nicolás. *El manual de los inquisidores.* Barcelona: Muchnik Editores, 1996.

Febrero, Josef. *Libreria de escribanos, e instruccion juridica teorico practica de principiantes,* 6 vols. Madrid: en la imprenta de Antonio Perez de Soto, 1769–81.

Fernández Giménez, María del Camino. *La sentencia inquisitorial.* Texto impreso. Madrid: Editorial Complutense, 2000.

Fiume, Giovanna. *Schiavitù mediterranee. Corsari, rinnegati e santi di età moderna.* Sintesi. Milano: B. Mondadori, 2009.

______. *Schiavitú, Religione e libertà nel Mediterraneo tra medioevo ed età moderna.* Cosenza: L. Pellegrini, 2008.

Flynn, Maureen. "Mimesis of the Last Judgment: The Spanish Auto de Fe." *Sixteenth Century Journal* 22, no. 2 (1991): 281–97.

Fosi, Irene. *Convertire lo straniero. Forestieri e Inquisizione a Roma in età moderna. la Corte Dei Papi.* Roma: Viella, 2011.

Franklin, Julian H. *Jean Bodin and the Sixteenth-Century Revolution in the Methodology of Law and History.* New York: Colombia University Press, 1963.

Friedlander, Alan. *The Hammer of the Inquisitors: Brother Bernard Délicieux and the Struggle against the Inquisition in Fourteenth-Century France. Cultures, Beliefs and Traditions Medieval and Early Modern Peoples.* Leiden, Boston, MA and Köln: Brill, 2000.

Friedman, Ellen G. *Spanish Captives in North Africa in the Early Modern Age.* Madison: University of Wisconsin Press, 1983.

Galván Rodríguez, Eduardo. *El secreto en la Inquisición española.* Gran Canaria: Universidad de Las Palmas de Gran Canaria, 2001.

______. *El Inquisidor General.* Madrid: Dykinson, 2010.

García Cárcel, Ricardo. *Herejía y sociedad en el siglo XVI: la Inquisición en Valencia, 1530–1609.* Barcelona: Ediciones Peninsula, 1980a.

______. "Número y sociología de los familiares de la Inquisición valenciana." In *La Inquisición española. Nueva visión, nuevos horizontes,* edited by Joaquin Pérez Villanueva, 271–84. Madrid: Siglo XXI, 1980b.

______. *Orígines de la Inquisición española: El tribunal de Valencia 1478–1530.* 2nd ed. Barcelona: Ediciones Peninsula, 1985.

______. *La leyenda negra: Historia y opinion.* Madrid: Alianza, 1998.

García Hernán, Enrique. *Irlanda y el rey prudente.* Madrid: Ediciones del Laberinto, 2000.

______. *Irlanda y la monarquía hispánica: Kinsale, 1601–2001: Guerra, política, exilio y religión.* Madrid: Universidad de Alcalá: Consejo Superior de Investigaciones Científicas, 2002.

Garcia, Pablo. *Orden de processar en el Santo Oficio, Recopilado de las instrucciones antiquas y modernas*. Madrid: la imprenta Real, 1628.
García-Arenal, Mercedes. *Conversions islamiques: Identités religieuses en Islam Méditerranéen*. Paris: Maisonneuve et Larose, 2001.
Gellately, Robert. *The Gestapo and German Society: Enforcing Racial Policy 1933–1945*. Oxford: Clarendon Press, 1990.
______. "Denunciation as a Subject of Historical Research." *Historical Social Research* 26, no. 2/3 (2001a): 16–29. https://doi.org/10.12759/hsr.26.2001.2/3.16-29.
______. "Denunciations in Twentieth-Century Germany: Aspects of Self-Policing in the Third Reich and the German Democratic Republic." *Journal of Modern History* 68, no. 4 (2001b): 931–67.
Gibson, Charles. *The Black Legend: Anti-Spanish Attitudes in the Old World and the New*. New York: Knopf, 1971.
Gil Fernández, Juan. *Los Conversos y la Inquisición Sevillana*, 8 vols. Sevilla: Fundación El Monte, 2000.
Gironés Guillem, Ignasi. "Relación de los morisquillos y morisquillas presentados en los diferentes pueblos desde la ciudad de Valencia hasta Orihuela, según el bando de 1611." In *30 Años de mudejarismo: Memoria y futuro (1975–2005): Actas [Del] X simposio internacional de mudejarismo, Teruel, 14–15–16, Septiembre, 2005*, 289–96: Teruel: Centro de Estudios Mudéjares, 2007.
Given, James B. *Inquisition and Medieval Society: Power, Discipline, and Resistance in Languedoc*. New York: Cornell University Press, 2001.
Goñi Gaztambide, José. *Historia de la bula de la cruzada en España*. Victoriensia Publicaciones Del Seminario de Vitoria. Vitoria: Seminario de Vitoria, 1958.
González del Valle, José M. *Derecho eclesiástico español*. 4th ed. Oviedo: Universidad de Oviedo, 1997.
González Novalín José, Luis. *El inquisidor general Fernando de Valdes (1483–1568). 1. Su Vida y Su Obra*. Oviedo: Universidad de Oviedo, 1968.
______. *El inquisidor general Fernando de Valdes (1483–1568). 2. Cartas y Documentos*. Oviedo: Universidad de Oviedo, 1971.
______. "Las instrucciones de la Inquisición Española. De Torquemada a Valdés (1484–1561)." In *Perfiles Juridicos de la Inquisición Española*, edited by José Antonio Escudero, 91–109. Madrid: Instituto de Historia de la Inquisición, Universidad Complutense de Madrid, 1989.
Gonzalez-Raymond, Anita. *La croix et le croissant: Les inquisiteurs des îles face à l'Islam, 1550–1700*. Collection Sud. Paris: Editions du Centre national de la recherche scientifique, 1992.
Guibovich Pérez, Pedro M. "Custodios de la Ortodoxia: Los calificadores de la Inquisición de Lima, 1570–1754." *Revista de la Inquisición: (intolerancia y derechos humanos)*, no. 10 (2001): 213–29.
Haliczer, Stephen. *Inquisition and Society in the Kingdom of Valencia 1478–1834*. Berkeley: University of California Press, 1990.
______. *Sexuality in the Confessional. A Sacrament Profaned. Studies in the History of Sexuality*. New York: Oxford University Press, 1996.
Hamilton, Bernard. *The Medieval Inquisition*. London: Edward Arnold, 1981.
Henningsen, Gustav. "I Inkvisitionens Net." *Skalk*, no. 5 (1980a): 18–27.
______. *The Witches' Advocate: Basque Witchcraft and the Spanish Inquisition*. Reno: University of Nevada Press, 1980b.
______. "The Archives and Historiography of the Spanish Inquisition." In *The Inquisition in Early Modern Europe. Studies on Sources and Methods*, edited by Gustav Henningsen and John Tedeschi, 54–78. Dekalb: Northern Illinois University Press, 1986.
______. "La legislación secreta del Santo Oficio." In *Perfiles juridicos de la Inquisición española*, edited by José Antonio Escudero, 163–72. Madrid: Instituto de Historia de la Inquisición. Universidad Complutense de Madrid, 1989.

______. "The Database of the Spanish Inquisition." In *Vorträge Zur Justizforschung, Geschichte Und Theorie, Band 2*, edited by Heinz Mohnhaupt and Dieter Simon, 43–85. Frankfurt am Main: Vittorio Klostermann, 1993.

______, ed. *The Salazar Documents*. Leiden: Brill, 2004.

Hillgarth, J. N. *The Mirror of Spain, 1500–1700: The Formation of a Myth*. Ann Arbor: University of Michigan Press, 2000.

Hordes, Stanley M. "The Inquisition as Economic and Political Agent: The Campaign of the Mexican Holy Office against the Crypto-Jews in the Mid-Seventeenth Century." *Americas: A Quarterly Review of Inter-American Cultural History* 39, no. 1 (1982): 23–38.

Jiménez Monteserín, Miguel. *Introducción a la Inquisición Española: Documentos básicos para el estudio del Santo Oficio*. Biblioteca de visionarios, heterodoxos y marginados. egunda Serie. Madrid: Editorial Nacional, 1981.

Kagan, Richard. *Lawsuits and Litigants in Castille 1500–1700*. Chapel Hill: University of North Carolina Press, 1981.

Kamen, Henry. *The Spanish Inquisition: A Historical Revision*. New Haven, CT: Yale University Press, 1997.

Kelly, Henry Ansgar. "Inquisition and the Prosecution of Heresy: Misconceptions and Abuses." *Church History* 58, no. 4 (1989): 439–541.

______. "The Right to Remain Silent: Before and After Joan of Arc." *Speculum* 68 (1993): 992–1026.

______. "Lollard Inquisitions: Due and Undue Process." In *The Devil, Heresy and Witchcraft in the Middle Ages: Essays in Honor of Jeffrey B. Russell*, edited by Alberto Ferreiro, 279–303. Leiden: Brill, 1998.

Kieckhefer, Richard. "The Office of Inquisition and Medieval Heresy: The Transaction from Personal to Institutional Jurisdiction." *The Journal of Ecclesiastical History* 46, no. 1 (1995): 36–61. https://doi.org/10.1017/S0022046900012537

Knutsen, Gunnar W. "Where Did the Witches Go? Spanish Witches After Their Trials." In *Pathways of the Past: Festschrift to Sølvi Sogner on Her 70th Anniversary*, edited by Hilde Sandvik, Kari Telste, and Gunnar Thorvaldsen, 197–207. Oslo: Novus Forlag, 2002.

______. "Religious Life in Seventeenth Century Norway Seen through the Eyes of the Spanish Inquisition." *Arv: Scandinavian Yearbook of Folklore* 61 (2005): 7–23.

______. "El Santo Oficio de la Inquisición en Barcelona y soldados protestantes en el ejercito de Cataluña." *Estudis* 34 (2008).

______. *Servants of Satan and Masters of Demons: The Spanish Inquisition's Trials of Superstition, Valencia and Barcelona, 1478–1700*. Turnhout: Brepols, 2009.

______. "Topics of Persecution: Witchcraft Historiography in the Iberian World." In *Writing Witch-Hunt Histories: Challenging the Paradigm*, edited by Marko Nenonen and Raisa Maria Toivo, 167–90. Leiden: Brill, 2014.

______. "Después de la condena: Supuestas hechiceras y brujas en Valencia después de sus procesos inquisitoriales." In *Mulieres inquisitionis: la mujer frente a la Inquisición en España*, edited by María Jesús Zamora Calvo, 287–308. Vigo: Academia del Hispanismo, 2017.

______. "Witchcraft and Slavery in Cartagena de Indias." *Magic, Ritual, and Witchcraft* 15, no. 2 (2020): 173–93.

______, Mauricio Drelichman, Gustav Henningsen, and Jean Pierre Dedieu. "Early Modern Inquisition Database." *Bergen*. emid.h.uib.no

Knutsen, Gunnar W., and Daniel Muñoz Navarro. "Prosecuting the French: Patterns of Trials against French Defendants in Valencia, 1566–1686." *Continuity and Change* 25, no. 3 (2010): 357–76. https://doi.org/10.1017/S0268416010000275.

Krstić, Tijana. *Contested Conversions to Islam: Narratives of Religious Change in the Early Modern Ottoman Empire*. Stanford, CA: Stanford University Press, 2011.

Langbein, John H. *Torture and the Law of Proof*. Chicago, IL: University of Chicago Press, 1977.

Lea, Henry Charles. *A History of the Inquisition of Spain*, 4 vols. New York: Macmillan Co., 1906–08.

Llorente, Juan Antonio. *Histoire critique de l'inquisition d'Espagne*, 4 vols. chez Treuttel et Wurtz . . . [chez] Delaunay . . . [chez] P. Mongie ainé, 1817–1818.

______. *The History of the Inquisition of Spain, from the Time of Its Establishment to the Reign of Ferdinand VII: Composed from the Original Documents of the Archives of the Supreme Council and from Those of Subordinate Tribunals of the Holy Office*. G.B. Whittaker, 1826.

Luque Muriel, Francisco. "Los abecedarios como fuente para estudio de la legislacion." In *Perfiles juridicos de la Inquisición española*, edited by José Antonio Escudero, 147–61. Madrid: Instituto de Historia de la Inquisición, Universidad Complutense de Madrid, 1989.

Lynn, Kimberly. *Between Court and Confessional: The Politics of Spanish Inquisitors*. Cambridge: Cambridge University Press, 2013.

MacKay, Ruth. *'Lazy, Improvident People': Myth and Reality in the Writing of Spanish History*. Ithaca, NY: Cornell University Press, 2006.

Maltby, William S. *The Black Legend in England: The Development of Anti-Spanish Sentiment, 1558–1660*. Durham, NC: Duke University Press, 1971.

Mandosio Quintiliano, Pietro Vendramini, and Damiano Zenaro. *Repertorium Inquisitorum prauitatis haereticae: in quo omnia, quae ad haeresum cognitionem ac S. Inquisitionis forum pertinent, continentur* . . . Venice: apud Damianum Zenarum, 1575.

Maqueda Abreu, Consuelo. *El auto de fe*. Madrid: Ediciones Istmo, 1992.

______. "Extranjeros, Leyenda negra e Inquisición." *Revista de la Inquisición*, no. 5 (1996): 39–102.

Martinez, François. "La permanence morisque en Espagne après 1609 (Discours et réalités)." Unpublished doctoral dissertation, Université Paul-Valéry – Montpellier III, 1997.

Martínez Gomis, Mario. "El control de los niños moriscos en Alicante tras el decreto de expulsión de 1609." *Revista de historia moderna: Anales de la Universidad de Alicante*, no. 1 (1981): 251–80.

Martínez Navas, Isabel. "Un manual para fiscales del Santo Oficio." *Revista de la Inquisición: (intolerancia y derechos humanos)*, no. 24 (2020): 11–35.

Martínez Torres, José Antonio. "El alimento para ir más alla: Fernand Braudel, el mundo turco-berberisco y los estudios sobre cautivos renegados (Siglos XVI y XVII)." *Hispania Sacra* 53, no. 108 (2001): 761–85.

Mea, Elvira. "O Santo Ofício português: Da legislação à prática." In *Estudos em homenagem a João Francisco Marques*, edited by Luís António de Oliveira Ramos, Jorge Martins Ribeiro, and Amélia Polónia, 163–74. Porto: Universidade do Porto, Faculdade de Letras, 2001.

Meccarelli, Massimo. *Arbitrium: Un aspetto sistematico degli ordinamenti giuridici in età di diritto comune*. Pubblicazioni Della Facoltà Di Giurisprudenza. Milano: A. Giuffrè, 1998.

Menchi, Silvana Seidel. "The Inquisitor as Mediator." In *Heresy, Culture, and Religion in Early Modern Italy: Context and Contestations*, edited by Ronald K. Delph, Michelle M. Fontaine, and John Jeffries Martin, 173–92. Kirksville, MO: Truman State University Press, 2006.

Mendoza García, Isabel. "El inquisidor general don Diego de Arce y Reynoso." Unpublished doctoral diss., Universidad Autónoma de Madrid, 1993.

Meseguer Fernández, J. "Los Hechos." In *Historia de la Inquisición en España y America*, edited by Joaquin Pérez Villanueva and Bartolomé Escandell Bonet, Vol. I, 281–370. Madrid: Editorial Cátolica, 1984.

Minkov, Anton. *Conversion to Islam in the Balkans: Kisve Bahasi Petitions and Ottoman Social Life, 1670–1730*. Leiden: Brill, 2004.
Molina Martinez, Miguel. *La leyenda negra*. Madrid: Nerea, 1991.
Monter, William. *Frontiers of Heresy: The Spanish Inquisition from the Basque Lands to Sicily*. Cambridge: Cambridge University Press, 1990.
______. *Judging the French Reformation: Heresy Trials by Sixteenth-Century Parlements*. Cambridge, MA: Harvard University Press, 1999.
Moreno Martínez, Doris. "Una apacible idea de la gloria: El auto da fe barroco y sus escenarios simbólicos." *Manuscrits: Revista d'història moderna*, no. 17 (1999): 159–77.
______. "La discrecionalidad de un inquisidor. Francisco Vaca, ¿El primer abogado de las brujas?" *Revista Internacional de los Estudios Vascos, RIEV*, no. 9 (2012): 202–14.
Murphy, Martín. "Estudiantes y comerciantes irlandeses en Sevilla, 1598–1798." In *Los extranjeros en la España moderna: Actas del I coloquio internacional, celebrado en Málaga del 28 al 30 de noviembre de 2002*, edited by Pilar Pezzi Cristóbal and María Begoña Villar García, 565–71. Málaga: Ministry of Science and Innovation, 2003.
Nalle, Sara Tilghman. *Mad for God: Bartolomé Sánchez, the Secret Messiah of Cardenete*. Charlottesville: University Press of Virginia, 2001.
National Research Council. *Identifying the Culprit: Assessing Eyewitness Identification*. Washington, DC: The National Academies Press, 2014. https://doi.org/10.17226/18891.
O'Banion, Patrick J. "For the Defense of the Faith? The Crusading Indulgence in Early Modern Spain." *Archiv fur Reformationsgeschichte* 101 (2010): 164–85.
O'Callaghan, Joseph F. *Reconquest and Crusade in Medieval Spain*. The Middle Ages Series. Philadelphia: University of Pennsylvania Press, 2003.
Ortega Gómez, Lorena. "La Inquisición en el mundo rural: Los familiares del Santo Oficio del tribunal de Toledo durante el siglo XVII." In *Campo y campesinos en la España moderna; Culturas políticas en el mundo hispano*, 1181–92. Madrid: Fundación Española de Historia Moderna, 2012.
Ortego Gil, Pedro. "Innocentia praesumpta: Absoluciones en el antiguo régimen." *Cuadernos de historia del derecho*, no. 10 (2003): 71–125.
______. "El arbitrio de los jueces inferiores: Su alcance y limitaciones." In *El arbitrio judicial en el antiguo régimen: España e Indias, siglos XVI-XVIII*, edited by José Sánchez-Arcilla Bernal, 133–94. Madrid: Dykinson, 2013.
Paiva, José Pedro. *Bruxaria e superstição num país sem 'caça às bruxas' 1600–1774*. 2nd ed. Lisboa: Editorial Notícias, 2002.
Paramo, L. *De origine et progressu Officii Sanctae Inquisitionis ejusque dignitate et ulititate, de Romani Pontificis Potestate et delegta inquisitorum edicto fidei et ordine judiciaris Sancti Officii quaestiones decem*. Typographia Regia, 1598.
Pastore, Stefania. *Il vangelo e la spada: L'inquisizione di Castiglia e i suoi critici (1460–1598)*. Roma: Edizioni di storia e letteratura, 2003.
Pedrós Ciurana, María Luisa. "Inquisición, magia y sociedad en la Valencia del siglo XVIII." Unpublished PhD dissertation, University of Valencia, 2015.
Peña Díaz, Manuel. "Sobre expurgos y calificadores. Debates en torno a la censura inquisitorial (siglos XVI-XVII)." In *Edición y literatura en España (siglos XVI y XVII)*, 95–110. Zaragoza: Universidad de Zaragoza, 2012.
Pène, Matthieu. "Le temps des archives et la périodisation historique: Une histoire découpée en boîtes?" *Questes* (2016): 31–43. https://doi.org/10.4000/questes.4315.
Pérez, Joseph. *The Spanish Inquisition: A History*. London: Profile Books, 2004.
Pérez García, Pablo. *la Comparsa de los malhechores: Valencia 1479–1518*. Valencia: Diputació de València, Centre d'Estudis d'Història Local, 1990.

______. "Perspectivas de análisis del proceso penal en el antiguo régimen: El procedimiento ordinario de Valencia foral (ss XVI y XVII)." *Clío & Crímen: Revista del Centro de Historia del Crimen de Durango*, no. 10 (2013): 35–82.
Pino Abad, Miguel. *La pena de confiscación de bienes en el derecho histórico español.* Madrid: Editorial Dykinson, S.L., 2014.
Plakotos, Georgis. "The Venetian Inquisition and Aspects of 'Otherness'. Judaizers, Muslim and Christian Converts (16th-17th Century)." D Phil, University of Glasgow, 2004.
Posadilla, J.Á. *Practica criminal por principios, Ó modo y forma de instruir los procesos criminales de las causas de oficio*, Vol. 2. Madrid, 1815.
Prosperi, Adriano. *Tribunali della coscienza. Inquisitori, confessori, missionari.* Biblioteca Di Cultura Storica. Torino: G. Einaudi, 1996.
______. "Notas sobre Inquisición." *Manuscrits: Revista d'història moderna*, no. 17 (1999): 31–37.
Pulido Serrano, Juan Ignacio. *Injurias a cristo: Religión, política y antijudaísmo en el siglo XVII: (Análisis de Las Corrientes Antijudías Durante la Edad Media)*. Alcalá de Henares: Instituto Internacional de Estudios Sefardíes y Andalusíes, 2002.
______, and William Childers. *La Inquisición vista desde abajo: Testificaciones de gente corriente ante el Santo Oficio*. Edited by Juan Ignacio Pulido Serrano and William Childers. Madrid: Iberoamericana, 2020.
Rábade Obradó, María del Pilar. "La toma de decisiones en relación con las denuncias de criptojudíos ante los tribunales de Ciudad Real y Toledo (1483–1504)." *Revista de la Inquisición: (intolerancia y derechos humanos)*, no. 22 (2018): 159–84.
Reguera, Iñaki. "Las Cárceles de la Inquisición de Logroño." In *Perfiles juridicos de la Inquisición española*, edited by José Antonio Escudero, 415–38. Madrid: Instituto de Historia de la Inquisición, Universidad Complutense de Madrid, 1989.
Roberts, Simon. *Order and Dispute: An Introduction to Legal Anthropology*. Classics of Law & Society Series, 2nd ed. New Orleans: Quid Pro, LLC, 2013.
Robinson, Daniel N. *Wild Beasts and Idle Humours: The Insanity Defense from Antiquity to the Present*. Cambridge, MA and London: Harvard University Press, 1996.
Rodríguez Besné, José Ramón. *El Consejo de la Suprema Inquisición*. Madrid: Editorial Complutense, 2000.
Ross, David Frank, J. Don Read, and Michael P. Toglia, eds. *Adult Eyewitness Testimony: Current Trends and Developments*. Cambridge: Cambridge University Press, 1994.
Rostagno, Lucia. *Mi faccio turco: Esperienze ed immagini dell'Islam nell'Italia moderna*. Supplemento N 1 a 'Oriente Moderno'. Roma: Istituto per l'Oriente C.A. Nallino, 1983.
Rouland, Norbert. *Legal Anthropology*. London: Athlone Press, 1994.
Rudt de Collenberg, W. H. *Esclavage et rançons des chrétiens en Méditerranée: 1570–1600: D'aprés les litterae hortatoriae de l'Archivio Segreto Vaticano*. Paris: Léopard d'or, 1987.
Sánchez-Arcilla Bernal, José, ed. *El arbitro judicial en el antiguo régimen: (España e Indias, siglos XVI-XVIII)*. Madrid: Dykinson, 2013.
Sánchez Rivilla, Teresa. "Biografía de la cúpula del Santo Oficio: Inquisidores generales y consejeros de la Suprema: Documentación biográfica." In *Historia de la Inquisición En España y América*, edited by Bartolomé Escandell Bonet and Joaquín Pérez Villanueva, Vol. 3, 228–440. Madrid: BAC, 2000.
Sarrión Mora, Adelina. "Clérigos torpes y mujeres solicitadas en los procesos de la Inquisición española." *Arbor: Ciencia, pensamiento y cultura*, no. 611 (1996): 25–50.
Scaraffia, L. *Rinnegati: Per una storia dell'identità occidentale*. Rome: Laterza, 1993.

Schaposchnik, Ana E. *Under the Eyes of the Inquisition: Crypto-Jews in the Ibero-American World (Peru, 1600s)*. Madison: University of Wisconsin, 2008.

Schnapper, Bernard. "La répression pénale au XVIe siècle au Bordeaux." *Recueils de mémoires et travaux publiés para la Société d'Histoire du Droit* VIII (1971): 17–20.

______. "Peines arbitraires du XIIIe Au XVIIIe Siecle (Doctrines savantes et usages francais)." *Tijdschrift voor Rechtsgeschiedenis* 42, no. 3–4 (1974): 81–112.

______. *Voies nouvelles en histoire du droit. La justice, la famille, la répression pénale, XVIe-XXe siècles*. Publications de la Faculté de Droit et des Sciences Sociales de Poitiers. Paris: Presses universitaires de France, 1991.

Scholz, Johannes-Michael. "Relatores et magistrados. De la naissance du juge moderne au XIXe siècle espagnol." In *Les figures de l'administrateur: Institutions, réseaux, pouvoirs en Espagne, en France et au Portugal, 16e-19e siècle*, edited by Robert Descimon, Jean-Frédéric Schaub, and Bernard Vincent, 151–64. Paris: Éditions de l'École des hautes études en sciences sociales, 1997.

Schwedt, Herman H. *Die Anfänge der Römischen Inquisition: Kardinäle und Konsultoren 1542 bis 1600. Römische Quartalschrift für Christliche Altertumskunde und Kirchengeschichte*. Freiburg: Herder, 2013.

______, Jyri Hasecker, Dominik Höink, Judith Schepers, and Hubert Wolf. *Prosopographie von Römischer Inquisition und Indexkongregation 1701–1813*, 2 vols. Paderborn: Ferdinand Schöningh, 2010.

Seitz, Jonathan. *Witchcraft and Inquisition in Early Modern Venice*. Cambridge: Cambridge University Press, 2011.

Shennan, J. H. *The Parlement of Paris*. London: Eyre & Spottiswoode, 1968.

Smail, Daniel Lord. *The Consumption of Justice: Emotions, Publicity, and Legal Culture in Marseille, 1264–1423*. Ithaca, NY: Cornell University Press, 2003.

Starr-LeBeau, Gretchen D. *In the Shadow of the Virgin: Inquisitors, Friars, and Conversos in Guadalupe, Spain. Jews, Christians, and Muslims from the Ancient to the Modern World*. Princeton, NJ: Princeton University Press, 2003.

Stradling, R. A. *Philip IV and the Government of Spain, 1621–1665*. Cambridge: Cambridge University Press, 1988.

______. *The Spanish Monarchy and the Irish Mercenaries: The Wild Geese in Spain, 1618–68*. Dublin: Irish Academic Press, 1994.

Tausiet, María. *Ponzoña en los ojos. Brujería y superstición en Aragón en el Siglo XVI*. Zaragoza: Institución Fernando el Católico, 2000.

Thomas, Werner. *La represión del protestantismo en España, 1517–1648*. Leuven: Leuven University Press, 2001a.

______. *Los protestantes y la inquisición en España en tiempos de reforma y contrareforma*. Leuven: Leuven University Press, 2001b.

Torres Arce, Marina. "Comisarios, familiares y calificadores en el distrito del tribunal inquisitorial de Logroño (1690–1705)." In *Política, religión e Inquisición en la España moderna: Homenaje a Joaquín Pérez Villanueva*, 647–70. Madrid: Universidad Autónoma de Madrid, 1996.

Trusen, Winfried. "Der Inquisitionsprozeß: Seine Historischen Grundlagen Und Frühen Formen." *Zeitschrift der Savigny-Stiftung für Rechtsgeschichte. Kanonistische Abteilung* 74, no. 1 (1988): 168–230. https://doi.org/10.7767/zrgka.1988.74.1.168.

Verdet Martínez, Nuria. "Francisco Jerónimo de León. Cultura, poticia y prática administrativa en la Valencia de los austrias menores." Universitat de Valencia, 2014.

Wakefield, Walter L. *Heresy, Crusade and Inquisition in Southern France 1100–1250*. London: G. Allen & Unwin, 1974.

INDEX

Note: Page numbers in *italic* indicate a figure and page numbers in **bold** indicate a table on the corresponding page.